The Making of The Other Half

Dag Petersson

The Making of The Other Half

Jacob A. Riis and the Mutation of Tenement Poverty

Aarhus University Press

The Making of the Other Half

Graphic design and cover: Carl-H.K. Zakrisson
Type: Lyon
Paper: 130 g Arctic Volume
Cover photo: Jacob A. Riis,
"A 'Scrub' and her Bed—The Plank,"
[90.13.3.48] 1890. Museum of the City of New York (MCNY).

Printed by Narayana Press, Denmark
ISBN 978 87 7124 164 8

Printed in Denmark 2015

Aarhus University Press
Langelandsgade 177
DK-8200 Aarhus N
Denmark
www.unipress.dk

International distributors:

Gazelle Book Services Ltd.
White Cross Mills
Hightown, Lancaster, LA1 4XS
United Kingdom
www.gazellebookservices.co.uk

ISD
70 Enterprise Drive, Suite 2
Bristol, CT 06010
USA
www.isdistribution.com

Published with support from
New Carlsberg Foundation
Dronning Margrethe og Prins Henriks Fond
Kulturministeriets Forskningspulje
Landsdommer V. Gieses Legat

Contents

Acknowledgments

This book I owe to friends, colleagues, peers, teachers, and students, past and present, and of course to the never unfailing support from my family. Over the years, as the manuscript has progressed, halted, retrogressed, recoiled and twisted into ever new shapes, I have benefited tremendously from the advice, the patience, and the suggestions you all have offered me. Thank you.

Writing has been a slow and uneven process with few roadmaps at hand and no clear destination in sight. I therefore owe much to Sanne Lind Hansen at Aarhus UP for guiding this project to its conclusion. I owe the birth of the project to Ingrid Fischer Jonge, who, as the former director of the Dept. of Maps and Images at the Royal Danish Library suggested the topic to me. Jens Erdman Rasmussen, former curator of the Danish National Museum of Photography, was always generous in sharing both knowledge and advice, and proved a great friend and collaborator while mounting the Jacob A. Riis exhibition in 2008.

Along the way I have received invaluable criticism and help from scholars of various fields, ranging from the history of photography to visual culture, literary studies, media studies, and critical theory: Bonnie Yochelson, Elizabeth Edwards, Martin Lister, Andrew Fisher, Gottfried Boehm, Mika Elo, Geoffrey Batchen, Sean Corcoran, Frederik Tygstrup, Asger Sørensen, Klaus Bruhn Jensen, Rasmus Helles, Tom Buk-Swienty, Louise Wolthers, Anna Dahlgren, Nina Lager Vestberg, Henrik Dupont, John T. Lauridsen, Roy Sellars, Graeme Gilloch, and Erik Steinskog; these and many others have offered valuable views and insights that directly or indirectly have shaped this book. I am deeply grateful to you all. Particularly, I wish to thank the members and directors of the Nordic Network for the History and Aesthetics of Photography (2003-07) and participants of the Study Group 4 (2002-2010) at the Nordic Summer University.

Archive employees at the Museum of the City of New York and the Library of Congress were extremely generous and helpful during my research visits and deserve my deepest gratitude. I also wish to thank William Stingone, the Charles J. Liebman Curator of Manuscripts at the New York Public Library for pointing out relevant areas of research and suggesting materials that cast a new light. Also, I wish to thank the staff at the National Archives in Copenhagen and the custodians of the Riis collections in Ribe for remarkable generosity and assistance.

My deepest gratitude must be addressed to my close friend, Axel Koenzen for reading portions of the manuscript at various stages of completion, always with a fresh perspective and tirelessly probing for undeveloped areas and overlooked questions.

This project has received financial support from Kulturministeriets Forskningspulje, Dronning Margrethe og Prins Henriks Fond, Ny Carlsbergfondet (twice) and Landsdommer V. Gieses Legat. I wish to thank them all.

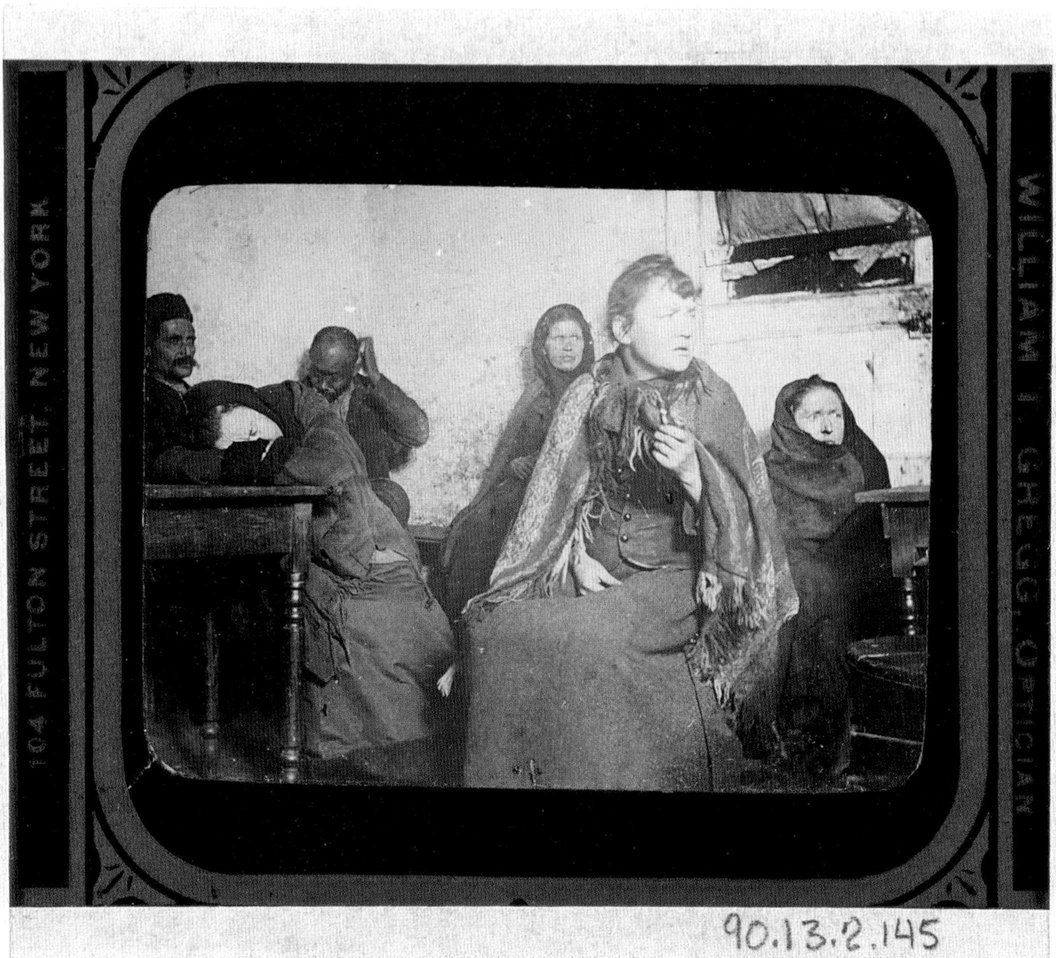

Figure 1. Richard Hoe Lawrence and Jacob A. Riis, "Hell. A Flashlight of a Low Basement Dive. Look at the Girl's Face," [90.13.2.145] ca. 1895. Museum of the City of New York (MCNY).

Introduction

> "They were not thieves by heredity; they were made. And the manufacture goes on every day. The street and the jail are the factories."
>
> Jacob A. Riis, "The Making of Thieves in New York," *Century Magazine*, Nov. 1894, 49:1, 116.

The environment makes the man. In the lower wards of New York, once infamous for their dark and overcrowded tenement blocks, their labyrinths of cluttered backyards, foul alleys, clamorous streets, clandestine networks of reeking cellar-dives, fetid lodging houses, hideous all-night restaurants, and sordid brothels, a milieu of misery had emerged that could only produce bad men, lost children, and dishonorable women. A social factory was reared in the tenements, nurtured by a corrupt municipal administration, a steady stream of immigrants, a pervasive dream of prosperity for all, and a deeply exploitative housing and labor market. In the eyes of the young immigrant police reporter Jacob A. Riis, closely covering the world of crime and misfortune for the *New York Tribune*, this factory of post-bellum Gotham churned out a city population that he was to label 'The Other Half.' Worse still: not only did the metropolis produce this terrifying inferior populace, it also deprived the unfortunates of any real chances to improve their lot. The Other Half comprised the socially immobilized day workers, the unemployable loafers, worn-out housewives, homeless street urchins, ailing grandparents, barefoot prostitutes, and criminal gangs. In the absence of effective and informed assistance, prosperity would never befall their kind.

Environments may make the man, but the slums of New York were entirely man-made. In his pursuit to uncover the truth of their proliferation, Riis identified several individuals and organizations that sustained the tenement system. Some could trace their own roots back to the tenements, but most of them hailed from other sectors of society and had been attracted to the lower wards for their fertile business opportunities. Only a few "absentee landlords" were found blissfully ignorant of the state of their property. The vast majority were fully aware of the dire effects of their investments, yet more concerned with securing their piece of the pie. In part self-sustained, in part fed by external interests, the tenement slums came across as a ferocious urban machine that produced useful political constituencies, an easily exploitable labor class, and a stable source of revenue. On the other hand, as a by-product, it also produced disease, depravity, illiteracy, crime, and occasional riots. As long as the political and economic assets outweighed the social problems, and as long as the profit-makers managed to hide the truth from public view, Riis reckoned that New York would remain unjustly divided, with one half infinitely better off than the other.

Such appeared to be the city's inequitable tenement equilibrium, the evil balance that Riis strove to overturn by disseminating—in his own words—"the truth as I saw it."[1] Truth, as Riis saw it, was always something more and other than a neutral and objective description, however correct it might be. Throughout his career, from local newsman to author celebrity and president affiliate, he agitated for a truth to be found in practical charity initiatives and enforceable reform policies; he agitated, perhaps primarily, therefore, in the direct sense of stirring up the all-pervasive tenement status quo, which he found resting safely in the complacency of the middle and upper classes. In order to shake up his bourgeois audience, Riis produced gruesome photographic evidence and minutely substantiated contentions, underpinned by morally irrecusable principles delivered through groundbreaking rhetorical narratives. His stories of the slums cast

1. Jacob A. Riis, *How the Other Half Lives* (Dover, New York: 1971), 229.

the audience as necessary compatriots in an inescapable battle against the pervasive and ubiquitous fabrication of evil. Eventually, and inadvertently, Riis's accumulating knowledge and constant argumentation developed into a coherent conceptual system aimed at better understanding and effectively changing the ill-begotten cities of the new world. A new social theory emerged. 'Truth' was then understood as a performative locution. For a description to be true, it must do something; it must perform in and have an effect on the world. Moreover, truth must act in accordance with the good. Truth cannot be objective, neutral, and free from values, as prescribed by the prevailing ideals of journalism. To speak the truth must instead be inseparable from acting for the common good; truth can only be spoken for a universally just cause. It is never to be dissociated from justice. Increasingly, it became clear to Riis that tenement life could not be truthfully described in mere objective terms. To content oneself as a journalist with reporting objectively on obscene tenement injustices must in itself be intrinsically unjust and logically inconsistent with the truth.

In this book, I will analyze this truth, its conceptual construction and its capacities for establishing new knowledge, and in so doing I will also engage in a tacit dialogue with Michel Foucault's well-known genealogy of knowledge. I will look at how other truths about poverty were produced and upheld in Riis's time; I will identify the places that truths were gathered from, the techniques with which different truths sustained their legitimacy, who and what their objects were, and who, by contrast, were entitled to claim these truths as their property. Moreover, I will look at how established truths interacted with each other, and how they responded to and mutated with Riis's work. Against the backdrop of these premises I will try to portray Riis's truth, with its particular logic, powers, origins, and position in the American public sphere. Foucault once declared that for him, the most important task had always been to show how "a particular regime of truth [...] makes something that does not exist [madness, disease, delinquency, sexuality, etc.] able to become something."[2]

2. Michel Foucault, *The Birth of Biopolitics: Lectures at the Collège de France 1978-1979* (Palgrave Macmillan, Hampshire: 2008), 36.

Whatever practices and rules had once enabled doctors, teachers, politicians, scientists, and priests, "to say and assert a number of things as truths"—thus also to bring about the very object of this truth—this had always been Foucault's scholarly objective. A regime of truth, he says, is not some univocal law of truth. It amounts rather to a dynamic and historical structure of "rules" which, during a limited epoch, enables certain subjects to judge the true from the false and to issue general declarations of truth and falsehood regarding certain objects. These structured unstructurables, that is, these relational sets of enforced and enforcing regulations that do not formally regulate themselves but are that under which veridiction is exercised, these are what should be analyzed and outlined. From such a genealogical perspective, it certainly appears that late nineteenth-century journalism involved a complex set of motley rules that permitted reporters and editors to speak a certain truth about certain matters. The reporter's 'field', for example, emerged as a site of veridiction as did the editor's exclusive right to issue statements of an opinionated or politicized nature. Elsewhere, certain other rules allowed different forms of tenement truths to develop, for example among associated philanthropists, preachers, anthropologists, and doctors; even dime museums and theaters could claim certain exclusive rights to the truth about tenement life. Needless to say, the question of veridiction is not merely a question of how to produce truth, it is equally a question of the right to assert the truth. In this book, I will examine how Riis's writings, public lectures, and photographs effectively challenged existing regimes of veridiction and their resilient truths about tenement life and reform possibilities. I will look particularly at the ways in which his outpourings defied conventional rules pertaining to charity and journalism. Moreover, I focus on how the groundbreaking photographs produced a new visual truth with its own mode of representation, i.e. a new modality of evidence, or valid testimony. Taken together, Riis's words and photographs mutated the established truth of tenement poverty.

The present method of investigation focuses on the impact that Riis's publications had on American philanthropy and journalism during the 1880s and 1890s. This transforming impact will be analyzed in terms of a confrontation of truth regimes. Discursive trajectories will be traced and assessed, crises will be measured, and the subsequent reorganization of rules will of course be minutely described. For reasons that will soon be given, this mutational event requires an approach that combines two vantage points. While one perspective accounts for the assembling of Riis's new forms of presentation (rhetorical, photographic, verbal-iconic) and their respective capacities to voice and to make visible a number of new and unfamiliar objects, the other perspective deals with the stabilizing architecture of concepts that enabled the individuation of a new modality of truth.

The first perspective may be called revolutionary. It details the creation of new forms of presentation, that is, the establishing of unprecedented apparatuses through which to bring matters of interest before a reformist public. Heuristically, these forms of presentation were fabricated and designed for probing into cracks and crevices of established discourse. Of course, the photographic forms of presentation were Riis's most revolutionary and later most acclaimed probing device, but his writings and public lectures contain many rhetorical and conceptual novelties that reach into language with equal power and prowess. Photography and rhetoric: Riis took advantage of both to pry into charity's visual and verbal orders of truth, always in view of a different perspective from which to cast new light on already familiar objects. It is well worth noting that Riis did not show his audiences anything they had not, in a strict sense, already seen before. What he presented in terms of disastrous tenement conditions, ruined families, and self-corrupting lifestyles had long since become commonplace. However, Riis's new forms of presentation allowed the well-known to appear in unfamiliar ways, open to new readings. This is key to understanding Riis's impact. Familiar things were presented in a new light—a light that made them appear as if properly uncloaked for the first time. Riis discovered these illuminating forms of presentation by experimenting not only with photography, but also with argumentation, literary tropes, concept development, image reproduction, mass-media dissemination, and captions. Such experiments were not undertaken for their own sake or without guidance from previously established forms of presentation. While in pursuit of a new truth of tenement poverty, Riis borrowed and revamped forms of presentation from other discourses and practices even if these belonged to socially alien domains. Although frequently at odds with each other and with conventional philanthropy, each such form of presentation brought with it particular capacities or forces to produce and reproduce truth, what Foucault refers to as "technologies of power."[3] Riis was no stranger to unconventional amalgama-

3. Technology of power is one of the central concepts in Foucault's later work. To appreciate it, one must first accept that power is never conceived of as a possession or an object: it is not owned by anyone, it does not reside anywhere, and it is never hidden from anyone. Power translates from the French *pouvoir*, which also means capacity. Power exists only as exercised and comes into play in view of doing something. It permeates all knowledge and all political bodies, and is what enables any of us to execute arguments and programs in a field of conflicting interests. The analysis is greatly indebted to Nietzsche; the technologies of power (or techniques of power) signify those operations and methods that various bodies may have recourse to for doing things, and which one might use and employ but never properly possess. Cf. *Security, Territory, Population: Lectures at the Collège de France, 1977-78* (Palgrave Macmillan, Houndmills: 2009), 16, 71, 101-109, and above all 162-163: "This kind of method entails going behind the institution and trying to discover in a wider and more overall perspective what we can broadly call a technology of power. In the same way, this analysis allows us to replace a genetic analysis through filiation with a genealogical analysis—genealogy should not be confused with genesis and filiation—which reconstructs a whole network of alliances, communications and points of support." See also *Discipline and Punish: The Birth of the Prison* (Penguin Books, London: 1991), 26-28. Here, Foucault describes how technologies of power enable discursive formations and observational practices to reach and maintain their form: a certain program of variations, disputes, conflicts and novelties is thus ordered and maintained within a given 'diagram.' Of the panopticon, which was a technology of disciplinary power, Foucault wrote that it is not "a dream building: it is the diagram of a mechanism of power reduced to its ideal form; [...] it is in fact a figure of political technology that may and must be detached from any specific use." ibid., 205. In *The Will to Knowledge* (Pantheon Books, New York: 1978), Foucault states that his "main concern" while undertaking an analysis of sexuality is to examine the "polymorphous technologies of power" (11). He also refers to "the 'economy' of discourses" to emphasize the plethora of technologies employed as operative functions of truth production (68).

tions of distinct technologies and he embraced the various possibilities pertaining to journalism, evangelism, statistics, morality, anthropology, entertainment, satire, photography, political ideology, and personal experience: each provided its own particular authority and its own capacity for knowledge production, yet many of them, if not all, were mutually incompatible. Uneasily welded together, they endowed Riis's presentations with an often reported jagged atmosphere and an unmistakably kaleidoscopic apprehension of the tenement problem. This appears to have rekindled public interest in the tenement cause, but it also spawned the precarious problem of incompatible authorities.

To counter this problem, Riis designed a conceptual architecture capable of buttressing and validating a new truth, an undertaking that must be viewed from a second, 'conservative' perspective. Irreducibly distinct technologies were made to find accord through a conceptual structure that redistributed their distinct veridictional powers and prevented the emerging truth from shattering into rhetorical inconsistencies. Distinct technologies for exercising veridictional power found mutually fortifying justification and authority as their already viable forms of presentation proved able to establish a differently concerted distribution of rights to the truth. Certain claims to universality had to be made. Some absolute notions and invariants had to be established. But only a well-composed presentation could order the various technologies and make it possible to reconcile the formal veracity clashes between, say, an earnest political cause and an ironic joke or a sinister photograph and a statistical mean. The capacity to reconcile sequestered truths while maintaining, even exploiting their differences, is probably what characterizes Riis's architecture more than anything else. Therefore, one of the main questions concerns precisely the invention of this architecture and its conceptual design relative to irreducibly multifarious technologies. Invariants would have to be positioned and modified so as to effectively validate and unify truths established within different technologies. It follows, however, that the absolute nature of these new invariants must not compromise the essential normative variance between different technologies of truth by validating every articulation the same way. How could Riis present familiar things in a new light without collapsing different technologies into each other, or else causing the concerted presentation to fall apart? This is the question of reconciliation that haunts Riis's work.[4] Only a mobile construction of conceptual relations (see chapter 2) could endow Riis's truth technologies with a concerted validity while sustaining the veridictional distinctions and their normative variance. The lion's share of the analysis ahead will be about unearthing these conceptual relations, which are remarkably simple and yet unique to Riis. It is important not to be mistaken here: although many, perhaps all of his concepts are homonymic with many of the most common philanthropic notions of the time, it is not a matter of identical concepts. Riis relates his concepts to each other in new and particular ways, and these new relations distinguish his concepts from their conventional meaning and use. They produce a unique architecture, which in turn endows each concept with new powers, functions, and possible meanings. The question, once again, must therefore be: how did this architecture come about? From where or what did it emerge? Perhaps the most important hypothesis of this study suggests that Riis's unique conceptual architecture came about in part from his adolescent migration from Denmark to America.

I venture the idea that a conceptual migration took place along with Riis's migration to the new world—not as an import of some Danish social theory or as a transplant of any concepts or ideologies, but by the means of a softer, simpler, non-linear form of migration. A locally developed, mundane Danish way of apprehending and articulating tenement concerns migrated with Riis—on the tip of his tongue, in his pocket, somewhere in the back of his mind. A statement, as Foucault famously has it, "is like the over-familiar that constantly

4. On the intended concept of reconciliation, see the author's *The Art of Reconciliation: Photography and the Power of Dialectics in Benjamin, Hegel and Derrida* (Palgrave Macmillan, Basingstoke: 2013).

eludes one."[5] I find this nearness, this non-phenomenal and ungraspable nature of statements to be crucial for the present hypothesis of a conceptual migration. Their alleged 'over-familiarity' to anyone who speaks implies that the agency of creating new forms of presentation should in this case be attributed to other agents than Riis himself. He need not, in fact he *must not* have been actively engaged in Danish philanthropy for its rules to have travelled with him across the Atlantic. The experiments in New York which later led to new forms of presentation had as their primal resource and wholly anonymous agent "the operational domain of an enunciative function." This operational domain of the over-familiar statement is obviously distinct from, being prior to and conditional of, any actual articulation of sentences, words, or meaningful propositions. The 'enunciative function' operates by limiting what sentences, words, and propositions are able to say in any given social, economic, geographic, or linguistic domain. Imagine how, while in Copenhagen as a young carpenter's apprentice, Riis was situated in the city's discursive practices—not, of course, by authoring expressed ideas or opinions of his own, but rather insofar as he, like everyone else, was subjected to "a body of anonymous, historical rules." These rules, being what "defines the conditions of operation of the enunciative function,"[6] effectively delimited what could be said and imagined in Copenhagen about labor, immigration, housing, hygiene, poverty, etc. These limits would then for Riis also have offered the most immediate and humdrum framework for apprehending the tenement situation in New York. Suppose then a clash between a native and a foreign enunciability: between an immediate, non-articulated Danish positivity and another, American one, which delimited these subject matters in a rather different way. The ensuing disequilibrium implied considerable potentials for new forms of expression and new conceptual relations to evolve, especially when pressurized by

5. Michel Foucault, *The Archaeology of Knowledge* (Routledge, London: 1972), 111.

6. Ibid., 117.

positive moral indignation and political incentives. For sure, no such novelties could emerge from a discursive clash alone; only from a persistent public feedback process of writing and reading, speaking and listening, seeing and showing could the prospect of bringing out distinct new technologies ever bear fruit. A non-linear discursive migration would only take place during such cyclical moments of imparting a new truth and only insofar as Riis and others consistently wrote, published, and reconsidered their positions before each new publication.

All of this notwithstanding, the present book begins prior to the moment of actualization. Without embracing an abstract historicist chronology, it opens with an analysis of the tenement situation in Copenhagen. Based on reports and debates published during the years of Riis's residence in the city, the first chapter describes the political and economic situation in such detail as is necessary to provide a background for the later emergence of distinct tenement problems in Riis's work. I hope it will then become clear why the stagnant charity discourse in New York—suffering as it was from declining powers to spur the middle class into action—eagerly welcomed new enticing narratives and new engaging forms of presentation. Riis's conceptual migration meant an opportunity for a new way of speaking the truth, a truth that established itself by affirming otherwise certain indisputable absolute values, thereby also rather acting upon the current state of affairs than being content with mere objective descriptions. This truth would only prove itself by affirming the values that are concomitant with the invariants that enable its expression, that ratify it, and impel it to act.

Previously, I identified two irreducible vantage points, two methodological perspectives on the mutating veridiction regimes. These two viewpoints bring together irreducibly different aspects of a truth formation: the revolutionary side and the conservative side. Both perspectives are necessary, because new forms of presentation do not by themselves erect a structure of buttressing validity, and conversely, a structure's conceptual relations do not exhaust the technologies of power. But their irreducibility does not mean that the two perspectives are disconnected or isolated from each other. They rather supplement each other in revealing the fabrication of a new singular statement and, in this case, a novel consistent truth about tenement life. Nonetheless, their mutual irreducibility to the historian is absolutely essential for retracing the production of this new whole, this new univocal truth. Depicting the performative quality of this truth depends on their distinction. What is ultimately at stake, what must be respected, is what Riis's work could do: the extent of its performative capacity. The double perspective alone permits historical questions to target its operational domain. For example: which truths were The Other Half actually able to establish, what conditioned them, and how did they affect existing charity conventions and the targeted tenement apparatus? How did different media impact on Riis's presentation of facts and how could his output reach such a dominant social position, and as quickly as it did? Which materials and processing techniques were found to agree with what sort of representational machines, and what kinds of bodies would then appear to testify against the prevailing political system? Questions like these—vital for understanding Riis—may not be answered from one vantage point alone. Only by carefully describing one aspect with a view toward the other, by installing the analysis in the middle, so to speak, will the performative quality of Riis's truth have a chance to appear.

I have said that I will attempt a dialogue with Foucault's genealogy of knowledge. Several reasons prevent me, however, from truly following or appropriating some strict Foucauldian protocol. A proper theoretical appropriation would not, first of all, be entirely true to Foucault's own thinking, sensitive as it was to problems that also modified the theoretical position. Secondly, there is in the present study a difference in object which must be respected: whereas Foucault tended to investigate veridictional orders as such and the genealogical thresholds between them (e.g. orders of madness, punishment, or painting before and after the modern episteme, or orders of economy relative to orders of language or life), this study deals with events and dynamics within a singular epoch and thence without any claims of explicating an epistemic revolution. It is only attentive to minor mutations in language and visuality, provoked by migrations from one established set of rules to another.[7] What is at stake on this level is the formation of a new discursive object (i.e. The Other Half) and its remarkable growth into dominance over related objects within the same discursive family.

What I present here, in other words, is a micro-genealogy of a single statement: a new curve appearing within the discursive modality of a group of signs and propositions. This modality is, as the *Archeology of Knowledge* famously puts it, what allows signs "to be in relation with a domain of objects, to prescribe a definite position to any possible subject, to be situated among other verbal performances and to be endowed with a repeatable materiality."[8] I study Riis's diction and photography insofar as they produced a new statement and a new visibility, enabling together a number of new communicative operations. His famous photographs, those first social documentary photographs, are here considered a new way of seeing rather than the origin of a photographic genre. I treat them as a modified non-discursive modality of appearance, one that, in the words of Gilles Deleuze, would be able to "contest discourse with its own form."[9]

Would it be misleading to say that Riis *invented* a new statement, or a new visibility? Only if his proper name would designate the historical person as constitutive of a genius of creation. Rather than a point of origin, I will let the name Riis—as the *general* name for a number of texts and images—name an emerging inflection point on

7. The need for small-scale analysis was noted already by Gilles Deleuze and Félix Guattari in *A Thousand Plateaus* (Athlone, London: 1888); see in particular the chapter "1837: Of the Refrain", 310-350, where they suggest that "Deformations destined to harness a great force are already present in the small-form refrain or rondo." (350). Deleuze also pointed to this minor scale in his book on Foucault, see *Foucault* (Athlone Press, London: 1986), 106ff. Another philosopher, Gilbert Simondon, should also be mentioned for his keen awareness of the need for minor scale analysis, see for example the Introduction to *L'individuation psychique et collective* (Aubier, Paris: 1989).

8. Michel Foucault, *The Archeology of Knowledge*, 107.

9. Gilles Deleuze, *Foucault*, 50.

the curve that represents all that was possible to know about tenement poverty and charity initiatives at the time in New York. Deleuze put it succinctly, when he argued that an approach like ours would be dealing not with named authors, but with practices that mutate regimes of veridiction:

> It is not necessary to be someone to produce the statement, and the statement does not refer back to any Cogito or transcendental subject that might render it possible, or to any ego that might pronounce it for the first time [...]. What counts is the regularity of the statement: it represents not an average, but rather the whole statistical curve. [... It] is neither axiomatic nor typological, but topological. [...] Foucault examined the diagrams of power as places of mutation [...]. For discursive practices are real practices, and far from being a universal logos their languages are transient and tend to promote and sometimes even to express mutation.[10]

Mutation Theory, as I venture to call the methodological procedure of this study, tries to explicate how a new statement is conceived from micro-discursive migrations and dynamics. The discovery and general explication of micro-genealogical mutations may be attributed to Deleuze and Félix Guattari; in this book, however, I will attempt to describe such a mutation process exclusively by following the relevant historical documents.

Challenging Riis

Riis himself would probably have scoffed at these efforts to understand his words and images rather than to continue his cause. "I don't care"; "I have no use for it" were standard responses to critical comments on his elliptical prose, his questionable method of research, or polemical tone. If ever he spoke about writing, rhetoric, or the use

10. Ibid., 3, 4, 106, 13.

of media, it was only to denounce its pertinence relative to communicated content.[11] For him, as a reporter and a photographer, all that mattered were the poor and their tenement life: their dark and unfit apartments, the reeking cellar dives, the dangerous labor conditions, their lost and tattered children, the recruiting gangs, the dirty streets and menacing alleys. He was concerned with the stale air that the tenement families were forced to breathe inside the damp and cold dens where they slept together with too many boarders; he worried about their lack of privacy, the shortage of schools, the shamelessly low wages, and it all came down to uprooting and reforming the system. Words and images were the mere means—of interest and value only insofar as they achieved these political objectives. Once, after a particularly thundering call against charity's general affluence of impotent words, Riis had to calm down and assure his listeners that "I am not a hater of books. I have written some myself."[12]

For my part, here, I do not take these occasional histrionic fits too literally. Riis had a way with words. In fact, and contrary to household knowledge, it is perfectly arguable that his reform achievements were largely confined to the area of communication: a tireless writer, lecturer, and admittedly a less persistent if nonetheless groundbreaking photographer, Riis's charity contribution involved the poor above all else as representations of poverty.

Perhaps, the time has come to critically examine what Riis's writings and photographs actually accomplished in terms of reforming the city. What evidence is there for his ceaseless publishing efforts leading to concrete political reform? A direct link can in fact be substantiated only in a couple of cases, namely the city's purchase of the Croton watershed and the abolishment of police lodging houses.[13] Except for these two, it seems that Riis's writings only played a

11. For a particularly colorful statement, see Jacob A. Riis, *The Making of an American* (Scribner's, New York: 1901), 223.

12. "Riis Talks Wisdom to The Trainer Graduates," in *New London Telegraph*, June 14, 1911 (1901?), Library of Congress (from now on: LC), Riis Papers, Box 17.

13. Cf. Bonnie Yochelson, "Jacob A. Riis: Photographer After a Fashion," in *Rediscovering Jacob Riis: Exposure Journalism and Photography in Turn-of-the-Century New York*, eds. Yochelson and Czitrom (New Press, New York: 2007), 179-197.

minor role in bringing about any actual reform initiatives. Perhaps one should be ready to confront a centennial myth that has heralded Riis's work as the decisive cause of a long list of effective reform initiatives in New York. Lincoln Steffens, a muckraking reporter and one-time assistant of Riis, listed these political achievements already in 1903.[14] Their attribution to Riis is still being vigorously attested by defenders of the hero figure who stubbornly cling to Riis's historical persona. A closer look at his univocally acclaimed "greatest triumph,"[15] the tearing down of the Mulberry Bend tenements for a public park, may suffice for disrupting the narrative. It was a complex case that requires a rather lengthy digression, but it is one that must be allowed, if we are ever to successfully bracket the exaggerated and substantially mistaken nature of Riis's influence. It is time to confront Riis himself and all of his defenders in order to revisit history and clear the way for a genealogical starting point.

14. "It was Riis who exposed the contaminated state of the city's water supply, and thus brought about the purchase of the whole Croton watershed. It was Riis who forced the destruction of rear tenements, and thus relieved the hideous darkness and density of life among the poor. It was the reporter with his nagging that wiped out Mulberry Bend, the worst tenement block in the city, and had the space turned into a park. Riis spoke the word that incited Commissioner Roosevelt to abolish police station lodging-houses. Riis fought for and secured a truant school, where boys who played hookey are punished—they used to be imprisoned with juvenile criminals. Riis did the work that won small parks for bad spots in the city; he labored years for enough schools; he drove bake shops with their fatal fires out of tenement basements; he demanded light for dark tenement hallways, got it, and thus opened one hiding place of vice, crime and filth. He worked for the abolition of child labor, and, when a law was enacted, compelled its enforcement. Playgrounds for schools and the opening of schoolrooms to boys' and girls' clubs were his work. And he raised the cry for flowers for the healthy as well as the sick poor." Lincoln Steffens, "Jacob A. Riis, Reporter, Reformer, American Citizen," in *McClure's Magazine*, Aug. 1903, 21:4, 419.

15. Grace Meyer, print curator at the Museum of the City of New York and curator of the first photo exhibition of Jacob A. Riis's photographs in 1947, played a role in the post-war making of Jacob Riis that has been greatly underestimated. In the press release for the exhibition she called the razing of Mulberry Bend Jacob Riis's "greatest triumph," undoubtedly in order to emphasize and to prove the political effectiveness of social documentary photography. Museum of the City of New York, Jacob A. Riis collection, Exhibition File for 'Battle with the Slum 1947', press release: "Jacob A. Riis – America's First Journalist Photographer, 1849 – 1914.

Ever since the Mulberry Bend Park opened to the public in the summer of 1897, it has been commonly known that Riis was instrumental in bringing it about.[16] His friends and supporters praised him for the accomplishment, obituaries reiterated it and passed the knowledge on to later biographies; exhibition catalogues have frequently restated it as an example of a photographer causing social change, and eventually, grand textbooks of urban development have assumed it as fact. In one of the most impressive examples, *New York 1880: Architecture and Urbanism in the Gilded Age*, one may read that, "it was not until Jacob A. Riis, the Danish-born journalist, dedicated an entire chapter of his 1890 book, *How the Other Half Lives*, to the conditions of this notorious area that action was finally taken, leading to the construction of Columbus Park on the site of Mulberry bend in 1894-96."[17] At this point, hearsay has turned into historical fact. Riis's book did not lead to the demolition of the tenements in question. Evidence is irrefutable: firstly, the application to condemn them had been submitted to the New York Supreme Court more than two years prior to the publication of Riis's book.[18] Secondly, once approved by the Supreme Court, the park project was for many years a strictly juridical case, dealing mainly with determining the cost of expropriating each of the Bend's many private properties; then, for some years more, it was a matter of pushing the project through the city's underdeveloped bureaucracy. What influence could Riis possibly have had on these affairs?

It all began during the opening ceremony of the Park on June 15, 1897. Toward the end of the proceedings, Commissioner George E.

16. Mulberry Bend Park is known today as Columbus Park and is located between Bayard St. and Worth St. on the southern end of Manhattan.

17. *New York: Architecture and Urbanism in the Gilded Age*, eds. Stern, Mellins, Fishman (Monacelli Press, New York: 1999), 496.

18. The Board of Street Opening and Improvement submitted the application to the New York State Supreme Court on July 26, 1888. *How the Other Half Lives* was published in November 1890.

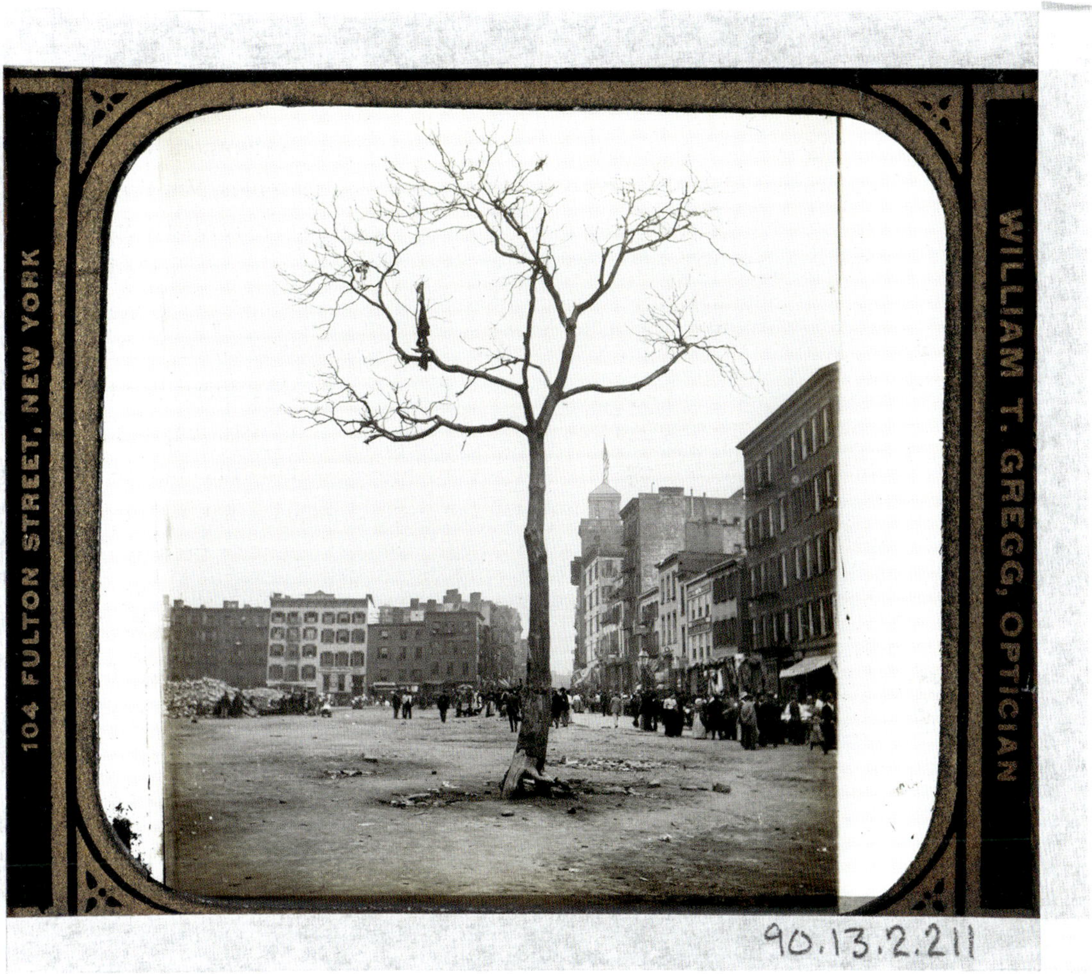

Figure 2. Anonymous photographer, "Mulberry Bend Park Under Construction," [90.13.2.211] ca. 1895. MCNY.

Waring Jr. of the Street Cleaning Department gave a brief speech which he closed, in the words of a *New York Times* reporter, "by calling for three cheers for Jacob A. Riis, to whom, he declared, the chief credit for getting the park was due. The cheers were given with a will."[19] Riis's autobiography corroborates the description and supplies further detail:

> My scrap-book from the year 1883 to 1896 is one running comment on the Bend and upon the official indolence that delayed its demolition nearly a decade after it had been decreed. But it all availed nothing to hurry up things, until, in a saggering moment, after four years of that sort of thing, one of the City Hall officials condescended to inform me of the real cause of the delay. It was simply that "no one down there had been taking any interest in the thing." I could not have laid it out for him to suit my case better than he did. It was in the silly season, and the newspapers fell greedily upon the sensation I made. The Bend, moreover, smelled rather worse than usual that August. They made "the people's cause" their own, and shouted treason until the commission charged with condemning the Bend actually did meet and greased its wheels. But at the next turn they were down in a rut again, and the team had to be prodded some more. It had taken two years to get a map of the proposed park filed under the law that authorized the laying out of it. The commission consumed nearly six years in condemning the forty-one lots of property, and charged the city $45,498.60 for it.[20]

It is true that Riis wrote about the planned park at the time and that a few other journalists joined him, but a proper press campaign was never launched. Moreover, Riis's reminiscences contain several improbable accounts and intriguing inconsistencies. The anonymous city official who informed Riis about the municipal indifference must

19. "Mulburry Bend's Park," in *The New York Times*, June 16, 1897, 7.

20. Riis, *The Making of an American*, 275-77.

have done so in the early summer of 1887, but his charges are hard to substantiate. For one thing, the Small Parks Act, which provided the municipality with the necessary legal instrument for the condemnation application, had been drafted that spring and was passed on May 13. According to the *Times*, signing it was, "one of the first improvements of general public benefit undertaken by Mayor Hewitt after his induction into office."[21] The mayor's four months in office preceding the Act were reportedly spent "devising a plan for keeping the control of the matter in one of the governing boards of the city," namely within the Board of Street Opening and Improvement, where the mayor himself was chairman. Having both ratified the legislation and submitted the application for the Mulberry Bend Park, it seems that the honors for the park should rather be awarded to mayor Abram Stevens Hewitt.[22] A rebellious Tammany Hall associate, Hewitt would have been as disinclined to listen to Riis—a self-proclaimed Republican—as Riis was unwilling to acknowledge Hewitt's reform efforts. Not least as their respective agendas for pursuing the park were very different. Hewitt's main motivation was the prospect of expanding and consolidating New York into one great city. A delegation from the influential Chamber of Commerce of the State of New York met with the Mayor in the fall of 1887 "to complain about the crowded, dirty state of the city and to encourage civic improvements."[23] Six months later, their annual report celebrated the mayor's reform initiatives and declared the Chamber in support of the consolidation. Possibly, Mayor Hewitt and Mr. E. Henry Lacombe of the Corporation Counsel, who had drafted the legislation and who were

21. "More Small Parks Wanted," in *The New York Times*, Oct. 21, 1888, 11. Mayor Hewitt's term in office lasted from Jan. 1 1887 until Dec 31. 1888.

22. The Small Parks Act had been drafted already by the Tenement House Commission of 1884, which, as pointed out by Joseph J. Varga, must be considered instrumental in bringing it about. See Varga, *Hell's Kitchen and the Battle for Urban Space: Class Struggle and Progressive Reform in New York City, 1894-1914* (NYU Press, New York: 2013), 67.

23. The Virginia Division of Legislative Services, "New York City: organization and governmental structure", available at: http://dls.virginia.gov/groups/consolidation/meetings/092204/NYCity.pdf. Accessed June 13, 2014.

responsible for the condemnation handling, may even have targeted Mulberry Bend for a park already when the law passed in May, 1887.[24]

The summer of 1887, when Riis's Mulberry Bend stories allegedly prodded a sleeping commission into action, is remembered quite differently elsewhere in Riis's own autobiography: "I wrote, but it seemed to make no impression."[25] This account is probably more correct as the commission was not appointed until November 1888, and with a strictly regulated protocol of procedure. Furthermore, the rule map for the park had already been submitted on May 28, 1888, not in the summer of 1889, as Riis has it. A series of early resignations from the commission meant that it was not fully functional until February 14, 1889. Given the strict protocols of procedure, particularly the extremely thorough hearings to be undertaken with numerous different stakeholders in each of the 41 parcels intended for condemnation (remarkable documents that await historical analysis![26]), four years seem reasonable for a body of private citizens with personal and professional duties on the side that often delayed the proceedings.

24. A news item, "More Small Parks Wanted" in *The New York Times*, Oct. 21, 1888, 11, suggests that this was the case. While explicating "chapter 320 of the Laws of 1887" it says: "By its provisions the Board of Street Opening and Improvement was empowered to determine upon such small parks their location and number, and for that purpose to expend a sum not to exceed $1,000,000 per annum. In pursuance of this authority the Board of Street Opening and Improvement, of which the Mayor is Chairman, has taken all the steps within its province to establish three such parks and to extend and develop others.
The Mulberry Bend Park has thus been located and the Corporation Counsel has taken the necessary steps to have Commissioners of Condemnation and Assessment appointed to condemn the necessary land and to assess the benefits and award the damages."

25. Riis, *The Making of an American*, 267.

26. The hearings are kept at the New York Municipal Archives, Dept. of Old Records, #17-1888 Parks Mulburry Bend Park. The first hearing began Tuesday Mar. 4, 1890, and the last hearing ended on Feb. 2, 1893. Questions dealt with ownership, maintenance, history, rents and mortgages, why the parcels had been bought and sold, for how much, when, and to whom. Detailed usage of the premises, lease contracts to bars and saloons were offered and interviews held with owners and subletters. Real estate agents were heard for an estimate of the market value. Interestingly, photographs were offered and accepted as evidence in the case of parcel 10, 53 Mulberry Street on Jan. 7, 1892.

Hundreds of complaints were then filed and registered in the period between November 1892 and February 1893. On May 29, 1893, the commission submitted its final report to the Supreme Court. Subsequently, with the report filed and under pressure from the many complaints, the legal procedure of assessing and compensating the commission members began; several tomes of stenographed hearings and protocols were presented before judge Henry R. Beekman Esq., along with a detailed invoice. Only on November 21, 1893 could he release the commission members from public duty.

Once the condemnation procedures were finalized, certain consequences followed that, in Riis's view, further shamed the city of New York. He wrote: "In 1894 the city took possession and became the landlord of the old barracks. For a whole year it complacently collected the rents and did nothing."[27] Reminiscing thus in *The Battle with the Slum* (1902), Riis attacked in hindsight with full knowledge of the legal and moral predicaments that the city officials had faced. He knew very well that the city had been forced by law to take ownership of the Bend and to collect rents. In fact, an immediate eviction with no alternative housing options would have been disastrous. He also knew about a legal technicality that in 1894 had delayed and complicated matters further. On December 20 that same year, Riis had publically rebuffed the administration's efforts to overcome the problem, calling it "a history of indifference and incompetency that are nothing less than treason."[28] What mandated this verbal assault was a failure on the part of Corporation Counsel William H. Clark to respond to a formal inquiry from the Comptroller Ashbel P. Fitch in August, regarding the $1,522,055.60, which, being the full cost of the condemnation, exceeded the legally stipulated limit of $1,000,000 to be paid per annum according to the Small Parks Act (see note 24). Fitch's letter had arrived at Clark's office in August, says Riis, who then wonders how the counsel could have failed to respond in four months time and, upon inquiry, renounce all responsibility

27. Riis, *The Battle with the Slum* (Macmillan, New York: 1902), 275-76.

28. Riis, "The Small Park Problem—A Way Out," in *The New York Evangelist*, Dec. 20, 1894.

as well as interest. Riis, however, fails to report that only two days after his visit at the counsel's office, Mr. Clark issued an opinion to the comptroller's office about "his powers in the matter of paying for the property taken for the Mulberry Bend Park."[29] Mr. Fitch then responded with an open letter to the newly inaugurated Republican mayor, Mr. William Lafayette Strong, published in *The New York Times* (Jan. 22, 1895), in which he voiced a desperate call for immediate legislation. He said: "Under the law, as it stands to-day, I am without power to provide for the payment of these awards [...]. One of the most embarrassing features of this unfortunate event is the position in which the city has been placed as landlord of the premises thus acquired. The buildings [...] are among the most undesirable species of tenement-house property in the city."[30]

Contrary to Riis's account, these documents convey awareness and urgency if not, perhaps, perfect accord among the municipal officials. Their univocal call for legislation resulted in an immediate amendment proposal to the Small Parks Act, which was submitted only two days later by Richard Watson Gilder of the Tenement House Committee, with particular mention of the Mulberry Bend Park. The amendment allowed the issuing of bonds "as may be necessary"[31] for the construction; bonds were then issued in March 1895 to pay the owners, and a lawful public auction was held in June, recovering any material value of the buildings before demolition. Unfortunately, it was then the new owners' responsibility to tear down the buildings at their own expense and to clear away the debris within 30 days. As this failed to happen, the city was again in a fix, resolving at first to prod the owners and then to look for a contractor to expedite matters. Once hired, this anonymous entrepreneur made no hurry during the busy season, knowing that the city was forced by law to stick to the agreement. The city pressured the contractor throughout the fall and was forced, in the winter, to appoint a special police force to keep people away from the dangerous rubble. In December, a series of

29. "Mulberry Bend Park Property," in *The New York Times*, Dec. 8, 1894, 3.
30. "Pay for Mulberry Bend Park," in *The New York Times*, Jan. 22, 1895, 9.
31. "Parks in Crowded Districts," in *The New York Times*, Jan. 24, 1895, 3.

unrelated events occurred that again would make it appear as if Riis had a decisive hand in the matter. Riis, angry about the lack of progress, filed an official complaint on December 20 with the Health Board. A few days later, an accident occurred when some neighborhood children rode a cart down a cellar hole among the rubble.[32] Clearance began shortly afterwards, which Riis attributes to his own intervention underscored by the tragedy. It is, however, very unlikely that a complaint to the Health Board would have impressed a contracted external partner. The slow season, possibly the accident, and any number of attendant factors may have determined the date. What, then, could possibly explain the cheers for Riis at the opening festivities? By that time, Riis had become something of a media celebrity. Waring had good reasons and a perfect opportunity to ally publically with the popular reform reporter. In return, Riis rewarded him by frequently referring to his street cleaning initiatives as examples of successful tenement reform projects.[33]

Riis's greatest feat is hardly to have effectuated a great number of urban reform projects. Nor is it, as far as sources can reveal, to have been his swaying of public opinion. His greatest documentable achievement—which I will return to in a moment—is rather to have pushed the limits of what could be said, seen, and imagined with regard to tenement reform. Riis made other thoughts, words, and

32. This event has not been possible to verify in the press archives from the time; it appears in fact, exclusively in Riis's accounts.

33. There are numerous examples of how political affinities laid the grounds for Riis's interpretation of events. Mayor Hewitt was a Tammany Hall Democrat who had beaten reformists Henry George and Theodore Roosevelt in the 1886 mayor election. This was likely sufficient reason for Riis to exclude Hewitt's contribution to the park. In 1895 Riis had amassed enough political independence to harangue the Republican administration of mayor Strong, whom Riis otherwise endorsed. Strong had broken the Tammany dynasty and had appointed both George E. Waring and Theodor Roosevelt as Commissioners of Street Cleaning and The Police respectively. The triple cheers for Riis in 1897 got Commissioner Waring publically close to the rising media star already associated with Police Commissioner Roosevelt. Waring's celebration was repaid in Riis's *A Ten Year's War*, in *The Battle With the Slum*, and in countless lectures where Riis showed photographed streets before and after his street cleaning initiatives.

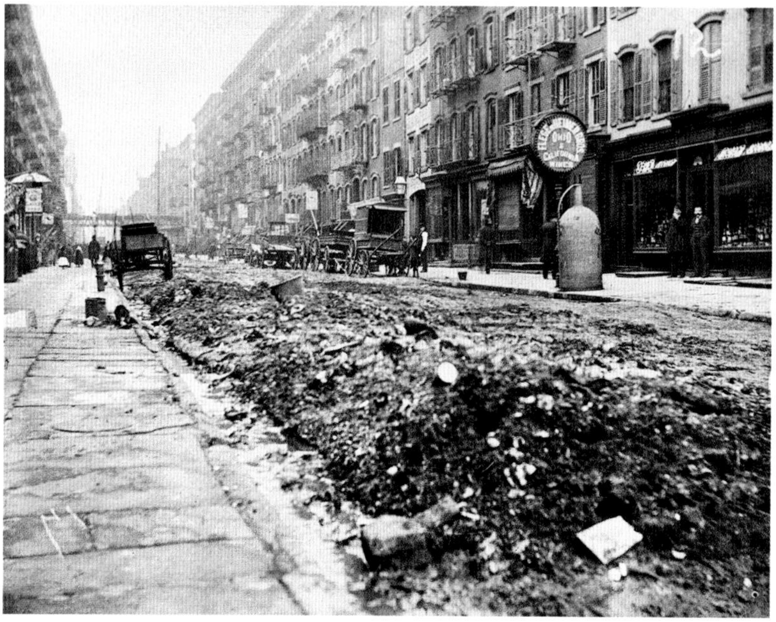

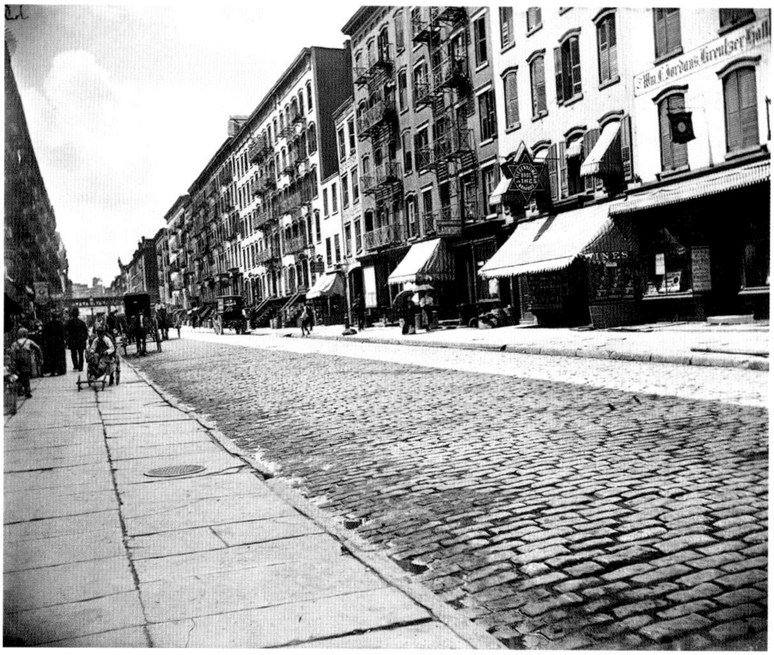

Figures 3 and 4. Anonymous photographer, "A Tammany-swept East Side Street Before Colonel Waring's Broom," [90.13.1.319] c. 1895 and "The Same Street when Colonel Waring wielded the Broom," [90.13.1.318] c. 1895. MCNY.

appearances possible. Although redrawing these limits obviously played into the hands of reformist peers, it was also a welcome target for political opponents. Tammany officials, lawyers, and businessmen would gleefully dismiss Riis's moral idealism and his naïve disregard for legal and economic realities. For us, however, it is not very important to decide exactly how his campaign was received in different political camps. The relevant observation is rather that with new and powerful means to present reformist ideas, more things could be said about reform—from all sides. The public sphere as such did not expand on the subject of charity and public reform, but a multitude of new analyses and interpretations were suddenly made possible. The implication of this was a discursive intensification; hardly, however, the beginning of a great epistemic turn.[34]

Methodology

Mutation theory is a genealogy of continuously changing knowledge regimes. Focus is on significant movements and transformations within the conditional modalities of language and appearance that form and regulate knowledge (i.e. statements and visibilities). These transformations do not necessarily amount to any great epistemic revolutions. The research procedure is based on surveying large quantities of historical documents and publications in pursuit of deviations from conventionalized forms of language and appearance. Particular care is devoted to identifying the genealogical forces that pertain to different knowledge protocols and to establish how dispute and dissent have nurtured, maintained, and delimited certain distinct public concerns. A public concern in our terminology is an agonistic hot spot marked by a relatively high discursive intensity. During the second half of the nineteenth century, the so-called 'tenement problem' emerged as a growing public concern in New York. It was the subject of increasing controversy and debate, frequent public

34. For a seminal account of the great turn, see John Tagg, *The Burden of Representation: Essays on Photographies and Histories* (Minnesota University Press, Minneapolis: 1988), 1-33; 153-183.

meetings, a great variety of philanthropic initiatives, and numerous reform proposals. It was taken up in almost every genre of publication: from the simplest magazine cartoons to alarming newspaper editorials, from lengthy charity pamphlets to romantic novels, and from scholarly reports to gothic slum-guide tomes. The social and economic causes of the tenement problem were identified negatively in wealthy neighborhoods and positively in poor ones; its symptoms and signs were noted and observed everywhere: in homes and in various industries, in markets and in shops, in entertainment venues, in dress codes, and housing design, in police records, lodging houses, brothels, and correction facilities, in schools and in orphanages. One could say, with no exaggeration, that any apartment, boarding room, cellar, and street in New York, any park and courtyard, any neighborhood, bar, and theater, in short, any public or private space in the city would constitute by its appearance, code of bodily display, and verbal conduct, a variation of the tenement problem.

A public concern expresses itself only through other things. It does not articulate itself as an object or even as a perceivable phenomenon. The tenement problem was never captured as such, in itself. The public concern should rather be considered a singularity, a non-phenomenal event, which gathers all there is to say about the tenement problem.[35] Its existence and its fluctuations in power are historically reflected only in the shifting intensities and ongoing undulation of public disputes and visual displays. These disputes always concern particular things, but the concern itself appears only as a gathering whose pertinence ebbs and flows with observable rhythm in the public domain. Concerns are then measured by the intensity and the extensivity of its disputes and displays. It is possible to analyze the power fluctuations of a public concern by observing the saturated space of its argumentative variations and their topical trajectories. In other words, one analyzes a public concern's ability to sustain debates by looking at the dynamic, the resources, and the directions of arguments and propositions, for these may both invigorate and destroy

35. Gilles Deleuze, *Logic of Sense* (Athlone Press, London: 1990), 52-57.

problems by curving away or bifurcating into autonomous sustainable offshoots. A trajectory is then understood as the distribution of variations in argument, passing through—and at the same time creating—discursive space. Public concerns mutate with redistributions provoked by probing variations. The space of a trajectory may be represented topologically as a curve analogous to the concern. The curve is an image of everything that is possible to say about a given issue at a given time. The statement is a mutable curve: a space of trajectories traversed by conflicting forces that afford and limit the enunciability of a regime of veridiction. A statement must be considered a whole: not a synthetic sum of its parts, but a full infinity of limited enunciability. A limited whole. There are always other curves developed elsewhere—discursively and non-discursively—and at other historical times with different, perhaps communicable concerns. Both formal and informal institutions serve to bind, or to 'territorialize' these concerns, often through feedback processes between authorized or otherwise legitimized apparatuses.[36] Thus a territorial boundary of knowledge is drawn, a petrified circumscription that is only more or less coextensive with the space itself. From within a knowledge perimeter (and scientific knowledge is always thus situated), the exterior may appear as a negation. Seen from elsewhere, it offers epistemic potentialities instead. For what from a bound problem's perspective appears as its defining limits are, topologically speaking, possible changes of the whole.[37] This present study focuses on a few

36. Gilbert Simondon, *L'individuation psychique et collective* (Aubier, Paris: 1989), note particularly Simondon's proposed 'energetics' for the human sciences and the distinction between area and domain, 64, which I appropriate below as a distinction between concepts of limit.

37. One should clarify that this stance on supplementary perspectives can only be described as dialectical in a particular, indeterminable sense: what is negative to knowledge, i.e. the unknown, things we are ignorant of or have forgotten, belongs, topologically speaking, to the given series insofar as one may easily recognize them as unknown or unimaginable within one's mode of knowledge. It is thus not a true 'outside.' One is never 'becoming aware' of this outside in a dialectical turn toward one's propositional presumptions. A dialectical turn, on the other hand, which itself is hard to dialectically determine, is to topology no more than a transformation of shape that maintains its invariants. To the one who knows, therefore, the negative is potential knowledge.

particular trajectories, a couple of distinct spaces, and their propensity to be affected. In short, one might say that the study measures how each one maintains its own limited resilience. When a given distribution of variations interacts with another one, there may sometimes occur, if conditions are favorable, a transformation event. In less than favorable circumstances the initial volatile phases may run out of energy or be externally annulled, whereby the space and the concern revert to their previous state. If this does not happen, the disequilibrium is allowed to pass into a second phase: a creative, disorienting, and 'deterritorializing' phase, where exterior singularities may be probed for their capacity to operate on the spatial structure. This phase is critical, dangerous, and highly consuming. A mutating concern may here exhaust itself, come unhinged, its trajectories may wither and die, but it may also eventually settle into a new form by passing through a phase of 'reterritorialization,' which essentially integrates a new apparatus for the mutated series of variations. If that happens, we witness a transformation of a public concern. This is essentially what happened to the tenement problem with the introduction of Riis's foreign and probing variations: it transformed with a process that we will analyze both from the vantage point of new forms of presentation and from the perspective of a new settling architecture of truth.

When transforming variations take hold of a given set of trajectories, it is common for affected institutions to enter a mode of crisis. As their stabilizing functions cease to be effective, crises tend to deepen, thence furthering the chances of transformation. Ironically, a common result of any self-protecting strategies that are based on the assumption that discursive change follows from new elements being *added* to a familiar set of variations, is that the transforming process tends to speed up even further. Because a curve is irreducible to the sum of its parts and rather forms a whole in the Bergsonian sense, it does not modify by way of partial additions but only through exterior impact directly upon the distributed variations. A curve can only reconstitute itself in its entirety, as it undergoes a topological transformation; however, when it does, it nevertheless maintains some of its code, a set of rules that are needed during the initial stages of the ensuing individuation phase. In other words, the process needs some continual codification to resume the production of variations—however different that production may turn out to be. This is why I find the word 'mutation' an apposite one.[38] Mutations of statements and visibilities occur more or less frequently and may be more or less violent. Some mutations last longer than others. Because Riis's work instigated durable mutations of both statements and visibilities, one may say that he invented at least two new curves, and in that sense a correlative new truth of urban poverty. The word 'invented' means here that trajectories were made to interact in a fortuitous way under certain circumstances that intensified a public concern, which, through a complex process, bifurcated, deterritorialized, and reassembled into a new problem.

I should perhaps again remind the reader of Deleuze's distinction between Foucauldian visibilities and statements as two irreducible fields of archaeology.[39] This to help us remember that, in spite of the statements' active and dominant role, they will never exhaust the visual regime of veridiction.[40] Truths of perception, of passion, cannot be reduced to the truths of argument. Accordingly, I will deal with the mutation of what could be said and the mutation of what could be seen in two separate analyses, the latter of which will also account for their relationship. These mutations will, in short, be the central topic of my analysis.

38. Cf. Dag Petersson, "Transformations of Readability and Time: A Case of Reproducibility and Cloning," in *Actualities of Aura: Twelve Studies of Walter Benjamin*, eds. Petersson and Steinskog (NSU Press, Göteborg: 2005), 49-76.

39. Deleuze, *Foucault*, 64; see also Joseph P. Tanke, *Foucault's Theory of Art* (Continuum, New York: 2009).

40. In this respect I also find reason to follow Roland Barthes, "The Photographic Message" in *Image, Music, Text* (Fontana, London: 1977), 16; As will become apparent in chapter 6 and 7, my analysis of photography and word is greatly indebted to this collection of essays, in relation to which I nonetheless seek to offer an alternative approach.

Procedure of Investigation

The first chapter begins not in New York, but in Copenhagen, and with the profound social and political transitions that the city underwent during the mid-nineteenth century. In 1866 Riis moved from his rural hometown of Ribe, a small ancient village on the windswept western coast of Jutland, to try his luck as a carpenter's apprentice in the bustling Danish capital. The fact that the analysis commences here, with a portrait of a young man plunging headfirst into a turbulent social environment does not necessarily imply a protagonist-driven narrative. It is rather an attempt to outline a socio-economic situation and a public concern which, as it were, held potential conditions in reserve for a possible mutation process to take place much later, far away, in the police reporter's headquarters on Mulberry Street in New York. It could almost seem as if Riis had contracted a strange condition in Copenhagen, as if the city had infected him with a language virus, that lay dormant until it found the proper conditions for becoming communicative. If I am principally barred from describing the virus itself, at least its habitat should be sufficiently detailed. Hence the first chapter describes the social, political, and economic climate changes in Copenhagen that took place after the termination of Danish monarchic sovereignty in 1849 and the later abolishment of the guilds' market control in 1862. A new kind of urban proletariat grew strong under the influence of liberalist reforms, nurtured by a steady influx of labor force and the many cultural challenges that rural workers faced while adapting to urban life. As a correlate, an emerging privatized philanthropy faced the new situation and its unfamiliar organizational demands by revising core charity values. Describing the new climate means to portray a volatile public concern intensifying dramatically with the forces of demographic movements, political decisions, urban developments, economic crises, social reform, medical breakthroughs, military defeats, financial investment schemes, and social networks.

This opening could of course be criticized on the grounds that an adolescent apprentice, like Riis, would neither have been aware of, nor concerned with the current charity issues of his time. The local discourse could therefore not have influenced his later American writings. Two arguments will be submitted in response: first, and already intimated, a 'passive' stance with regard to the intense debates and controversies in Copenhagen was not a hindrance, but rather a requisite for discursive interactions to occur much later in New York. Had Riis engaged more actively in the social welfare disputes of Copenhagen, certain views and opinions would inevitably have settled with him, and these would rather have reduced any ability to affect the tenement concern in New York. What migrated successfully were not some fully formed opinions or concepts, but quite simply a mode of mundane understanding. Its capacity to affect charity in New York was certainly not present or recognizable to anyone in Denmark. Nothing 'happened' in Copenhagen, nothing but a virtual event: a set of potentialities assembled, conditioning what might someday become—in the future perfect tense and with a throw of the dice—the inaugural moment of a mutation process. Second: although Riis did not engage personally in the debate, he was certainly not impervious to the matters at stake. Any young apprentice in Copenhagen would know that the prevalent polemics over urban poverty also touched on issues concerning one's own future livelihood and prospects for social mobility. Labor organizations for journeymen, affordable good housing for workers, loans for small-scale businesses, available private savings accounts and health insurances: these were disputed novelties at the time whose political maturation might alter livelihood opportunities for young men like Riis. Public debates on the future of the working class could not have eluded him.

The second chapter moves ahead to describe the fertile mutant, so to speak. Conceptual analyses serve here to outline the most fundamental tenets pertaining to The Other Half, describing also the invariants and the universals that buttress Riis's blend of distinct truth regimes. At first is identified three absolute, but nonetheless nominal values: the family home, the proper division of labor, and neighborliness. Together, they form three interconnected axes: a triangular diagram. While objectively absolute, these nominal values are also real and, furthermore, phenomenally dynamic whenever the triangle is attributed to a social body. Each nominal value is in other words universal and yet individually variable—indeed measurable by appraisal—wherefore the diagram is introduced as a socio-ethical diagnostics instrument. A body's fluctuating capacity to agreeably affect other bodies and to be agreeably affected, i.e. through interaction to realize what good it is capable of is indexed as movements of that body's diagram. Riis observes that individual real values are strengthened or weakened with real social and physical interaction—that is, with every sequential affect and its ensuing alteration of one's capacity to affirm the good. Given their concurrent absolute nature, these changes in real values (affirming or negating) may be registered without an exterior 'measuring rod'. Alterations are measured relative to the ideal reality of each nominal value. From a measured increase or decrease in a body's real values, Riis deduces its further capacity to be affected agreeably by another body (affirming the ideal) or disagreeably (negating the ideal). Such is the diagnostic function of Riis's conservative triangle. It will provide comprehensive evidence of a general atrophy of values in the tenements. As a conceptual device, the construction serves furthermore to hold together incongruous truth regimes and modes of presentation. As already mentioned, Riis's kaleidoscope offered a multitude of incompatible perspectives on the social interactions in the tenements, but their ethical measure, i.e. the truth of those interactions, was obtained through the conservative triangle. Riis often applied it to scale-differentiated bodies. The smallest social body was for Riis the singular family member—no human being is considered isolated from a family. The family is the social atom. Domestic units of a family with boarders represented a somewhat larger social body. Larger still, a tenement house with shared facilities was considered a social body in its own right, in other words, a distinct body, and one with exterior relationships to the families who lived there. The same was true of a neighborhood, a social network, a sweatshop with its markets and even the entire city or 'the system'. They all related externally to their 'parts'. Furthermore, each body possessed an essentially indeterminable capacity for interacting otherwise with exterior bodies, and while each body would seek to interact with others in pursuit of some good or advantage, individual persons often found themselves simultaneously on conflicting sides, as parts of several different social bodies. To Riis, the advantages fought for in the tenements appeared morally misconceived out of widespread greed and egotism, serving consistently to negate the ideals. Against the common pursuit of these corrupting pseudo-advantages, Riis worked out five 'principal propositions' which this chapter outlines in some detail. As the pillars of his political program, they represent the necessary reinforcement of conservative values in the tenements.

In the third chapter, the analysis returns to Copenhagen for a close reading of local public disputes over charity and poverty aid. The aim is to reconstruct some important trajectories of a developing public concern. Disjunctive, as the course of analysis might seem, this return is prompted by a discovery conveyed in the preceding chapter: Riis had found a unique way to conceptually bridge materialist sociology and Christian ontology. Materialism and Christianity: two regimes of veridiction severely at loggerheads in the American charity discourse at the time. Even a mere theoretical reconciliation would have profound effects on a mutation process. The construction of Riis's conceptual bridge was founded upon public disputes in Copenhagen concerning the so-called 'unworthy poor'. A specific aim of this third chapter is thus to analyze the Danish public concern about the unworthy, that is, the question of what to do with the forlorn paupers who had lost the will to help themselves. The question of the unworthy emerged at the heart of a cluster of related issues: how to restore a broken will, how to diagnose it, how to include those without will in a social order, etc. It is important to note that the arguments brought to bear in Copenhagen were never backed by religious tenets, however acute the ethical problem appeared to all parties involved. With Riis's publications in New York a decade later, these strictly secular conceptual variations of worthiness and will from Denmark probed deep into a profoundly religious charity discourse in America and its rather uncontested pious notion of worthiness. For one thing, the Danish trajectory allowed Riis to erode the discursive configuration that maintained the abyssmal American distinction between Christian faith and socio-economic apathy. But more importantly, the Danish variations led to the individuation of a new concept of will, a concept with which Riis was able to bridge Christian altruistic neighborliness and the fundamental social desire to improve oneself. This mutated notion of will—the will to honesty—whose ethical function emerged with its insemination into an American discourse, did not imply an exterior addition to the American statement. To the contrary, it stabilized the process of a mutating discursive object and offered a powerful new way of articulating a stagnant tenement problem.

The fourth chapter acknowledges immediately that the capacity to alter the American charity discourse was not exclusively a matter of introducing a new conceptual structure. It was equally a matter of pathos. Thus, I turn to Riis's sense of humor and his elliptical mode of writing. Although jokes about the poor were not uncommon in the American press at the time, Riis's amusing ironies and sarcasms differed formally from the established norms and served other purposes as well. Similarly, a notoriously jagged eloquence was being copied from the Yellow Press and from the literary entertainment industry, but with Riis the style would find a different expression, and again not least by serving a different purpose. Within the framework of charity, Riis's humor and style broke sharply with the philanthropic tone, which was sober, factual, sometimes pathetic, but always sincere. The effect was a deep discursive destabilization which opened up ample opportunities for reorientation. Dark humor and a craggy diction were effective weapons against the resilience of traditional charity, but they also offered possibilities to reconfigure the entire kaleidoscope. It is as if they not only opened opportunities for experimenting with new forms of presentation, they also protected Riis's discursive probings and warded off criticism with biting ridicule and snappy retorts. Riis's pathos represents the most creative, risky, and affirming phase of the mutation process. A new modality of expression developed for charity under its wings.

Chapter five accounts for the construction of a new performative idiom of truth. This performativity was secured through the interplay of new forms of presentation and relational invariants. In the first step of the analysis, I find that the discursive bridging effectuated by the will to honesty was also what positioned the concept of will as the structural keystone in the tertiary diagram of a body's ethical capacity. God-given in every person yet corruptible by physical experience, the will expresses itself through the weakening and strengthening of values in the conservative triangle. Only the movements of these values reveal the bridge between social materialism and Christian ontology. A nominal value, which is universal and absolute, yet only more or less realized in a social body, is at the same time an unconditional edict for the Christian republic that to Riis's mind includes all bodies. Riis's conservative values (neighborliness, the family home, and the division of labor) are in that sense real, nominal, and absolute at the same time. An individual's will to affirm these values is equal to his ethical capacity to agreeably affect and be affected by other individual bodies. An increase in capacity affirms the individual's will to honesty and strengthens the nominal values, which then, through interaction, spread to members of the surrounding community. Hence, in the second step of the analysis I find that Riis's techniques of communication were designed to strengthen those values in his audience. The performative function of his words and photographs, i.e. their effect upon the conventional veridiction of the tenement problem, was coextensive with their capacity to strengthen the conservative values in his audience. This proposition concludes the investigation of Riis's discursive mutation.

Chapter six changes the perspective. Here, the task is to investigate the prevailing visibility of tenement bodies as it too branched off in a unique direction with Riis's photographs. What is at stake here are the reproductions of photographs and their manifold abilities to make the already well-known tramps, urchins, and laborers appear in the public light anew, as if never seen before: harshly, in a new kind of blinding, fixating light. In particular, their ability to engage with Riis's discourse is scrutinized. At first, I distinguish between the photographs' semantic and non-semantic qualities, and I do so by examining their capacity to form syntagmatic and paradigmatic complexes. I then commence a survey of the different ways in which syntagmatic relationships were forged between texts and images. Noticing that illustrated lectures with magic lantern projections offered different possibilities for verbal-visual syntagma than did either books or magazine articles, I work out the relevant communicative affordances of each medium while taking due note of the semantic mutability offered by each photograph. Since many photographs were used and reproduced differently across a range of different media while also circulating in a variety of different contexts establishing a great variety of meanings, I argue that Riis's photographs enjoyed a remarkable degree of semantic freedom, restricted merely by the requirement that they engage with the discursive strenghtening of conservative values. It is therefore also argued that the primary role of his photographs was to affirm the performative force of his truth, and not simply to add visual evidence to verbal narratives. The observed semantic freedom proves that the photographic veridiction was not first and foremost descriptive, based on a photographic 'that-has-been-there.' Riis's photographs rather spoke the truth syntagmatically, and particularly by affirming the values of the conservative triangle.

The final chapter looks at the non-semantic qualities of Riis's photographs, and it identifies two visual trajectories that situate his work within two already established paradigmatic regimes. First, a powerful entertainment industry was already disseminating a rather multifarious vision of tenement life, one which Riis tapped into and developed in a new direction. Categories had emerged of urban underdevelopment and aberrant daily conduct in the tenements; playwrights, for example, had recourse to an entire catalogue of readily detectable symptoms of stereotype diseases, of mental exhaustion, of intemperance and malnutrition; there was also a recognizable typology of criminals, urchins, workers, drunkards, and the exceptional moral heroes. These signs and typecast figures had already been visually coded by the slum-horror entertainment industry. Riis's photographs belonged paradigmatically to this chilling trajectory of tenement drama, however much their context of display and several unignorable details implied a firm deviation from the entertainment industry. Riis exploited its iconic allure but rejected its reduction to mere curiosity. The strength to uphold that distinction was gathered from a second paradigmatic visibility.

While charity lectures were normally presented unaccompanied by visual illustrations, a budding genre of visually enhanced anthropological lectures was about to establish a photographic code of display for the globally uncivilized 'Other Half'. Photographed human specimens from exotic cultures were shown laboring, playing, trading, housekeeping, and engaging in strange rituals on hundreds of canvas screens in public lecture halls across the country. Anthropological lectures were publically advertised as enlightening events —a form of scholarly civic education that sharply sequestered its mode of presentation from the offensive displays of the amusement industry. Riis's non-academic, but no less enlightening lecture setup copied the formats and the ceremonials of those respectable sessions. As a result, the visibility of The Other Half was neither more nor less academic than it was entertainingly spectacular. It created its own consistency while undulating from one regime to the other in rhythmic intervals. That seesaw movement was perhaps one of the most important visual features of Riis's photographic display. A common visual advertising scheme at the time was based on such a visual rhythm, on the swinging from problem to relief, from doubt to clarity, from ambivalence to assertion. With this technique, Riis once more supplemented and underpinned the discursive performativity of truth. It would only occur, however, during illustrated lectures. Here, a purely visual rhythm supplemented the discourse with a performative truth of its own: a play on security and danger that paralleled the mobility of values with the sense that the bottom had not yet been reached, that there would still be more to see, that there will always be another turn.

CHAPTER 1

A New Beginning

> "We know that things and people are always forced to conceal themselves, have to conceal themselves when they begin. What else could they do? They come into being within a set which no longer includes them and, in order not to be rejected, have to project the characteristics which they retain in common with the set."
>
> Gilles Deleuze, *Cinema 1: The Movement-Image*, 3

> "Lane is wrong on [...] the psychology of Danish welfare legislation. Ultimately, Riis cannot be made a Danish-American reformer; he is an American."
>
> Daniel Levine, review of James B. Lane's "Jacob A. Riis and the American City" in *The Journal of American History*, 62:1, 1975, 158.

Much like the Introduction made an attempt to revise the historically attested causality between Riis's agitation and the realization of urban reform initiatives, this chapter begins with an even more deep-seated myth that deserves similar scrutiny. It concerns not the alleged effects of his writings as much as their origin and cause. Readers of Riis have always been told that the decisive impetus for his work came from earlier personal experiences of poverty and deprivation, suffered while vagabonding the north-eastern roads in search of odd jobs during the early 1870's. As a newly arrived immigrant to America, Riis learned the hard way about famine, exploitation, and hopelessness, and it was ostensibly these first hand experiences that provided him with the incitement, the insight, and the unique approach that would later distinguish his writings from peer publications. Carol Schloss explained Riis's unique qualities by pointing out that this writer "found others in distress, recognizing their destitution as an analogue of his own earlier disinheritance as an immigrant."[1] Peter Lubove, a much earlier interpreter of Riis, voiced the same idea already in the early 1960s: "Seven lean years flittering from one unsatisfactory job to another, more than a decade as a police reporter exploring the life of the outcasts, criminals, and the poor of New York—these were the experiences which Riis distilled into his book."[2] More recent variations on this recognition motif can be located in works by David Leviathin, Peter Hales and Tom Buk-Swienty.[3]

The appealing idea of a decisive link between Riis's own struggles and later reform writings was properly substantiated for the first time in his own autobiography, *The Making of an American* (1901). Although earlier suggestions of a formative relationship had been made during introductions to lectures and in printed review notices, at no time had it been as graphically and as persuasively elaborated as in his memoirs. Riis's own story about his first four years in America accounts minutely for dire conditions and deepening deprivation, but it also tells of steadfast faith and stubborn resolve in the face of growing miseries and increasing hardships. Eventually, these lean years form a personality of enough spiritual strength and moral authority to rise up against the social and moral corruption in New York. It's a wonderful story. Even a contemporary reviewer couldn't help mocking Riis's many burdens and the "necessity that he should be everlastingly bumping his head."[4] If I too dare to question the narrator's

1. Carol Schloss, *In Visible Light: Photography and the American Writer: 1840-1940* (Oxford University Press, New York: 1987), 107.
2. Peter Lubove, *The Progressives and the Slums* (University of Pittsburgh Press, Pittsburgh: 1962), 57.
3. David Leviathin, "Framing the Poor: The Irresistibility of How the Other Half Lives," in Jacob Riis, *How the Other Half Lives* (Bedford Books of St Martin's Press, Boston: 1996), 19; Peter Hales, *Silver Cities: The Photography of American Urbanization 1839-1915* (Temple University Press, Philadelphia: 1984), 165; Tom Buk-Swienty, *The Other Half: Jacob Riis and the World of Immigrant America* (W.W. Norton, New York: 2008), 170-1.
4. Anonymous, "Riis's Narrative," in *Clinton Daily Item*, May 7, 1901, unpaginated clipping. LC, Riis Papers, Box 16.

authority today, it is neither to deny that Riis felt passionately and personally about the tenement injustices, nor to suggest that prior personal experiences of life bereft of prospects did nothing to fuel his sentiments. If nonetheless I would opt for an alternative narration, it is certainly not because I think Riis lied about his past; the diaries that he kept during his first years in America corroborate the details of the autobiography. But I have found nothing to support the grand bearing idea of cause and effect, or, more precisely, the notion that personal experiences of life on the road would lead to pioneering political insights and convincing theorizations of metropolitan tenement problems, or that his written accounts would thereby be destined for a groundbreaking contribution to a tightly knit local charity network. It is very difficult to substantiate that Riis's experiences would somehow account for his later impact as a reformist writer. A closer look rather begets a paradox.

It is easy to observe how Riis's autobiography unfolds in the opposite direction of what his general sociology would predict for a downtrodden immigrant, yet, in a paradoxical way, as a typical example of what a hopeful and ambitious newcomer might expect. Riis says clearly and often enough that the path from destitution to accomplishment will always be exceptional. In the autobiography, however, destitution rather explains his later achievements—despite the overwhelming adversities that he faced and which, according to his own theory, ought to have smothered such opportunities at once. Riis never addressed this paradox at the heart of his own case and few commentators—if any—have since addressed it. Probably, the righteous recognition motif is still too welcome and too resilient to let the paradox be heard; strong rhetorical devices gloss it over in the autobiographic pursuit of a deserving personality. Innocently naïve, relentlessly seeking justice and truth, unselfishly devoted to the wellbeing of the fellow man—the rewards eventually reaped were then as well-deserved and as just as that civil society would be, that in these virtues recognizes its founding moral principles. The narrator's model personality naturalizes his exceptional story and keeps the paradox at bay. If one deliberately chooses not to let the narrative run its course, then what it explains needs rather to be explained. The task of working out a different narrative is hereby assumed. Let us therefore return to *The Making of an American.*

Most likely, Riis wrote his autobiography for career purposes. In 1899, he had quit his steady job at the *New York Evening Sun* to pursue a freelance career, but the popularity of his publications were beginning to wear thin and the books sold less impressively than before. *A Ten Year's War* was critically acclaimed in 1900, but as a mere review of reform accomplishments made since the success with *How the Other Half Lives* in 1890, it could neither point forward nor reach the sales figures of his first book.[5] The autobiography, which was due for publication in the following year, was rather a marketing project than a philanthropic contribution. As such it involved great risk. If Riis lost his footing here, like Ward McAllister had done with *Society as I Have Found It* earlier that year,[6] he might lose the authority and the reputation from which he now intended to make a living. An Illinois newspaper had identified his most essential asset to be "the knowledge and experience requisite to enable him to speak with authority" yet as "the most modest of men."[7] The risk of appearing immodest in an autobiography of extraordinary and undeniable success must be foreseen, calculated, and preempted.

Riis's choice of narrative was crucial. His journey from pauperdom to the pinnacle of society had to be made both humble and righteous. Riis cast himself as an ambitious, naïve, and overzealous young protagonist who endured physical challenges, mental stress, and spiritual doubt with quiet faith and inward resolve. Whether in doubt of himself, in want, or simply frustrated with the world, he always picked himself up, learned his lesson, and moved on. This essentially Protestant adventure implies a hero that pursues his journey in solitude.

5. Cf. Bonnie Yochelson, *Jacob Riis* (Phaidon, London: 2001), 11-15.
6. Cf. "A Wicked Four Hundred," in *Brooklyn Times*, Dec. 15, 1890, LC, Riis Papers, Box 16.
7. Unidentified and undated news clipping in LC, Riis Papers, Box 17.

Moreover, the economy of providence and its resulting moral justification require that the path to accomplishment is one of overcoming severe material privation and spiritual counterforce. The rhetorical goal was to outline a just and humble persona, one whose moral weight would be measured by the magnitude of obstacles overcome. Not only had the inhospitable American society a role to play here, the young narrator's unrequited love for hometown Elisabeth fulfilled a similar function. It is symptomatic that once the unattainable figure of Elisabeth is conquered in marriage, she disappears from the story with breviloquent promptness. Not at all by chance, this happens at the same time as the protagonist's fortune turns and a few social spearheads begin to take notice of the struggling police reporter.[8] Riis's inward endurance, faith, and resolve has by then proved strong enough to morally sanction his professional success, which, in turn, would likely not appear immodest or unjustified.

Reception was mixed. Riis's friend, Joseph B. Gilder, did not fully endorse his choice of narrator: "Nothing could be easier than to write a disparaging notice of this autobiography. In the first place it is egotistical: it bristles fairly with 'I's.' I did this; I did that; I thought so and so, and was right, and the world has come around to my way of thinking."[9] The strategy came dangerously close to failure. However, even Gilder found redeeming qualities, and the autobiography was generally received as planned. "Here was a man," wrote Julian Hawthorne for the *North American Book Supplement*, "unknown and unregarded, with not an atom of pull outside of his own personal strength and faith and indignation against evil."[10] Other reviewers also noticed with approval how Riis's solitary strength and unflinching resolve had turned the nomadic narrator into a generous and authoritative character who inspired trust and respect. The ordeals of his background even excused the frank and sententious language—even gave to its coarse-

8. Riis, *The Making of an American*, 150; 166; 179.
9. Joseph B. Gilder, "The Making of Jacob A. Riis" in *The Critic*, Jan. 1902, 40:1, 63.
10. Julian Hawthorne, "'Making of an American,' by Roosevelt's Friend and Fellow-reformer Jacob Riis," in *The North American Book Supplement*, 131, unpaginated clipping in LC, Riis Papers, Box 17.

ness a palatable tint of romance. Today, for our counternarrative, we highlight instead another important discursive rule, one which Hawthorne's remark suggests only negatively: that any unduly assisting element—any guidance or previous modeling—would lessen the moral right and authority to be gained by the suffering solitaire. Riis's path must not have been paved beforehand.

As already stated: what is challenged henceforth has nothing to do with the historical accuracy of the autobiography. Nor am I concerned with assessing the moral implications or the political incorrectness of Riis's method or views. What is under scrutiny here is the discursive emergence of a subject with new claims to knowledge, one whose radically enchanting veridiction could boost a reformer's market value, both as a lecturer and as an author. If one probes a little further into the precarious question of a previous model for Riis's work, something he had much reason to conceal, were there, in any sense, a precursor or some prior guiding element that got brushed aside in the autobiography? One period of his life is conspicuously disregarded and therefore worth looking into: the three years that Riis spent in Copenhagen before moving to America. The few paragraphs that represent this period in *The Making of an American* offer only a few casual anecdotes of amusing self-mockery. Would that really be all worth mentioning? If Riis owed more to his native capital than he concedes to, his silence can perhaps be explained by the ideology that underpins his chosen narrative.

Copenhagen 1866-1869

Jacob Riis moved to Copenhagen in May 1866. He returned to his native town of Ribe three years later with a certificate of apprenticeship signed by one of the biggest carpenter masters in the capital. In August 1870 he came back for a few weeks while waiting for a ship to take him to America. During many later return trips to Denmark he would occasionally revisit Copenhagen. The years of his apprenticeship, 1866-1869, are generally considered a turbulent period in

Danish history. Particularly for the capital, but also for the city of Ribe, this was a moment of painful transitions. In 1864 Denmark had lost a large part of its territory—the duchies of Schleswig, Holstein, and Lauenburg in the southern part of Jutland—to the Austrian-Prussian army led by Otto von Bismarck.[11] Ribe was suddenly very close to the new border and the small ancient market town lost a substantial part of its trade area to the Germanized territories. Denmark looked to England for a new export market, and the nearby town of Esbjerg developed an industrial harbor that soon attracted both labor force and railroad connections. Riis may have moved from Ribe for personal reasons, but many young men left the city as a direct response to its declining economy.

Denmark's military defeat meant that almost 40%, or a full million of the total population of 2,600,000 people had suddenly—and for the most part gladly—become Germans.[12] Fifteen years prior, during the so-called Three Year's War (1848-1851), a separation movement had been quenched in the duchies by Danish troops. The vast majority in the region, who spoke Low German and had long felt subjugated to an enforced second-rate Danish citizenship, celebrated the defeat in 1864 as a victory. Denmark's economy was in a shambles for years after the war, and only the country's strategically sensitive position at the mouth to the Baltic Sea kept England and Russia from allowing Bismarck to claim the entire nation as a German province.[13]

In the summer of 1849, in the midst of a civil war against the rebellious duchies, the state of Denmark abandoned monarchic government and ratified its first democratic constitution. Two political parties shared both chambers of parliament during the first decades

11. For literature in English about this episode, see Johs. Nielsen, *The Danish-German War 1864* (Tøjhusmuseet, Copenhagen: 1991) and Waldemar Westergaard, *Denmark and Slesvig 1848-1864* (Nyt Nordisk Forlag, Copenhagen: 1946)

12. Cf. Ole Degn, *Denmark, Ribe 1500-1950: Scandinavian Atlas of Historic Towns No.3* (Odense University Press, Odense: 1983). The figures are from the census of 1860.

13. Søren Mørch, *Den Sidste Danmarks-historie* (Gyldendals, Copenhagen: 2006).

of democracy. The National Liberals were in majority over the Conservatives and made sure that the economic interests of the bourgeois estate class prevailed over the traditional aristocracy. Leading liberals such as L.N. Hvidt and Orla Lehmann were architects behind the transition of government. Much later, as governing majority, the same liberals would bear full public responsibility for the military defeat against Germany and, even worse, for the failed peace conferences in London in April and June 1864. Their stubborn refusal to negotiate a new permanent German border is not one of Denmark's finest moments. It unleashed renewed Prussian attacks that led to the occupation of the entire Jutland peninsula; consequently, the new Danish government had to resign already in October and declare unconditional peace. This shameful defeat paved the way for increased conservative sympathies after the war, something that may have affected Riis's political views.

Prior to the war, theNational Liberals had steadily strengthened both their political power and their self-confidence. In 1862 they could celebrate their biggest victory since their entry into the Assembly of the Estates of the Realm in 1843 and the ratified June Constitution in 1849: they had now successfully disempowered the guilds and opened up a free market. The Act of Free Commerce had passed already in 1857, in the midst of the big international market crunch, but with the amendment that it would come into effect after a transition period of five years. In practice this legislative victory meant that as of 1862, letters of commerce could be issued freely without the guilds' approval. Anyone could apply to set up a shop or offer services or goods as they saw profitable. The price of labor dropped dramatically with the increased competition, and it was difficult for many to maintain the income necessary to support a family. Grain prices remained stable while housing shortage and ceaseless urban immigration helped to push up the rents. Traditional social security networks disintegrated or were forced to reorganize. Master artisans raged against abolished quality standards, unfair competition, and defunct insurance and pension systems. As for the carpenter's guild, a newly formed voluntary organization, The Association of Carpenters, protected the masters' financial interests, including health insurance, retirement pensions, and wage negotiations with the better-organized journeymen.[14] But for many, who were not used to the new conditions or unable to afford the new fees, a fall from prosperity into poverty could easily happen overnight. A bad deal or a contract lost to a cheaper competitor could be fatal. On the other hand, new construction and business initiatives were undertaken on a massive scale in the 1850s and 1860s. Aired grievances about the overall economic and political instability in Copenhagen intensified public awareness of the growing needs for poverty control and labor regulation in the years just prior to Riis's arrival. Furthermore, the territorial condition of the enclosed city made the housing situation particularly acute for the working class, to which Jacob Riis obviously belonged for three years.

For military reasons the city of Copenhagen had been walled in like a fortress since at least the 14th century.[15] A time-honored law that prohibited durable constructions outside the city ramparts was only lifted in 1852, despite its proven ineffectiveness during the English bombardment in 1807. Four boroughs quickly sprouted outside the city gates in the 1850s and -60s: North borough, West borough, East borough, and Amager borough with Christianshavn to the south. The late demilitarization of these exterior territories makes Copenhagen an exceptional case in terms of overcrowding. The 145,000 citizens that in 1850 lived inside the walls on an area of about 4 km^2 suffered tremendous deficiencies in space, sanitation, and hygiene. It is telling that the first health and sanitation regulations coincided with the construction of new boroughs. Open street sewers, backyard cesspool privies, rotten drainage pipes, and irregular renovation services were public grievances that slowly found their way into political disputes, then into development drafts, and finally appeared in budget calcu-

14. C. Nyrop, *Kjøbenhavns Tømmerlav: industrihistoriske meddelelser* (Nielsen & Lydiche, Copenhagen: 1887), 217.

15. *København før og nu – og aldrig*, ed. Bramsen (Palle Fogtdal, København: 1991), vol. 11 "Bykort, prospekter og byens historie", 11-19.

lations. In stark contrast to a tourist article on Copenhagen that Riis published in New York in 1881, the city that he had lived in reeked with filth and feces.[16] A cholera epidemic in the summer of 1853 killed nearly 5,000 inhabitants. The Health Commission of Copenhagen [*Sundhedskommissionen*] had been founded in 1851, and it developed quickly into a politically noticeable body that focused particularly on the city's sanitary condition. Its chairman was the young medical doctor Emil Hornemann, a vocal contributor to public health disputes, whose opinions and ideas reverberate in Riis's work.[17] Particularly, firm belief in sanitary model tenements and strong support of governmental rights to condemn bad tenements unite the two reformers.

Doctor Hornemann had completed his medical studies in Paris and London in 1841 with a dissertation on disinfectants. Armed with new socio-medical doctrines, developed at metropolitan institutions abroad, he returned to Copenhagen with demands of improved sewage and water facilities, street cleansing, and housing regulations, which included forced reconstruction, condemnation, and even expropriation.[18] As Riis would discover for himself much later, many of these demands conflicted with powerful private property rights. Hornemann's propositions were largely dismissed by the city council, particularly by liberals such as Jacob C. Jacobsen and L.N. Hvidt, but also by the more conservative Tage Algreen-Ussing.[19] With

16. Jacob Riis, untitled article in *The Traveller*, 1:8, July 2, 1881, unpaginated, in LC, Riis papers, box 12.

17. Emil Hornemann (1810-1888) published several newspaper articles, took active part in commissions and hearings and edited an annual publication on the need for improving hygiene and public health between 1856 until 1888, called *Hygieiniske Meddelelser*. In the late 1860s and early 1870s, Hornemann's work focused on the regulation of labor conditions and the abolishing of child labor. In 1872 children under 10 years old were no longer allowed to work in factories.

18. For more in Danish about Dr. Hornemann, see Dansk Biografisk Leksikon, ed. C.F. Bricka (Gyldendals Boghandels Forlag, Copenhagen: 1894), VIII, 91-97. This is also available at: http://runeberg.org/display.pl?mode=facsimile&work=dbl/8&page=0093. Accessed June 13, 2014. See also Klaus Pedersen, *C.F. Tietgen som Bygherre*, unpublished thesis, (Københavns Universitet, Copenhagen: 1980), 18.

19. Riis described the same conflict in *How the Other Half Lives,* 212: "It is to be remembered," Riis wrote, "that the health officers, in dealing with this subject of dangerous houses, are constantly trenching upon what each landlord considers his private rights, for which he is ready and bound to fight to the last. Nothing short of the strongest pressure will avail to convince him that these individual rights are to be surrendered for the clear benefit of the whole."

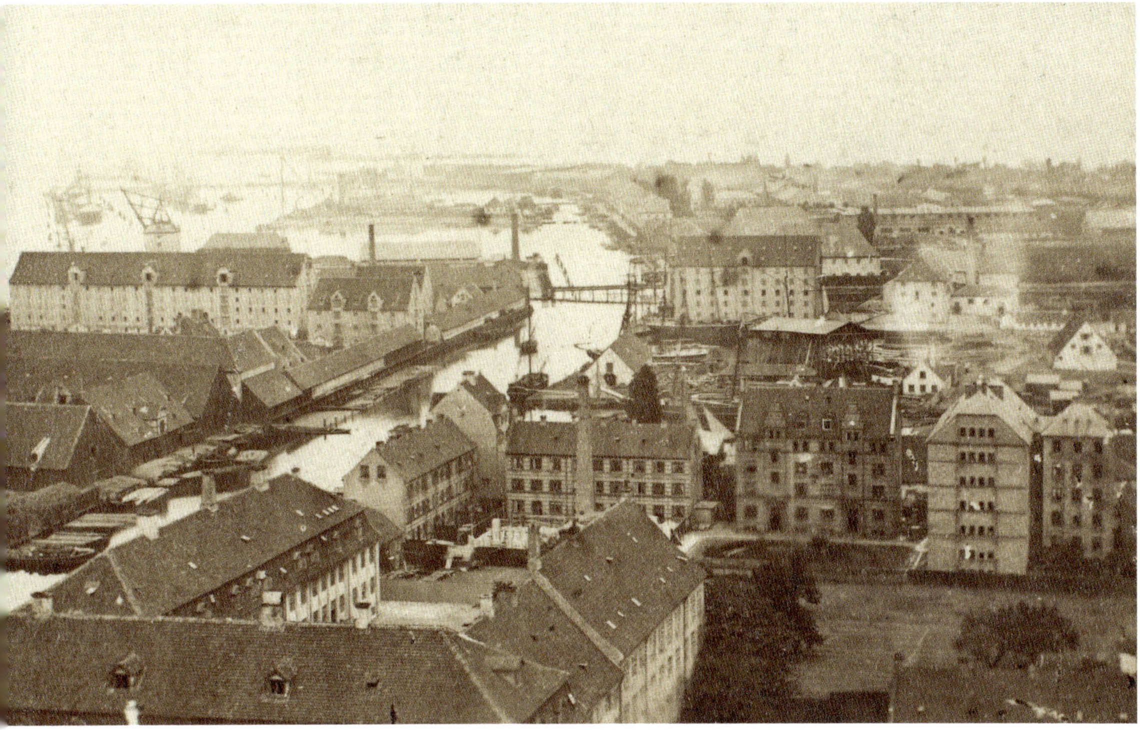

Figure 5. Anonynous photographer, “View over Christianshavn toward Holmen,” n.d. The Danish Royal Library, The Collection of Prints and Photographs.

the 1853 cholera epidemic, political conflicts intensified. In a peaking moment, on August 15, the city council rejected Hornemann's petition that the municipality should help finance new permanent homes for the 250 families who had been evicted from unsanitary apartments during the epidemic. Instead, the decision was made to refurbish and winterize the existing interim barracks. Carl Bille, editor-in-chief of the daily *Dagbladet*, commented bitterly on the decision and presented an argument which can also be found in Riis's later writings:

> [T]he conduct of the city council corresponds closely to the fact that all of its members are landowners. Every move toward an expansion of the city that might lead to a decrease in the value of land, every suggestion of limiting their right to squeeze as much advantage as possible out of their properties to the peril of the common good and public health, the city council will always resist them. And so it will continue until times have improved enough for public elections to provide the common will with a legitimate body of its own, or until the citizens follow the example of the city council and threaten it with "the self-help of despair."[20]

The warning issued between quotation marks refers to a possible uprising of the lower classes (a threat that Riis likewise would often remind of). As the Danish historian Karin Lützen has remarked, the famous trope is here ironically cited from L.N. Hvidt himself, who in 1848 had coined the expression in an address to Denmark's last absolute monarch, king Frederik VII, hinting at a possible bourgeois coup unless he acceded to abandon governing sovereignty.[21]

20. Carl Bille, untitled editorial, *Dagbladet*, Aug 17, 1853, 1. Author's translation.

21. Motivated by the separatist movements in the southern duchies, L.N. Hvidt and Orla Lehman had urged that the Danish regent should replace his cabinet of ministers with "men who might save the honor of Denmark and secure the freedom of the land; we advise Your Majesty not to push the nation to the self-help of despair." Quoted in Karin Lützen, *Byen tæmmes: sociale reformer og velgørenhed i 1800-tallets København* (Hans Reitzel, København: 1998), 37. Author's translation.

Bille's public threat mobilized little political leverage. Instead, it was a second cholera outbreak in 1857 that tipped the political balance. Although no more than a few cases were reported, the mere reappearance of the disease empowered the hygiene cause and shifted substantial political force to the Health Commission. Its growing clout became evident with the passing of the Interim Law of Precautions Against Cholera that same year. All public and private institutions were now forced to comply with their authority until a Health Police had been formed. Nothing became of this Health Police, but parliament introduced a Law of the Procurement of Health Regulations, which demanded that the Ministry of Justice draft health regulations for all major cities in Denmark. On October 26, 1860, the powerful Bill of Health for the City of Copenhagen and its Boroughs was passed. It was frequently used to condemn many of the worst houses; several private tenements and even sublet rooms were effectively subjected to forced reconstruction.

Whereas the corresponding New York Tenement House Code of 1867 was notoriously difficult to enforce, Danish building regulations were met with general compliance. Riis noticed with dismay that New York had to wait until 1895 for a law that effectively allowed the "seizure of buildings that were dangerous to the public health or unfit for human habitation."[22]

In the aftermath of the first cholera epidemic in Copenhagen, model tenements became increasingly attractive as objects of charity investments. Dr. Hornemann, being one of the prime initiators, was in a sense compensated for his rejected petition in 1853 with a council donation of a very attractive parcel, 8¼ acres of land, on *Østre fælled* north of the city. On this lot, he and the Association of Medical Doctors [*Lægeforeningen*] planned the construction of model tenements to be built in four increments: in 1854, 1857, 1867 and 1870 (more on this below). During the 1860s, several similar projects sprang up across the city, for example, *De Classenske Boliger* (1867-1869); *Arbejderforeningen af 1860 til Opførelse af Arbejderboliger*

22. Riis, *The Battle with the Slum*, 116

udenfor Staden (1860-1871); *Arbejderboliger i Nyboder* (1865); *Understøttelsesforeningen paa Christianshavn* (1869-1871); *Arbejdernes Byggeforening ved Burmeister & Wein* (1865-1875).[23] This multitude of model tenements, constructed while Riis resided in the city, offered on the one hand attractive moral investment opportunities for the upper class, and on the other a significant, if perhaps insufficient, number of low-cost, hygienic housing opportunities. Riis's firm belief in "philanthropy and five per cent"[24] can be traced to these successful experiments in Denmark. He often complained that "Model tenement building has not been attempted in New York on anything like as large a scale as in many other great cities, and it is perhaps owing to this, in a measure, that a belief prevails that it cannot succeed here. This is a wrong notion entirely."[25] Alfred White's model tenements in Riverside, Brooklyn, which Riis supported on numerous occasions, had been erected in 1872-77 on principles resembling Danish standards.[26] General opinion maintained that as investments they were unattractive and therefore not nearly efficient enough to battle mass poverty.[27] The fact that model tenements had multiplied in number and proven a viable form of charity in Copenhagen depended of course on the smaller urban size, the scale of available capital, and their acknowledged moral and philanthropic worth among investors.

Jacob Riis in Copenhagen

As an adolescent carpenter's apprentice in Copenhagen, Riis witnessed first hand the turbulent urban dynamics of the period. The political event that first impacted on Riis's professional career was a labor conflict. In March 1866, only weeks prior to his arrival, the carpenter's journeyman organization demanded a general raise of

23. Emil Hornemann, *Danske Arbejderboliger* (Bianco Lunos Bogtrykkeri, København: 1876).
24. Riis, *How the Other Half Lives*, 2.
25. Ibid., 225.
26. Cf. Richard Pluntz, *A History of Housing in New York City* (Columbia University Press, New York: 1990), 88-121.
27. David Ward, *Poverty, Ethnicity, and The American City 1840-1925* (Cambridge University Press, Cambridge: 1989), 64.

wages. The Association of Carpenters responded with an extended application of piece rates and special agreements with those with particular skills. This was not enough for some six hundred journeymen who, on May 19, 1866 laid down their tools. Two weeks later, the conflict had been settled with a general raise of summer wages. One should perhaps take note here of the Danish labor chronicler C. Nyrop, who described these events only two decades after they had taken place. Before socialism had arrived in Denmark—the first pamphlets being published by Louis Pio in 1871—he says disputes were conducted "with a mutual deference from both sides".[28] Jacob Riis was always explicitly skeptical of strike as a means of waging labor disputes, but these ostensibly courteous Danish negotiations were a form of agonism he would often advocate.

Riis's first home in Copenhagen was located in a neighborhood outside the ramparts, on Murergade 15, second floor.[29] This was in the North Borough, which had been erected in great haste in the 1850s. The parcel can be found registered in the name of Mads Larsen, a master carpenter who had owned the lot since 1857.[30] As it was customary at the time for apprentices to board with their masters, there is reason to believe that this was Riis's first employer. Larsen was one of the new kind of entrepreneurs who had set up shop without a guild

28. Nyrop, *Kjøbenhavns Tømmerlav* (Nielsen & Lydiche: 1887), 224. Author's translation. A further detailed account is interesting: "The free constitution of 1849 created no labor class movements; patriotism was at the time the overriding emotion, and the Free Commerce Act of 1862 was not to the liking of most working men. The old, still surviving labor organizations were falling apart; a lot of members left, even among the carpenter journeymen. With some measure of truth it has been said that, 'they instinctively felt there was a reason for the guilds, but to anyone with a sense of professional pride their hegemony was regrettable' This is why the working class was rather volatile when the social movement, which had to come, finally arrived in the early summer of 1871, when L. Pio began publishing the "Socialist Letters". The labor cause became related to social and political agendas, and the rising movement came into its own as it established permanent professional organizations."

29. *Lægdsruller for København 1866*, Q 2026. Provinical Archives of Zealand, Copenhagen.

30. *Maalebrev for parcel 36U6H, Murergade 15*, issued on March 11, 1856 to owner Mads Larsen, May 11, 1857. Copenhagen City Archives, Copenhagen.

membership. His letter of citizenship, which certified him as a master carpenter in the city of Copenhagen, is dated January 30, 1862,[31] only a month after the Act of Free Commerce had been effected as law. Four years later he joined the Association only to leave again in 1869.[32] Larsen had a couple of journeymen in his shop and produced a steady income of about 1500 Rigsdaler each year; his employers received an average of 7.60 Rd a week.[33] In 1875 Larsen gave up the construction business and opened a grocery store with license to sell distilled spirits. Larsen died in 1898, a fact that alone suffices to disqualify him as the master carpenter that Riis refers to in his autobiography and calls "a good friend." *The Making of an American* states that this master's name was in the newspaper obituaries in 1900.[34] His identity may now be revealed as Julius Andreas Blom. Blom signed Riis's certificate of apprenticeship on March 10, 1869, and died on June 18, 1900.[35]

The typewritten manuscript for *The Making of an American*, which is kept in the New York Public Library, contains a deleted passage suggesting that a vacancy had been found for Riis at his master's shop. It remains unclear when and why Riis decided to change his employment, and it is not really that important. What is of interest, however, is the social position that Blom enjoyed and the philanthropic activities undertaken in those circles. Blom would have been a role model to Riis rather than a good friend—what little is known about him fits well with Riis's profile of a model philanthropist, but as a prominent builder he is unlikely to have befriended his apprentices. Blom had had an altogether different career than Mads Larsen. He had risen socially among the artisans of Copenhagen with a seat in the city council between 1849 and 1855, and had meanwhile advanced in the city's voluntary fire department to eventually become its high-

31. *Borgerskabsprotokol 1860-1865*, Copenhagen City Archives, Copenhagen.
32. *Medlemsmatrikler*, Copenhagen Carpenter's Guild Archives, Copenhagen.
33. *Skattebøger for København, 1865, 1866, 1867, 1868, 1869*, Copenhagen City Archives, Copenhagen.
34. Riis, *The Making of an American*, 25-26.
35. *Svendeprøvekommissionen: Indtegninger 1862-1866*, Copenhagen City Archives, Copenhagen.

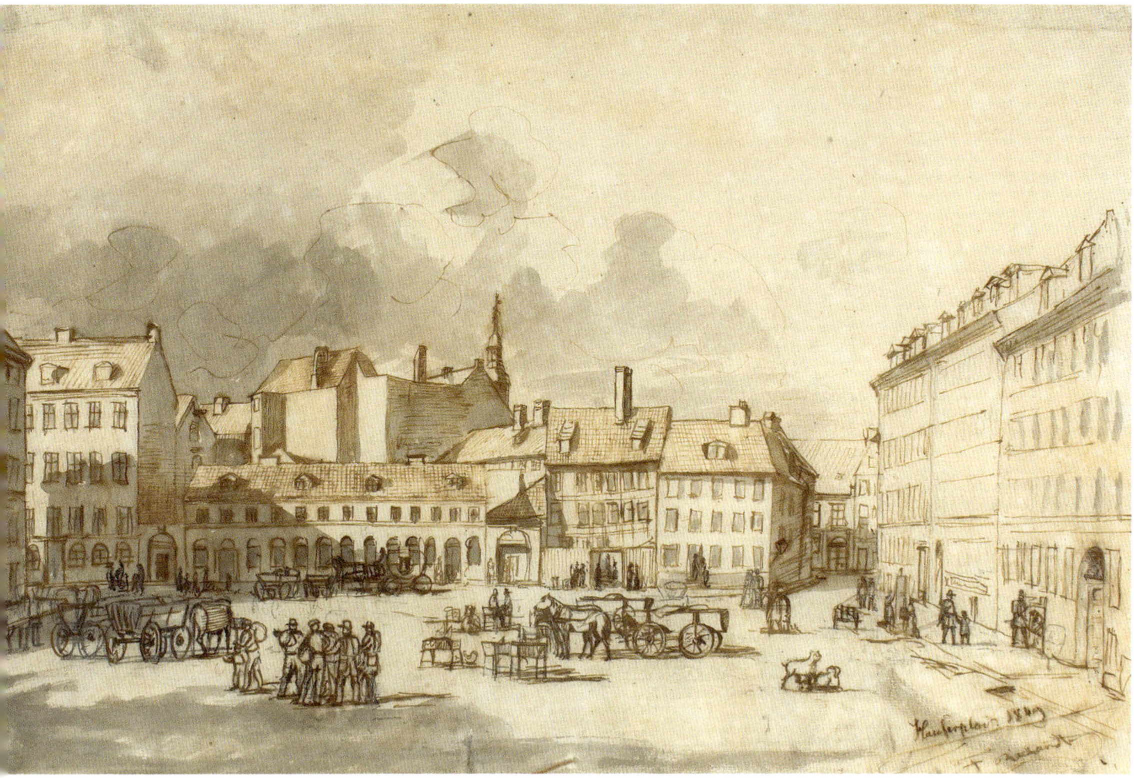

Figure 6. Anonymous artist, "Hauser Plads," 1850s. The Museum of Copenhagen. Jacob Riis's home was in the attic of the second house from the right.

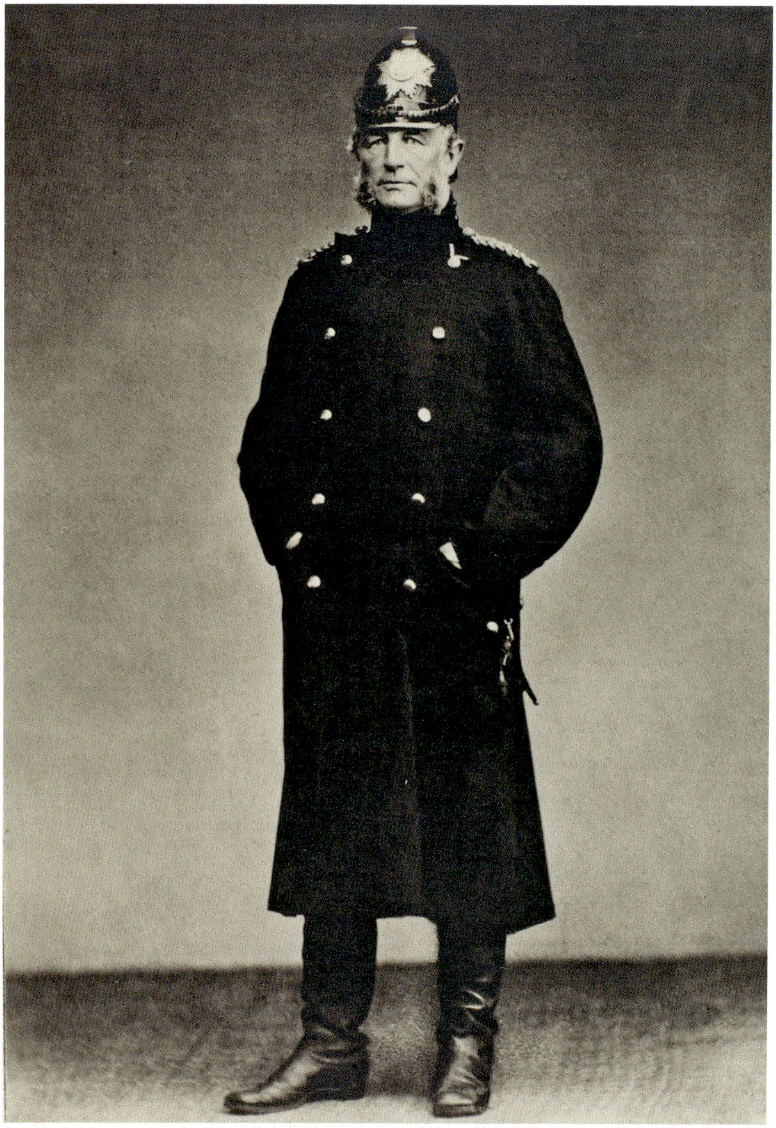

Figure 7. Anonymous photographer, "Julius Andreas Blom," 1868. The Danish Royal Library, The Collection of Prints and Photographs.

est ranking officer. Records of council proceedings reveal only a modest interest in political duties on his part, but he was nonetheless involved in decisions made during the period of hygienic reform, for example regarding street cleaning in 1851 and the rehousing of evicted families after the cholera epidemic in –53.

Philanthropy in the Circles of J.A. Blom

Blom's altruistic career was primarily within the city's fire brigade. He had received his first title as low-rank fire brigade officer in 1833,[36] and he retired with distinction as chief fire brigade officer in 1870. In a joint effort with Harald H. Kayser, Copenhagen's most active builder of model tenements, Blom founded a fire insurance company, *Nye Danske Brandforsikringsselskab*, in January 1864. He was respected for his social skills in the carpenter's guild[37] and was often engaged as board member in various charity organizations, e.g. Copenhagen's Home for the Aged and Sick [*Kjøbenhavn's Sygehjem*]; The Foundation for Elder Master Artisans [*Stiftelsen for gamle Håndværksmestre*]; The Home of Consolation [*Trøstens Bolig*]; The Deaconess Foundation [*Diakonissestiftelsen*], and The Savings Bank of Copenhagen and Surrounding Boroughs [*Sparekassen for Kjøbenhavn og Omegn*].

This latter organization, a philanthropic savings bank, had been founded in 1820 to cater especially to the working class. In its first letter of invitation, addressed to members of the "serving and laboring classes," the bank advised that "the impecunious might in their savings find an aid for unforeseen misfortunes" and, "when plight strikes need neither beg nor turn to unlawful means, but in their own saved assets find rescue from demise."[38] Blom joined the board in 1859 together with the philanthropist and publicist F. Hegel, who later would publish several of the most important works on charity reform,

36. P.B. Grandjean, *Medlemmer af Direktionen for Trøstens Bolig* (Schultz, Copenhagen: 1910), 2.
37. Nyrop, *Kjøbenhavns Tømmerlav*, 220.
38. H.L. Bisgaard, *Sparekassen for Kjøbenhavn og Omegn 1820-1920* (n.p., Copenhagen: 1920), 26-7.

such as Vilhelm Munck's *Om Fattigdommen i Kjøbenhavn* and Johan Christopher Holck's *Godgjørenheden i Kjøbenhavn*. Among Blom's first responsibilities as board member was to amend the statutes to allow a charity fund to be set up from the bank's accumulated surplus.[39] As a first project, the bank financed and managed its own soup kitchen, but experiences were discouraging, wherefore Blom redirected the bank's activities toward sponsorship of already established projects. Among these were orphanages, controlled pawn institutions, and health insurance associations for nurses and apprentices.

In 1865 the bank became the leading investor of a model tenement project. It was initiated by "The Association of 1865 for the Provision of Low-cost Homes for Workers" [*Foreningen af 1865 for tilvejebringelsen af billige Arbejderboliger*]. This association included a number of prominent board members, among whom were the major business tycoon in Denmark, C.F. Tietgen. The project coincided with another model tenement initiative, The Worker's Housing Association [*Arbeidernes Byggeforening*], founded by the workers of the Burmeister & Wain shipyard. The two projects make an interesting comparison. Whereas the latter raised the necessary capital from members' savings (35 øre a week), and then distributed the houses in an ownership raffle (unlucky members got their investments back with interest after ten years), the Association of 1865 solicited capital from wealthy citizens through an emission of shares at 1000 Rdl each and a fixed return rate of 5%. This model was soon copied by other initiatives and corresponds to Riis's famous dictum of "philanthropy and 5 per cent."

Executive responsibility for the Association of 1865 was concentrated to a body of three board members: C.F. Tietgen, H.H. Kayser and Counselor of State, Edvard D. Ehlers. Ehlers had a polytechnical degree and had in 1858 received one of the city's four mayoral titles. Furthermore, he was the son-in-law of the former chairman of the city council, L.N. Hvidt.[40] Blom, representative of the largest individ-

39. Ibid., 220.

40. Pedersen, *C.F. Tietgen som Bygherre*, 28.

ual shareholder with a total of 10 out of 41 shares spread between 25 investors, was not only acquainted with Tietgen, Hvidt, and Kayser, he also knew the second largest shareholder, the aging high-court attorney F.W. Treschow. Blom and Treschow were both in the board of The Home of Consolation, which provided housing for "morally sound, thrifty, and enterprising families" and "worthy old widows."[41] Other shareholders in The Association of 1865 included Jacob C. Jacobsen (founder of Carlsberg breweries) and former member of the city council, O.B. Suhr.

It was a friend of Blom's, Harald H. Kayser, who took the lead as the city's main housing reformer. Kayser had also been a member of the city council and was the chairman of the Industry Association in 1848-51; he had even sided with the National Liberals in the first constitutional assembly. Kayser would later represent Christianshavn in the common house of parliament and he voted for the Free Commerce Act in 1857. In spite of his liberal agenda, Kayser too would have represented a model philanthropist to Riis.

Along with the high-court attorney L.C. Larsen and Jacob C. Jacobsen, Kayser had been appointed on August 8, 1853, to assess the petition from Emil Hornemann's Association of Medical Doctors. The plea was, in detail, "to erect permanent, light, suitable half-timbered houses with planking, for 250 families of the working class, to be occupied before the winter by those who after the eviction from infected houses are living in tents or interim barracks."[42] In their opinion from August 12, Kayser and Larsen said the requested 55,000 Rd would be well spent, given that no empty buildings could be procured to house the evicted families. Jacobsen disagreed, however, arguing that the situation was insufficiently documented and that the plans were unrealistic. The council adjourned for three days after which, as we have seen, a decision was made to improve the existing interim barracks for winter lodging. Several council members voted against it, and only a small majority supported the decision to spend

41. P. Petersen, *Trøstens Bolig 1805-1908* (N. Herdahls Bogtrykkeri, Copenhagen: 1908), 69.

42. *Kjøbehavns Borgerrepræsentations Forhandlinger*, April 6, 1853 (Lars Kleins trykkeri, Copenhagen: 1855), 120.

12,300 Rd on 41 barracks, "a significant sum spent on something that neither fulfills its purpose nor is permanently useful," according to Keyser and Larsen.[43] Undeterred, Hornemann formed a new non-profit organization that, with the financial support from philanthropic investors and land donated from the city, erected 571 model tenement apartments for the working class on *Østre Fælled*, all with a small garden. This new organization, named "The Association of 1853 for the Construction of Sound and Inexpensive Houses for the Unwealthy Classes" [*Foreningen af 1853 for Opførelsen af sunde og billige Boliger for de ubemidlede Klasser*] had in spite of its non-profit status in 1876 accumulated a capital of 750,000 Rd. The chest was used to "buy bad, unhealthy, and unsanitary ramshackle tenements around the city, demolish them and construct good houses for the better part of the working class."[44] Hornemann's two partners in this initiative were F.F. Ulrik, an equally vocal doctor on hygienic reform, and C.E. Fenger, National-Liberal politician, medical doctor, minister, and brother of the priest P.E. Fenger on Christianshavn, the mentor of a certain Vilhelm Munck.

Blom was, in other words, very well established in the city's network of philanthropists. What is more, he was directly involved in some of the model tenement projects that were commonplace in Copenhagen at the time of Riis's arrival. "The Association of 1865" had already in its second year completed three model tenements, each with a total capacity of 148 apartments, known as "Kaysertown." It is quite inconceivable that Riis would not have known about such model tenement projects, or been unfamiliar with the ongoing discussions about them. As "a good friend," or rather, a close admirer of a man like Blom, Riis's knowledge of tenement housing projects, social control, and urban development were both intimate and most likely ideologically slanted toward the conservative. However, noth-

43. Ibid., 126.

44. Quoted in Pedersen, *C.F. Tietgen som Bygherre*, 19fn.

ing of what he knew or saw was at the time articulated in writing or otherwise preserved for posterity. It is curious that only one man from these circles left a trace in Riis's personal notebooks.

Because C.F. Tietgen, the wealthiest industrialist in Copenhagen, was childless, he and his wife Laura rented a stately apartment in the city's most prosperous neighborhood. The flat belonged to Blom's estate on Kronprinsessegade 30, where the owner also lived with his family. The two men were neighbors, friends, and business partners: Blom co-founded The Copenhagen Tram Company [*Kjøbenhavn's Sporvejsselskab*] with Tietgen in 1866, and he is reputed to have worked on projects for The Great Nordic and Tuborg as well. In 1883 the two men were partners in the foundation of the Faxe Limestone Quarry.[45] An unconfirmed source suggests that Blom provided the carpentry for the dome of Tietgen's great monument, the Marble Church, in the early 1890's.[46] In one of Riis's notebooks, kept at the New York Public Library, among things to do and people to see during a trip to Denmark, appears the name C.F. Tietgen.[47] Whatever business Riis may have had with the old philanthropic capitalist is not known, but a passage in *The Making of an American* may give us a clue. While reminiscing on his early hardships in New York, Riis mentions having brought with him from Denmark some letters "to friends of my family in New York who might have helped me, but hunger and want had not conquered my pride. ... I destroyed the letters."[48] Who, one might ask, were these friends in New York: friends of a school teacher's family in Ribe? Riis suggests in an earlier passage that the letters were addressed to the Danish consul and to a Mr. Goodall, "President of the American Banknote Company." Mr. Goodall, says Riis, had once been shipwrecked outside the coast of Jutland, and was rescued by "a friend of my family."[49] This addressee may thus be accounted for, but who might have recommended Riis to the Danish consul?

45. Ole Lange, *Stormogulen* (Copenhagen: Gyldendals, 2006), 411.
46. Wilhelm Wedell-Wedersborg, *Bogen om Ellen og Ferdinand Blom* (Thomas Blom, Pandrup: 2000), 242.
47. "Jacob Riis 301 Mulberry St. New York," undated notesbook in New York Public Library, Jacob Riis Papers, Box 5.
48. Riis, *The Making of an American*, 69.
49. Ibid., 39.

As an agent for shifting American concession holders in the North Atlantic Telegraph project, Tietgen had in the early 1860s made important business connections in New York.[50] When a competing trans-Atlantic cable project managed to establish the connection in 1866, Tietgen's ambitions only grew and he decided to seek telegraph concessions for a Danish-British-Norwegian cable, which in a second phase could develop into a startup hub for a competing global Russian-American cable, parts of which had already been laid down by the North Atlantic Telegraph Co. In the winter of 1869, Tietgen spent three months in New York and Washington trying to secure the necessary legal backing for his project. With the influential Danish Minister of War, W.R. Raasløff, as middleman, Tietgen managed eventually to win support for his plans from Western Union and to secure landing rights in Labrador from the Governor General in Canada, John Young. Raasløff's primary business in America, however, concerned the sales of the Danish West Indies; by his side in 1869 during negotiations with the American administration was of course the Danish consul in New York, Christian T. Christensen.[51] Christensen had fought in the American civil war under general Wool. Subsequently, he had earned the public's confidence and had powerful "ties to several major trade and finance houses in New York,"[52] as a Sunday magazine let Copenhageners know in July 1869. Tietgen knew consul Christensen through Raasløff, and public opinion regarded him "a reliable support to all of our countrymen in need." A visit from Riis would not have been inappropriate, and a letter of recommendation could very well have been signed by Tietgen.

Through Tietgen and Blom's philanthropic connections, Riis is also likely to have heard about two philanthropic clergymen on Christianshavn, Vilhelm Munck and Johan Christopher Holck. Both Kayser and Tietgen were financially involved in their Relief Associa-

50. Lange, *Stormogulen*, 183-88.
51. Frederik Skrubbeltrang, *Vore Gamle Tropekolonier* vol. 3, ed. Brøndsted, (Fremad, Copenhagen: 1967), 88-90.
52. *Illustreret Tidende,* July 4, 1869.

tion of Christianshavn [*Christianshavns Understøttelsesforening*]. Along with some 40 other private citizens and the industrial giant Burmeister & Wain, Kayser and Tietgen may be found listed as original investors in the association's model tenement corporation, founded in October 1868 on similar principles as "The Association of 1865."[53] Kayser bought two 200 Rdl shares in The Corporation for the Construction of Workers' Homes; Tietgen purchased five. Secretary of Corporation was Michael Funch, principal at The Danish Ministry of Finance and member of the Blom family through Julius' wife, Caroline. Its first tenement building was projected and built on Sankt Annægade 59, and in the summer of 1869 the apartments were ready to receive 100 families. Three more tenements were built on Prinsessegade and Dronningensgade in the following years, housing another 100 families. This too was "philanthropy and 5 per cent".

In spite of their success, Riis didn't honor these examples with a word's notice. When in *How the Other Half Lives* he wrote that "enough has been said to show that model tenements can be built successfully and made to pay in New York if the owner will be content with the five or six per cent,"[54] he referred exclusively to American examples: Mr. Alfred White's Riverside Buildings; Miss Ellen Collins's Water Street Tenements; Mr. W. Bayard Cutting of the Improved Dwellings Association, and Mr. Edwin R.A. Seligman of the Tenement-house Building Company. As already noted, Riis had plenty of reasons not to bring experiences from Copenhagen into the light. He knew first-hand about the power of model tenements "to change, gradually but surely, the character of a whole bad block."[55] But he learned soon enough that such projects were not generally supported by philanthropic investors in New York or elsewhere in America. Model tenements were considered inadequate, not least because investment plans offered too modest returns to be attractive. This widespread

53. "Vedtægter for det ved Bestyrelsen for 'Christianshavns Understøttelses-forening' Actieselskab til Opførelsen af Arbeiderboliger paa Christianshavn," in *Sager vedr. Arbejderboligerne*, Christianshavns Understøttelsesforening, (2-67-22). Provincial Archives of Zealand, Copenhagen.

54. Riis, *How the Other Half Lives*, 229.

55. Ibid.

skepticism may be compared to records of social impact in Copenhagen. In 1876, Emil Hornemann summed up a total of 1,859 model tenement apartments in the city. Not counting nine houses erected by Tuborg and a few smaller projects, Hornemann concluded that, "after 25 years of activity, homes have been provided for approx. 4 percent of Copenhagen's total population, or 13 percent of the entire poor working class , which is more than 10 percent of all the families of this class."[56] "I doubt," he added with a hint towards London, "that any other capital can do any better."

It is reasonable to conclude that Riis had closer ties to Copenhagen and its relief projects than what his writings suggest, and that individual philanthropists were within his range of attention. What I suggest, once more, is not that he was personally engaged in their projects at the time that he lived in the city. I have wanted merely to quickly portray the complex social and political situation that Riis lived in and was a part of: a situation of recurring epidemics, lasting labor conflicts, intense political turmoil, and acute and escalating tenement problems, all of which the city elite tried to battle on their own terms. Their engagement proves nothing with regard to Riis's later writings, and my account is certainly not meant to replace the narrated years of hardship. His situation in Copenhagen was not a cause. It provided nothing but a particular orientation toward certain political, moral, and social conflicts, and such an orientation is neither a cause nor an explanation for what would come. Portraying Riis as embedded in a particular situation in Copenhagen is nonetheless historically motivated, because it identifies important elements of the non-linear mutation process. The Copenhagen situation is relevant insofar as its orientation toward certain conflicts and problems would later become operative in a foreign situation, one whose rather stagnant order of charity made it particularly susceptible to be affected and transformed. From this historically non-linear perspective, Riis's migration mutated what Foucault has termed the "composition

56. Hornemann, *Danske Arbejderboliger*, 46.

of forces,"[57] that is to say, the politico-epistemological distribution of powers to say and to display a number of things as truthful accounts of tenement poverty. One foreign composition of forces impacted upon another, local one, changing what was possible to say and to show in New York as the truth of its tenements. Of course, long before Riis entered the public charity scene, a multitude of American institutions and private individuals were already maintaining an intense public debate on tenement poverty and social reform. Within its range of established discursive variations, the tenement problem was already being made understandable in a number of ways. Supporters and opponents of all shades established for the New York charity movement a certain vocabulary, a particular idiom, which identified the causes of poverty, diagnosed its different appearances, and suggested preferable methods of relief. Limited only by its 'composition of forces,' this idiom said all that could be said and presented every piece of evidence that could possibly be procured about tenement poverty. In the next chapter I will attempt to show that Riis then said a number of things that, for American reasons alone, could not yet be argued, proposed, suggested or demanded. What was possible to say actually changed. A different truth was made possible. Much of what would subsequently in New York be presented on the topic of unjust tenement conditions and fought over with great vigor and aplomb—and certainly not by Riis alone—could only follow from this modification of what language could and could not say. A strong and resilient modification allowed other philanthropic subjects, tenement objects, and public media to find their place in a restructured order of knowledge. Thus emerged a new public concern. A distinct mode of debating arose that did not belong to anyone, neither to the active debaters nor to the passive stakeholders in the controversy. Whatever share Riis had in this mutation, whatever it had to do with his deviant and compelling mode of addressing the tenement issues in New York and elsewhere, it must not be understood as an instruc-

57. Foucault, *Discipline and Punish*, 162-169; cf. Foucault, "Nietzsche – genealogy: history," in *The Foucault Reader*, ed. Rabinow (Pantheon, New York, 1984), 84.

tion or an 'import' arriving from Copenhagen. This cannot be emphasized enough. Whatever came across was never, strictly speaking, dispatched or received; if anything, a contraband of sorts pushed a pidgin to the surface with the force of a new public concern: a new argot emerged in response to favorably modified conditions of communicability. To explore these conditions, one should examine Riis's work closely. A diagram of its governing invariants, values, and normative prescriptions would be helpful. Only when its distribution of subjects, objects, performances, and materialities are established, and the veridictional apparatus is fully explored, will it be meaningful to approach the mutation event itself.

CHAPTER 2

A Diagram of Conservative Materialism

Riis often made a point of being both ignorant and disinterested in matters of scholarly writing. Consistency of argument, methodological clarity, even fidelity to logic—all such things mattered less to him than a deep-seated determination to change things. "I don't care two pins for all the social theories that were ever made unless they help to make better the men and women by bettering their lot."[1] Or, "Vigorous optimism, a stout belief in one's fellow man, is better equipment in a campaign for civic virtue than stacks of tracts and arguments, economic and moral."[2]

Despite his expressed disregard for social theory, Riis's own writings demonstrate considerable command of theoretical complexity and coherence. Behind the impressionistic, often kaleidoscopic style of composition and the, for today's readers, offensive excess of racist and sexist remarks, there hides a strangely beautiful and intricate political thought, waiting to be excavated. If it is difficult to recognize at first, it is in part because his approach differs only slightly, but on a fundamental level, from the charity conservatism of mainstream American philanthropy at the time, and in part because Riis adhered to none of the established political ideologies that we are currently most familiar with. His political thinking is no less dissociated from

1. Riis, *The Making of an American*, 68.

2. Riis, *A Ten Year's War* (The Riverside Press, New York: 1900), 257-58. Other examples may be found in *The Battle with the Slum*, cf. 136; 232; 285; 431. There are oral examples too. In July 1901, Riis delivered a speech at the Summer School of Philanthropic Work at the Charity Organization Society, which he opened by saying: "You may set up your theories, science may step in with its most approved plans, but you can't replace the mother's arms." Riis, "Children's Rights," in *New York Weekly Witness*, July 17, 1901, 9.

socialism than from liberalism, which, he said, "thinks the individual's interest superior to the public good," and therefore "is the thing we have got to fight till we die."[3]

Riis's political theory is a pragmatism *avant la lettre* and may be referred to, if a name were to be found, as 'Conservative Materialism.' In this chapter I will try to outline its basic conceptual structure. Most importantly, Riis's Conservative Materialism recognizes three nominal, yet absolute values: the value of a family home, the value of the division of labor, and the value of neighborliness. Moreover, it postulates five principal propositions, which must be politically adopted in order to develop and maintain a healthy working class in an industrialized metropolis. The five propositions are:

- The proposition of materialism: Any development of personal character depends on material surroundings. A favorable material milieu is a precondition for the ability to affirm the three nominal-absolute values.
- The proposition of conscience: Capitalism breeds prosperity, social thrust, and differentiation but also greed and selfishness. Civic conscience must constrain and balance it to avoid detrimental exploitation.
- The proposition of hope: Contrary to appearances, there is hope for all. The will to honesty in every man and woman cannot be extinguished, but it may become inert. It must be nursed and protected at all social levels.
- The proposition of solidarity: All of society has a share in the tenements. Unless changes in attitude are effected among the wealthy classes, nothing will improve in the slums, which is to the further detriment and danger of the middle-class.
- The proposition of aesthetics: The pauper's lack of self-esteem buttresses the inertia of the slums. Beauty and fun are powerful means to raise engagement in one's community and hence to build self-esteem.

3. Riis, *The Battle with the Slum*, 34

These five interlinked propositions, informed by the three absolute yet nominal values, set Jacob Riis's work apart from other American reform and charity programs. In the following, I will delineate each element in some detail and establish both their theoretical and their rhetorical functions. Together, they presented a novel image of the poor as well as a persuasive program for the facilitation of their self-improvement.

Three Absolute and Nominal Values: the Conservative Triangle

"By far the largest part—eighty per cent. at least—of crimes against property and against the person are perpetrated by individuals who have either lost connection with home life, or never had any, or whose *homes had ceased to be sufficiently separate, decent, and desirable to afford what are regarded as ordinary wholesome influences of home and family.*"[4] This opening statement of *How the Other Half Lives* is echoed in the book's conclusion: "Upon any other plan than the assumption that the workman has a just claim to a decent home, and the right to demand it, any scheme for his relief fails."[5] The value of a family home is not up for debate in Riis's writings. The workingman's right to a decent place to live is founded upon the idea that the home and the family are the sources of true citizenship, the origin of democracy, even "the rallying points of civilization."[6] It is not only for the isolated benefit of the individual worker that Riis argues this; it is for the sake of civil society. "How can the one who hardly knows what a home means be expected to have any pride or interest in his home in a larger sense: the city?"[7] As the family is the place for nursing and raising children, the home is also the factory for society to come:

4. Riis, *How the Other Half Lives*, 1. Riis's italics indicate a quotation taken from hearings held before a legislative committee investigating the draft riots of 1863. In the published lecture *The Peril and Preservation of the Home* (Philadelphia: George W. Jacobs, 1903), 19, it is attributed to the secretary of the New York Prison Association.
5. Riis, *How the Other Half Lives*, 212.
6. Riis, *A Ten Year's War*, 33.
7. Riis, *The Battle With the Slum*, 133.

> You cannot rob a child of its childhood, of its home, its play, its freedom from toil and care, and expect to appeal to the grown-up voter's manhood. The children are our to-morrow, and as we mould them to-day so will they deal with us then. Therefore that is not safe. Unsafest of all is any thing or deed that strikes at the home, for from the people's home proceeds citizen virtue, and nowhere else does it live. The slum is the enemy of the home.[8]

The ideal home, one reads elsewhere, is "that of a man with his feet upon the soil and his children growing up there. So, it seems to me, we should have responsible citizenship by the surest road. [...] I ask, above all, the mother who makes the home; I want the mother. Without her, home is but an empty name."[9]

One should note that, to Riis, a family home is not so much a safe haven, a place of tranquility and rest, as it is an engine for social momentum. Children receive fundamental social skills at home. It is the privileged site for rearing civic virtues, because home is where the personal and the social merge under the most intimate and sheltered conditions. Riis insists that the family needs internal privacy and firm structural coherence in order to aggregate externally, home by home, into a civic body capable of political self-governing. Family is the precondition of the possibility to build a democratic republic. For the worse, however, a family home is fragile and easily corrupted. Sensitive to deleterious heritage and to exhausting battles between personal desires, economic limits, and social demands, the home can easily foster resentment, conflict, and neglect. Unless it is duly guarded and its social value properly recognized and affirmed, the family home is where the individual and the common good first come unglued to the detriment of both.

8. Ibid., 7.

9. Riis, *The Peril and Preservation of the Home*, 24-25.

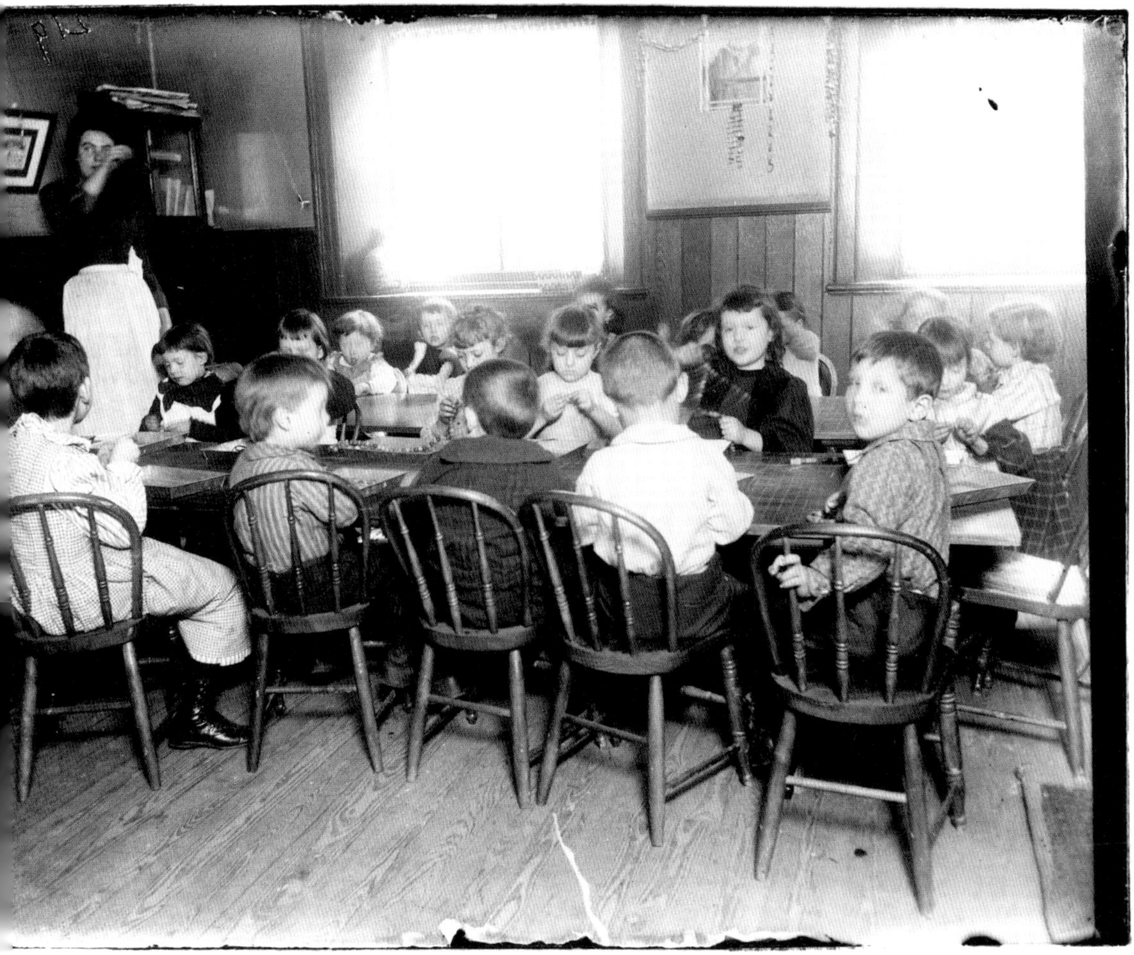

Figure 8. Jacob A. Riis, "King's Daughters Tenement Chapter; Threading Beads in the Kindergarten," [90.13.4.223] ca. 1897. MCNY.

Riis's plea for kindergartens, which intensifies in his later lectures, does not detract from the value of family. Quite the contrary, it supplements the home where a family is deeply corrupted and may work the miracle of restoring it. In an undated speech about kindergartens, Riis described the process:

> A child in tatters, dirty, begrimed [...] went to the kindergarten where the teacher received him, washed him, stitched together his rags and sent him among his fellows, a child like the rest, redeemed from the gutter. He went back to the hovel he called home carrying this silent rebuke on his clean face. Day after day he came and went, and the patience of the teacher did not give out. And at last there came a day, a bright and beautiful day, when he came to school with shining face and elbows mended, and that day the teacher thanked God in her heart for a new miracle wrought in her sight, than which none greater was done when our Savior walked the earth, a miracle wrought as in His day by love and steadfast devotion.[10]

Never suggesting that kindergartens can or should replace the family, Riis praises their value as educational institutions with corrective and therapeutic capacities. Often referring to the German pioneering pedagogue Friedrich Froebel, Riis found that kindergartens above all else should safeguard and stimulate the virtue of play, "through which [a child] begins to recognize moral relations."[11] Playgrounds, small parks, country homes and kindergartens were all part of children's institutions that, while not challenging the absolute value of the home, could work the remedy of families that in fact did not live up to the moral and political demands placed upon them.

10. Riis, "Speech on Kindergartens," in LC, Riis papers, Reel 4.

11. Ibid.

However fundamental, the value of a family home is but one of three absolute values tied into a conservative triangle. What defines the family home is not an intrinsic principle or essence. It is rather defined by external relations: to the division of labor on the one hand and to neighborliness on the other. Without a just division of labor, no home is able to manufacture civic virtues or nurture democratic governance. However, Riis did not understand division of labor in terms of increased specialization or alienating labor conditions, nor did he question capitalist ownership of the means of production, or even class society as such. Labor division in Marxist terms was not the issue. It is true that unrestrained exploitation of labor force in the tenements was for Riis associated with a cruel optimization of profits. But such a lack of restraint reflected rather a moral deficiency, a lack of conscience among employers and landlords, than a detrimental political compliance with capitalist interests. Individual selfishness and greed—not the unregulated methods of capital accumulation—was behind the evidently collapsed division of labor which, in Riis's opinion, invariably eroded the family home. From this perspective, Riis found that socialism, and particularly the labor unions' struggle for influence (or control) over the production apparatus, was as susceptible to selfishness and greed as liberal capitalism.[12] Neither one would be able to affirm the neighborliness and the genuine sense of human brotherhood that Riis identified as the third absolute and nominal value of the triangle.

A definition of labor culled from Riis's mode of reasoning could be formulated as 'the practice of the desire to better oneself.' (Riis's notion of the desire to better oneself—or "will to honesty" is a cornerstone concept that I will return to shortly.) Accordingly, a 'worker' is then no longer defined economically through the commodification of his labor. It follows from this that damaging labor exploitation is no longer coextensive with industrial alienation. The perils

12. "Capital seeks to crush out its neighbor." "But capital has no monopoly of wrong. Labor organizes its multitudes and instantly raises a club to keep out the man who does not think as the next man does, with violence if he will not go willingly." Riis, *The Peril and Preservation of the Home*, 38-40

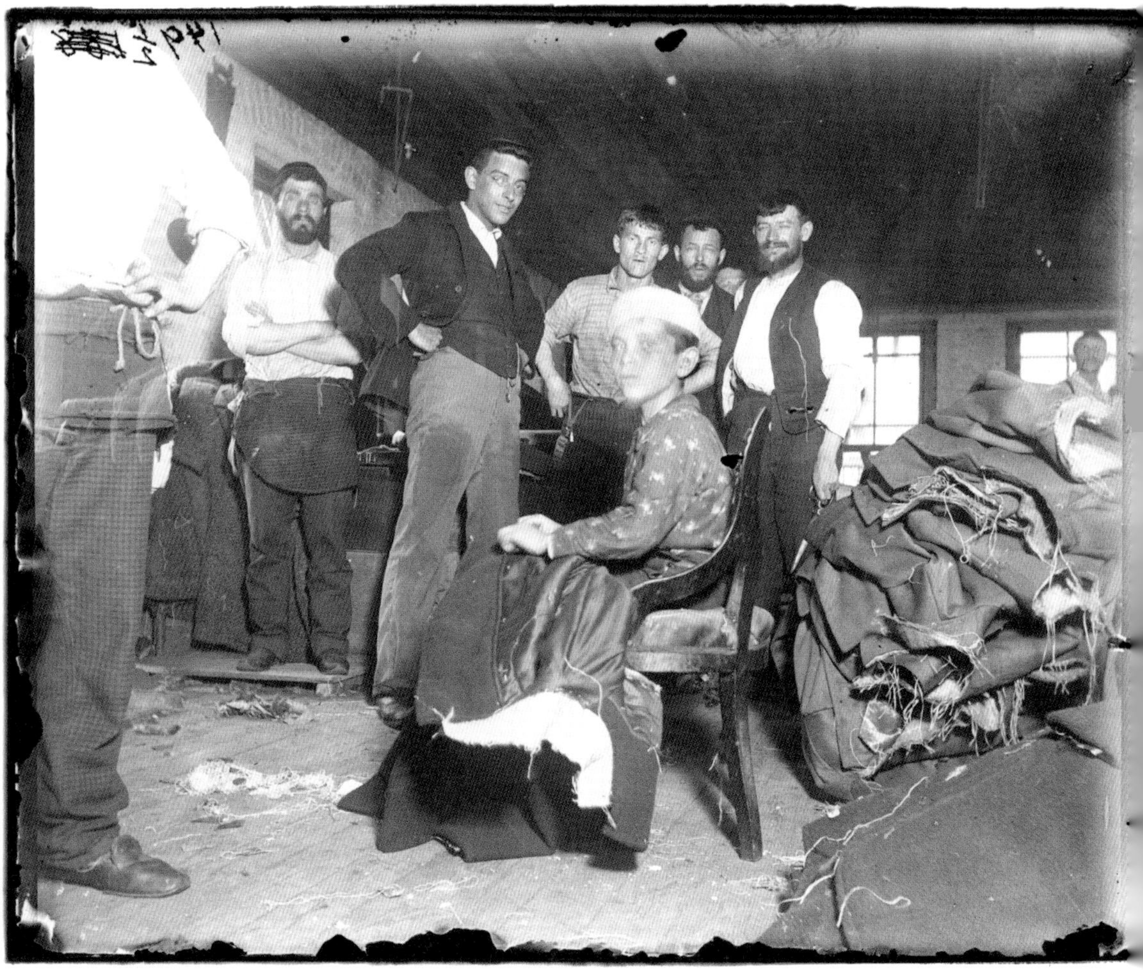

Figure 9. Jacob A. Riis, "12-year old boy at work pulling threads. Had sworn certificate he was 16—owned under crossexamination to being 12. His teeth correspond with that age," [90.13.4.152] ca. 1890. MCNY.

of labor exploitation are rather caused by labor market agents who ignore a worker's natural desire to improve him- or herself through work, and who therefore impair his or her ability to practice this desire. What does all this mean? By relating the value of labor division to the production of civil values in the family home, the *division* of labor becomes for Riis coextensive with the organization of the family. To work is to practice a God-given will in man to improve oneself (which is not restricted to material improvements). However, to different individuals belong different kinds of work, all depending on what best serves a neighbor, a spouse, another individual. When economic circumstances force all household members into wage labor, no one is improving. In a lecture from 1903, Riis put it schematically: "Where men alone work, they earn the support of the family; where men and women work, they together earn the support, with nothing to spare; and where men, women and children work, they do that and no more; so that nothing is gained and everything is lost."[13] (Note, in passing, that this gendered division of labor is not absolute and applies only to healthy working class families; single women who ventured out into the labor market were a widespread public worry, but Riis defended them and celebrated their industriousness.[14]) Riis's first concern was not with individual persons. The family was the atom of social life, and its 'health' depended on the division of labor between its members. Household chores were not considered less valuable than wage labor, and skills at expenditure and consumption were as crucial to any family as honest moneymaking. The universal desire to improve oneself must in every human being find a practical application, but to each in different ways. Not even child labor was an absolute taboo for Riis. Although never preferable to schooling or

13. Riis, *The Peril and Preservation of the Home*, 27-28.

14. Riis devoted a chapter of *How the Other Half Lives* to "The Working Girls of New York", generally praising women at honest labor and opening the analysis by quoting a recent demand for minimum wages, issued by the Working Women's Society: "'It is a known fact that men's wages cannot fall below a certain limit upon which they can exist, but woman's wages have no limit, since the paths of shame are always open to her.'" Riis, *How the Other Half Lives*,183.

to play, many simple tasks were preferable to playing hooky among the vicious temptations of the street. Riis's definition of labor means it cannot, any more than the family home, realize its nominal value through some fulfillment of an intrinsic essence. Affirmation of labor division is only possible under strict ethical observance, and it will only, like proper family homes, be realized through practice. Every man must be given a chance to prosper. As I will try to demonstrate later, the desire to better oneself is an ethical *a priori* precondition of social life. Riis invented a concept of will that is the expression of God's image in every human being. Labor, being the practice of this desire, may only realize its absolute value through affirmation of that divine brotherhood. Hence, the problem of labor exploitation is ethical, not political.

Damaging exploitation results from ethical indifference; particularly, this is easy to observe in the many instances of poor labor conditions which follow directly from individual greed and selfishness. The true enemy in the battle of the slum is an ethical adversary.[15] Therefore, Riis put little trust in judiciary means to fight poverty. In the chapter "What Has Been Done" in *How the Other Half Lives*, he wrote: "The law has done what it could. That was not always a great deal, seldom more than barely sufficient for the moment."[16] Ethical justice is not only valued above the legal system; it towers also above any mere formal moral argument. What actually benefits the fellow man: this is the only guiding principle that may sufficiently warrant political and social action. Industrial capitalists are no natural enemy of this principle—greed alone is. A conscientious market self-regulates according to the ethical justice that coincides with its own interest in long-term sustainable market relations. What Riis, at the end of the day, had to offer the tenement population was ethical-

15. "Problems confront us in the government of our cities; in the legislatures of our states; in the corruption of the franchise; in the growing inequality in the distribution of wealth. They all have one tap-root: human selfishness and greed, parading under many masks, but always to the same purpose. That is the enemy." Riis, "The Harlan Iowa Speech," 1907, 5. LC, Riis Papers, Reel 4.

16. Riis, *How the Other Half Lives*, 211.

ly astute businessmen: "The remedy that shall be an effective answer to the coming appeal for justice must proceed from the public conscience. Neither legislation nor charity can cover the ground. The greed of capital that wrought the evil must itself undo it."[17]

This remarkable suggestion from the introduction to *How the Other Half Lives* is an "appeal to the consciences of men."[18] It is an appeal that was further underscored in the Introduction to *A Ten Years War*, which chronicled the awakening of civic conscience during half a century of reform. The call for conscientiousness emerged from the third corner of the conservative triangle, from the idea of the Brother, or Neighbor. Riis would say: "We are brothers whether we own it or not, and when the brotherhood is denied in Mulberry Street we shall look vainly for the virtue of good citizenship on Fifth Avenue."[19] A notion of absolute neighborliness was crucial for rendering the gap to The Other Half as a reconcilable error committed not out of sheer evil but out of remediable greed and selfishness.[20] "Neighbors!" Riis once saluted a lecture audience, "Brothers, if we but knew it, made of the same clay, in the same mould, though we forgot it when we moved apart. The mould is the image of God that is in us all. It is that which makes us kin – the differences we dwell upon, petty, imaginary."[21] On another occasion he explicated schematically: "It is the Fatherhood of God that is warrant for the Brotherhood of man, nothing else."[22]

17. Ibid., 2.
18. Riis, *The Peril and Preservation of the Home*, 43.
19. Riis, *The Battle with the Slum*, 6. A similar phrase is found in *The Peril and Preservation of the Home*, 41.
20. Riis's final book was titled *Neighbors*. The Macmillan Company published it in 1914 as a collection of short stories subtitled, "Life Stories of The Other Half." This was the last in a series of collections of semi-fictional short stories from the tenements; *Children of the Tenements* and *Out of Mulberry Street* had both been published in 1897. These short stories are a substantial part of Riis's literary production but have been largely neglected by scholars. More than any other genre of Riis's oeuvre, these stories establish a parallelism between the religious realm and the political. A stunning 18% of them are Christmas stories, which offered Riis an opportunity to let divine benevolence override worldly justice. Many other stories deal with the limited worldly capacity to assess human qualities.
21. Riis, "My Neighbor," in LC, Riis Papers, reel 4; See also Riis, "Jesus my Savior and Redeemer," in LC, Riis Papers, Reel 4.
22. Riis, "Big Brother Movement," in LC, Riis Papers, Reel 3.

Just like the division of labor and the family home, the concept of neighborliness was defined through external relations. The fact that the realization of Christianity is dependent on social structure is perhaps the most provocative and stunningly materialist aspect of his work. Although a transcendental God warrants the *being* of a human brotherhood, any *actual recognition* of God depends upon human affairs. Neighborliness is therefore not warranted by inward faith in God, for, says Riis: "How shall the love of God be understood by those who have been nurtured in sight only of the greed of man?"[23] There is sometimes no "inner man" to appeal to, only a frail, possibly corrupt desire to better oneself. "You cannot expect to find an inner man to appeal to in the worst tenement-house surroundings. You must first put the man where he can respect himself."[24] That place is first and foremost the family home underpinned by a proper division of labor. Ethical development depends on the material nurturing of self-respect, a long and slow process through which an individual recognizes being part of the human Brotherhood. This recognition depends, in other words, upon social acknowledgement and material conditions. Where home and labor division are not corrupted, beauty and joy will nurture conscientious self-respect and promote neighborliness over selfishness. By contrast, the street and the saloon may not teach anyone how to respect the self or the rights of others. So on the one hand, conscience and neighborliness rest upon the universal image of God in all human beings. But on the other, conscience is actualized only through social and aesthetic acts of self-respect. Christianity as such is thus never wholly actualized: wherever it works, it affirms the processes that realize the proposition of conscience over greed.

The capitalism of modern civilization "implies a race, to get ahead."[25] In this race, some people inevitably fall behind while others advance. It is a neighbor's joy and duty to help a brother in need, but some who fall far enough behind do not appeal to the fellowship, nor do they arouse pity or even a desire to help. Riis leans

23. Riis, *How the Other Half Lives*, 2.
24. Ibid., 209.
25. Riis, *A Ten Year's War*, 1.

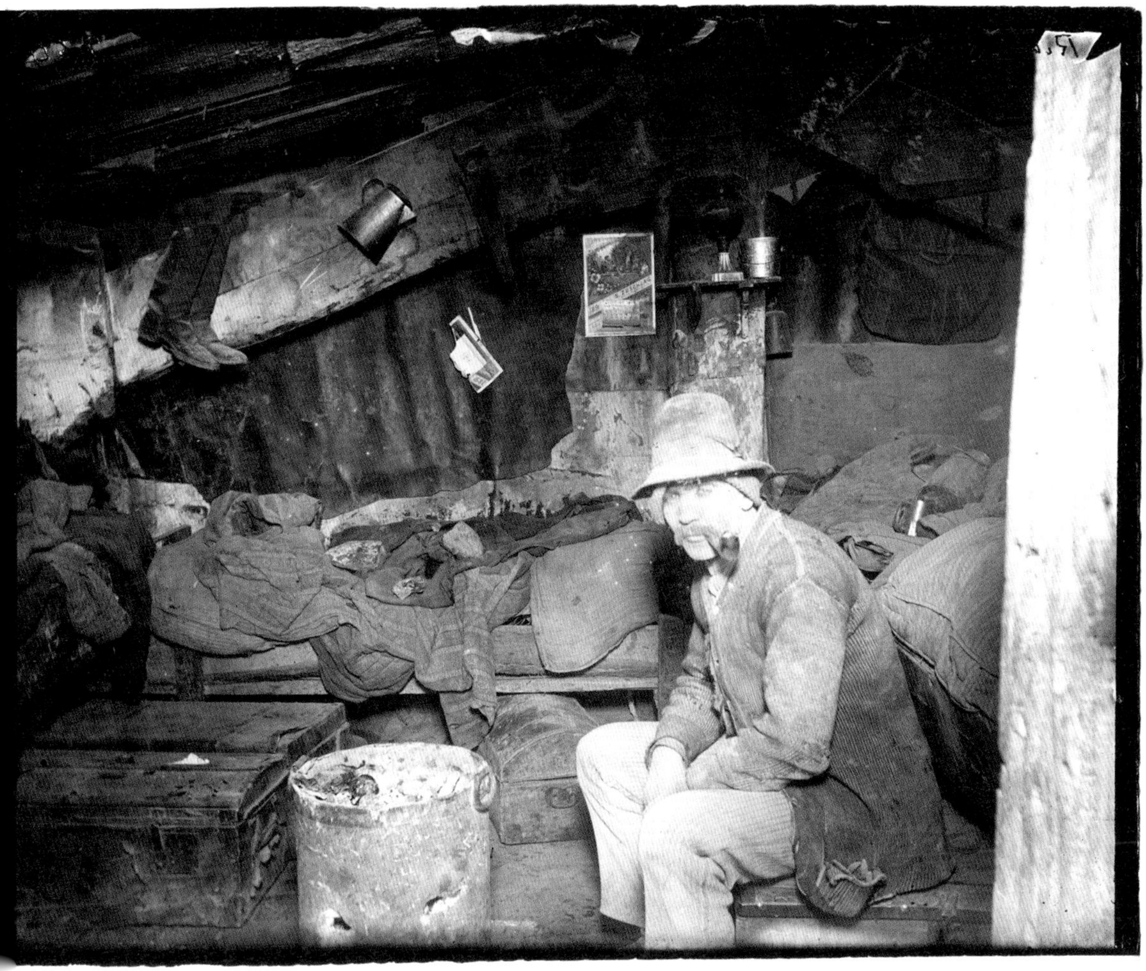

Figure 10. Jacob A. Riis, “Under the Dump at Rivington St.” or “An Italian Home Under the Dump,” [90.13.4.208] ca. 1890. MCNY.

heavily upon this well-known distinction between the worthy poor and the unworthy. The unworthy poor represented in America a category of people whom philanthropists considered personally responsible for their own destitution. They were usually regarded as hopeless. These were for example the decrepit alcoholics, the prostitutes, the murderous gang members or the homeless paupers, to all appearances unable to fend for themselves and their families. One of Riis's most unique measures was to include them in the reform agenda by introducing a new line of distinction. It separated two forms of assessment. Firstly—and entirely conventionally—Riis recognized an economic assessment of the poor and categorized their response to civilizing demands as worthy or not. But secondly, he also recognized a 'deeper,' religiously conditioned assessment that discarded unworthiness as such. A far more fundamental mode of judgment, this one allowed him to measure the recovery potentials of a damaged will to honesty on a nonfinite scale of inextinguishable hope. Although tramps and vagrants are "hopeless" when assessed socio-economically, they are still our neighbors. There is an ethical, indeed even a metaphysical obligation to assist anyone who has fallen behind, but the means of assistance must be suited to the task. Restoring the self-respect of a thief or a thug is a different task than helping to restore a tramp's eroded will to honesty. Assistance aimed at these two groups must work from different economies: one where investments could justifiably demand a return in terms of actual improvement, the other where an asymmetrical expenditure may only affirm hope and trust in divine providence.

The family home, the division of labor, and neighborliness are interconnected, absolute nominal values. It means one of them may not be denied without creating a negative effect upon the other two. Conversely, affirmation of one strengthens the others, and so, any act that affirms any single one of an individual's values will, according to Riis, help to improve life conditions in the slums. Their systematic negation has instead prevented the rise of effective self-help and rather deepened the hold of destitution. In this way, the three values underpin Riis's consistency of argument while guiding his views on various reform initiatives. As the three values also affect each other, Riis could heuristically suggest a set of political propositions in view of strengthening the relations between them. These propositions provide the most adequate description of what The Other Half really is.

Materialism

The first proposition maintains that a certain material standard is necessary for sustaining an individual's will to self-improvement. This will is absolutely central to Riis's argument. It exists *a priori* in all human beings as the image of God, that is, as an expression of God's perfection. (The will is not a value; it is rather a variable predicate of being human.) Riis mentions it only a few times, always very briefly and in a rush. He says, "The true line to be drawn between pauperism and honest poverty is the clothes-line. With it begins the effort to be clean that is the first and the best evidence of a desire to be honest."[26] Elsewhere in *How the Other Half Lives*, he declares that, "the poorest immigrant comes here with the purpose and ambition to better himself and, given half a chance, might be reasonably expected to make the most of it."[27] In *The Battle with the Slum* one may read: "The parents of 95.23 per cent [of the slum population] had come over the sea, to better themselves, it may be assumed."[28] And similarly in *The Children of the Poor:* "The working of the strong instinct to better themselves, that brought the crowds here, forces layer after layer of this population up to make room for the new crowds coming in at the bottom."[29] To the extent that Riis's work implied a turn in American philanthropy, it was conceived with this will to honesty that is always there, in every human being, albeit sensitive and corruptible, not least from material insufficiencies.

Riis did not himself use the term materialism. If it is employed here, it is in a restricted sense. Materialism refers to Riis's conviction

26. Riis, *How the Other Half Lives*, 41.
27. Ibid., 20, 218.
28. Riis., *The Battle With the Slum*, 176.
29. Riis, *The Children of the Poor*, 2fn.

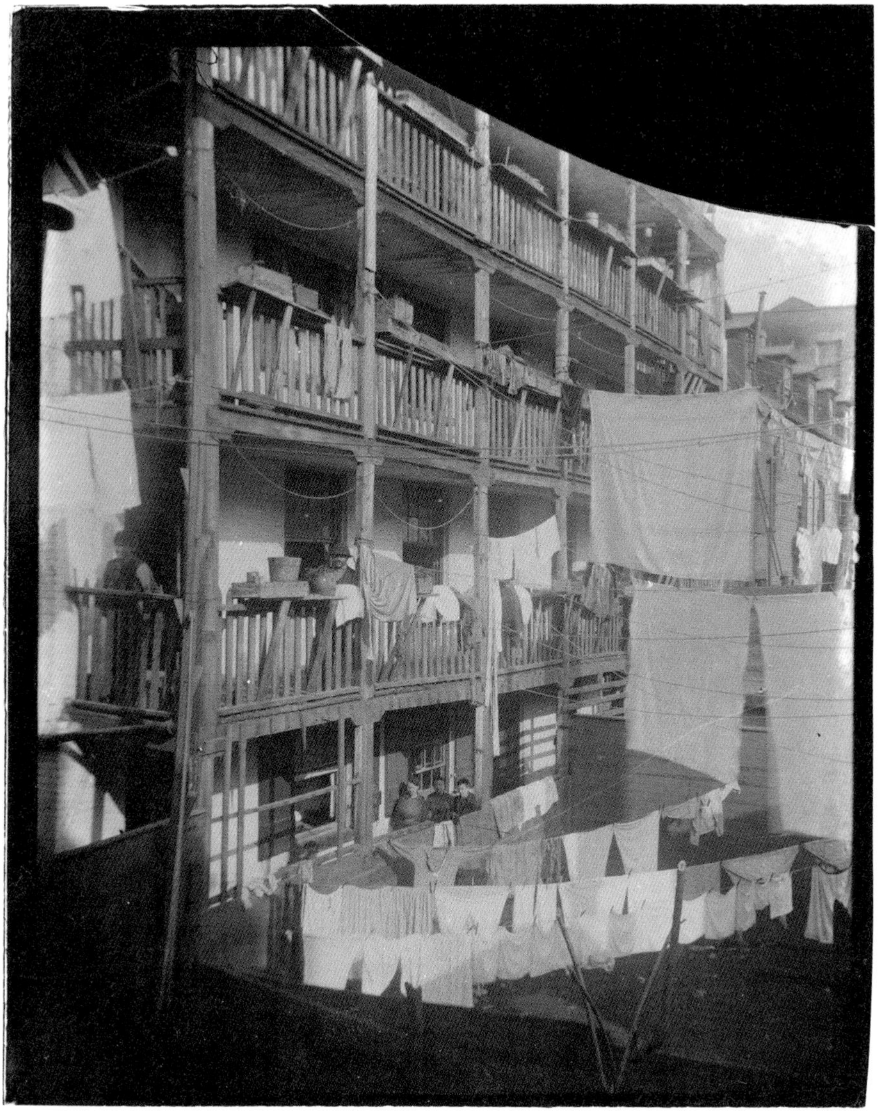

Figure 11. Jacob A. Riis, "Rear Tenement in Roosevelt Street," [90.13.4.100] ca. 1890. MCNY.

that effective social reform must begin with physical circumstances rather than spiritual principles: "Always remember that human souls live in bodies. If you want to reach the soul, you must reckon with the man in the body; or your preaching will be vain."[30] And elsewhere: "Soap and water are as powerful moral agents in their particular field as preaching."[31] The materialist perspective prioritizes physical improvements (both domestically and publically), but any such primacy must be understood in the light of the relational logic of the conservative triangle. Material improvements are effective only in rapport with acts that affirm neighborliness; in and of themselves they may instead rather limit the extent of possible social development.[32]

> I recall the discomfiture of a certain well-known philanthropist, since deceased, whose heart beat responsive to other suffering than that of human kind. He was a large owner of tenement property and once undertook to fit out his houses with stationary tubs, sanitary plumbing, wood-closets, and all the latest improvements. He introduced his rough tenants to all this magnificence without taking the precaution of providing a competent housekeeper, to see that the new acquaintances got on together. He felt that his tenants ought to be grateful for the interest he took in them. They were. They found the boards in the wood-closets fine kindling wood, while the pipes and faucets were as good as cash at the junk shop. In three months the owner had to remove what was left of his improvements. The pipes were cut and the houses running full of water, the stationary tubs were put to all sorts of uses except washing, and of the wood-closets not a trace remained. The philanthropist was ever after a firm believer in the total depravity of tenement-house people."[33]

30. Riis, *The Peril and Preservation of the Home*, 96.
31. Riis, *How the Other Half Lives*, 156.
32. Ibid, 218: "The moral effect is as great as the improvement of their physical health."
33. Ibid., 214.

If tenement dwellers are "shiftless, destructive, and stupid, in a word, what the tenements have made them,"[34] samaritan landlords have little choice but to take their stupidity into account and make sure to establish a working relationship between the tenants and their improved facilities—either by hiring a "competent agent on the premises"[35] or, preferably, by moving in together with the tenants. The neighborly act carried out by such settlement projects (owner-in-residence tenements) seemed to effectively strengthen the tenants' desire to improve, thus affirming also the real values of family home and division of labor. However, Riis is unequivocal: without material and physical improvements, neither teaching nor preaching will help to improve the tenements.

Conscience

It has already been suggested that Riis's materialism is paradoxically both at odds with and concomitant with Protestant morality. It contains a very unconventional interpretation of moral precepts. In contrast with for example Charles Loring Brace's claim that "Christianity is the highest education of character,"[36] Riis poses twice in *How the Other Half Lives* the uncomfortable question: "How shall the love of God be understood by those who have been nurtured in sight only of the greed of man?"[37] In context, this question suggests that although every human being is created in the image of God, the ability to receive God is nonetheless relative to the dealings of mankind, dealings in which basic material conditions of life cannot be denied to others. Riis says elsewhere that, "As a man does in dealing with his brother so it is the way of God that his children shall reap."[38] In other words, moral sin begets ethical sin: every single act of promiscuity,

34. Ibid., 214.
35. Ibid., 218.
36. Charles Loring Brace, *The Dangerous Classes of New York and Twenty Years' Work Among Them* (Wynkoop and Hallenbeck, New York: 1872), 23.
37. Riis, *How the Other Half Lives,* 2 and 209.
38. Riis, *Battle with the Slum*, 8.

social indifference, intemperance, and lawlessness breed selfishness and greed—the two cardinal vices for Riis. Worse still, they lessen the ability to recognize the kinship of one's neighbor. Vice, in all its autocatalytic forms, is that which obstructs the actualization of neighborliness. Whether it is the poor themselves that are greedy and selfish or, as is equally often the case, it is the upper and middle classes that protect their short-sighted interests in the slums, it makes little difference. Egotism and greed violate the only moral law that Riis's pragmatism allows: "When common sense and the golden rule obtain among men as a rule of practice, it will be over." Thus the introduction to *The Battle with the Slum,* and similarly in *The Making of an American*: "not alms, but the golden rule is what is needed in the tenements of the poor."[39]

The golden rule with its reciprocal morality is for Riis the *general* preceptive expression of neighborliness. Ecumenically universal, it affirms the human will to honesty across religious, social, and ethnic divides. The *individual* preceptive expression of neighborliness, however, is conscience. It is very likely that Riis appropriated this notion of conscience from his friend and associate, Felix Adler, but in Riis's architecture it bears upon a slightly different conceptual structure. For Riis, conscience belongs to an individual body. It is affirmed only through exterior interaction, as implied by the neighborliness that it expresses. Earlier it was suggested that conscience is actualized through various social and aesthetic acts of self-respect. If it is a neighbor's duty to help a brother in need, then one can say that the ability to recognize that duty as a joy is conscience. Capitalism, which in Riis's view is an indispensable engine of modern civic development, must be counterbalanced by the joys of affirming self-respect in the fellow man so as not to foster greed and selfishness. Again: "The coming appeal to justice must proceed from the public conscience. [...] The greed of capital that wrought the evil must itself undo it. Homes must be built for the working masses by those who

39. Riis, *The Making of an American,* 288-89.

employ their labor. [...] 'Philanthropy and five per cent.' is the penance exacted." In other words, conscience as a countermeasure to greed is intrinsic to healthy capitalism. Conscience is then not merely imparted onto the individual from church or from other moral custodians: it is recognized as a business interest. Neighborly relations are important for long-term political stability and hence also for long-term market stability. Conscience directs business toward continual moderate prosperity spreading across social classes. Capitalism has an interest in protecting itself against greedy tenement speculation and exploitative labor conditions that bring political imbalances to the market. Bad business is essentially bad for business. However, for a conservative businessman there can be no *duty* to act conscientiously. It would be absurd to appeal to duty, when conscience is rather what conditions the ability to recognize duty. The appeal to conscience is not based on duty, then, but on the golden rule, which Riis considers an axiom of the Christian republic.

Regarding everyday applications of the golden rule, Riis observes that its ethical tenacity requires a mutually shared minimum of will to honesty among all involved. Later, twentieth century invocations against the golden rule, such as Karl Popper's variation: "do unto others, wherever possible, as they want to be done by,"[40] would be firmly rejected by Riis, who remarked that "it is a dreary old truth that those who would fight for the poor must fight the poor to do it."[41] To correctly understand Riis on this issue, it is important to note that the golden rule only works as a moral imperative for someone who cares about his own improvement. Anyone who does not—a pauper, a tramp—is more likely to contaminate his surroundings than to affirm conscience. As an exception, Riis noticed a category of unworthy poor who actually cared for their material improvement: thieves and robbers. The golden rule applies to them, and that allows a new important distinction to be drawn between two forms of unworthiness: the unworthy idler and the unworthy criminal.

40. Karl Popper, *The Open Society and its Enemies*, vol. 2 (Princeton University Press, Princeton: 1966), 386.

41. Riis, *How the Other Half Lives*, 214.

"The thief is infinitely easier to deal with than the pauper, because the very fact of him being a thief presupposes some bottom to the man. Granted that it is bad, there is still something, a possible handle by which to catch him. To the pauper there is none. He is as hopeless as his own poverty."[42] Hopelessness means here that unlike the criminal, the tramp is excluded from the civilizing process, which, as we noted earlier, depends on the development of individual conscience. The Christian imperative to nevertheless recognize the tramp as a lost brother gives him a dangerous political position.[43] Just like the thief, the tramp thinks that "the world owes him a living," but it means something different to him, which is also what makes him so dangerous. Unlike the criminal, a tramp does not steal, rob, or kill for his own benefit. The tramp does not 'make a living' at all but lives from society's scraps, leftovers, and remains. Subsisting on that which is without value, tramps reside on society's fringes, without reciprocal relations to its norms and demands. Idleness is more dangerous to society than crime, because inertia cannot be reproached with moral justice, i.e. it cannot be corrected on the basis of the golden rule without the correcting actions becoming a reward in the idler's favor. Whereas a criminal's unlawful and selfish will to improve may be curbed into civil self-respect, the tramp, "the lazy man, is entitled only to be locked up. Only the other day," Riis told a seminar audience in Philadelphia in 1903, "I was invited to come up to Boston and join in a discussion of the tramp problem before a distinguished body there; I refused. I do not think there is a tramp problem which hard labor behind strong bars cannot solve."[44]

Assessed socio-economically, as Riis does here, a pauper's comatose will to honesty can only be awakened by forced labor. Labor, we

42. Ibid., 192; see also 153 for a definition of the golden rule as 'the handle' with which to grasp the petty criminals among the Street Arabs.

43. Walter Benjamin understood this dangerous position when he assumed for his own historical method the assemblage techniques of the rag-picker. See Walter Benjamin, *The Arcades Project* (Belknap/Harvard University Press, Cambridge, Mass.: 1999), 460 [N1a,8]. See also Irving Wohlfarth, "Et Cetera? The Historian as Chiffonier," in *New German Critique* Nr. 39, 1986, 143-168.

44. Riis, *The Peril and Preservation of the Home*, 108.

recall, is the practice of the will to honesty; it is that, says Riis, through which neighborly laws are taught and apprehended. "Through toil and tears we may make out the lesson which sums up all the commandments."[45] A curious theme this one: the danger of the tramp amounts to his non-reciprocal relation to society, which immunizes him from the demand to work and, worse, from his own desire to prosper, which in turn threatens to halt the forward-racing system of civilization. Such a bare protest can only be met with forced labor. But what is thus implied? "Hard labor behind strong bars"—does it not evoke a strange and terrible legitimacy of violence, a legitimacy of religious-political violence for morality's sake—violence, as it were, 'before' morality? Violence for the sake of morality, or perhaps, as condition for morality, for it to take effect on the idler: at the very least, Riis's refusal to recognize the problem measures the magnitude of the threat posed by paupers and tramps. It marks a limit to the socio-economic mode of justice.

Hope

Directly in line with the concept of conscience is a notion of inextinguishable hope. Hope, not as a general optimism, but as a radical supplement to the socio-economic assessment of worthiness. Riis often told the story about "The Kid" to illustrate the meaning of this hope, and it is worth quoting extensively.

> There was something underneath the hard crust that spoke to me of the image of God in which he was made. Overlaid by the slum, yes! hopelessly, you might have said; but there is no such thing as hopelessness where the spark of His life is. It may be quickened at any moment. It needs only the right thing to strike fire, and that is always the same. Love of God? He did not know what that was. He would have spurned you away

45. Riis, *The Battle With the Slum*, 8.

> had you come to him with it on your lips. But when, five minutes later, a cry of horror went up on Broadway where a little toddler baby had strayed out upon the railroad track with a runaway car not ten feet from the child, who crowed with delight at the sound of the bell which the gripman banged, sick with dread, for he was powerless to stay the car—when we stood frozen to stone with the despairing shriek of that mother whom men were holding back while they turned their heads away, with her cries ringing the doom of the child in our ears—where there seemed no help on earth, then it was the "Kid" who tore himself from the grasp of the policemen and sprang upon the car-track, saving the child at the risk of his own life a thousand times over! Thief, tough, indexed and hung in the Rogues Gallery; started fair for the jail and the gallows, he did not hesitate. The peril of the innocent child struck the spark, and the image came out which the slum had tried to smother. Plenty there are who, had they seen him, would not have thought it was there; for there are other things beside the slum that bury it deep, too deep for the spark to struggle through: too good a time, overindulgence, selfishness, for instance.[46]

To excavate Riis's notion of hope from this anecdote one might ask: is it conceivable that a tramp might substitute for the Kid as the story's protagonist? The answer must be negative. A tramp cannot act like the Kid and still be a tramp; if a tramp nevertheless did he would not have been a tramp to begin with. But being a tough—and one of the worst—only makes the Kid's unexpected heroism more meaningful. Common socio-economic assessment has already dismissed him ("plenty ... would not have thought [the image] was there"); but with unselfish bravery, The Kid proves such inferences unjustified. Riis's articulation of hope ("something ... spoke to me ...") voices by contrast a religious assessment, one that does not reckon with the convention-

46. Riis, *The Peril and Preservation of the Home*, 176-78.

al category of unworthiness, to which the criminal still belongs. The pious judgment is, however, sensitive to the applicability of the golden rule. The Kid acts out of conscience. His action can be measured by the golden rule; hence one can also nurture the processes of self-respect and reform him into a civil citizen.

Yet two formulations in this story also speak of hope for the tramp: "the image of God in which he was made," and "there is no such thing as hopelessness where the spark of His life is." Do they not indicate a door ajar also for the idle pauper? Earlier in the lecture Riis argued that, "a pigsty, in time, will make a pig even of man who is created in the image of God."[47] If Riis is understood literally, saying that a man may actually become an animal, an un-human, as the divine spark in him dies, then the pauper is truly hopeless. But he might also be read metaphorically, suggesting that the man may become *like* a pig, to all appearances hopelessly lost, but nevertheless always still human. The latter alternative is suggested in *The Children of the Poor*: "There was no trace there of a striving for better things—the tenement had stamped that out—nothing but darkness and filth and misery. From this hole, Giuseppe had come to the school a mass of rags, but with that jovial gleam in his brown eyes that made him an instant favorite with the teachers as well as with the boys."[48] Later on, while confirming that "even the dock-rat is human,"[49] Riis again expresses inextinguishable hope for all. But he never *declares* it. To the contrary, he says about the opium addicts in Chinatown: "From any other dissipation than that for which Chinatown stands there is recovery; for the victims of any other vice, hope. For these there is neither hope nor

47. Ibid., 76.
48. Riis, *The Children of the Poor*, 29. This story is inconclusive with regards to the matters discussed, as Giuseppe was never himself described as hopeless. Nor, however, is it said that he managed to elude the bad influences of his home environment.
49. Ibid., 257. Whether Riis with the term 'dock-rat' refers to the gangs of the piers or the tramps (Cf. his photographs "Dockrats in Quarters" (1887) and "A Child of the Dump" (1892)) remains unclear, which also renders this statement inconclusive. It is relevant here to notice Bonnie Yochelson's remarks about Riis's "ambivalent attitude toward the dump's inhabitants." in *Rediscovering Jacob Riis,* 181-184.
50. Riis, *How the Other Half Lives*, 83.

recovery—nothing but death—moral, mental, and physical death."[50] Now, one should note that the victims of the pipe are not the heathen Chinese: "The Chinaman", says Riis, flaunting tactical ignorance about the drug, "smokes opium as Caucasians smoke to'oacco, and apparently with little worse effect upon himself." Western souls, however, who shipwreck on the bunks are soon irrecoverably lost to the drug, but however lethal it may be to body, mind and morality, the addict is never wholly lost to the redeemer. Riis seems mindful not to speak of spiritual death, which, on another occasion, he made sure to explicitly exclude as such from mortal judgment.[51]

This playing with ambiguity may offer a clue, for the playing is not itself ambiguous. There is a pattern: whenever the most hopeless enter the stage, Riis's diction deflects. It sometimes expresses hope for an analogous example; it may contradict the present sense of hopelessness later on; it may invoke some neutralizing category; it occasionally turns description into a sinister joke, a metaphor, or an exaggeration which is later revoked. Such tropes express an uncertainty in language, a limit to communicable knowledge and judgment which plays an important role in Riis's political theory. His idiomatic deflections articulate a political position that is unreachable by conceptual understanding or intuition, but is all the more replete with rhetorical powers; it is a position unobtainable even through that "something" that spoke to Riis about the image of God in the Kid. Nonetheless, it belongs to the production of truth: it belongs as an epistemological state of pure potentiality. There is hope that cannot be verbalized or articulated in any other way than as a 'perhaps', hope communicated

50. Riis, *How the Other Half Lives*, 83.

51. Riis, "The Other Half and How They Live: Story in Pictures. Address by Jacob A. Riis, Washington Convention of Christians at Work" in *The Temple Builder: Christian Work and Methods in All the World*, 2:5, 1895. About the mass burials of the deprived on Potter's Field, Riis said: "Then the trench is closed, and the long sad story with it, as far as we can reach, or as our human knowledge goes. If, dear friends, it were really the end, if there were nothing beyond it, what would be the use of my standing here and talking to you? Thank God! There is something even beyond the Potter's Field, for out of its gloom and misery, and desolation, there comes a voice of our Saviour ..."

through the possibility and impossibility of communicated judgment. Judgment left undecided. Riis's appeal for the most hopeless rests upon this undecidability. It is never properly articulated; it holds no promise of reward; it provides no supporting community, no method, and no lasting improvements. It works under the aegis of a different economy.

Hope was thus expressed in three ways. First, as hope for the worthy poor, those who most certainly were able to lift themselves out of poverty with a little assistance. This sense of hope encouraged the common philanthropist, it found expression in the statutes of voluntary organizations, in labor market reforms, improved tenement standards, settlement house projects and other reasonable means to counter the increasing growth of unworthy poor. This hope was not for the criminals, idlers, and tramps. For them there was hope that *supplemented* certainty; hope against all odds, in the face of experience, reason, expectation. The second order of hope was extended to criminals, to ragamuffins and to the gangs; it also included the Chinese who shut themselves away from society, the greedy landlords, the moneylenders, and the selfish industrialists who exploited the tenement labor force. Riis offered no certain prognosis about their will to honesty, but hope demands action and action means transgressing the dominant socio-economic assessment in view of what Riis calls Christian Citizenship.[52] Third, there was perhaps hope also for those unreachable by Christian Citizenship, those who were beyond the golden rule, lost to the opium dens, the mental asylums, and the brothels. The third order of hope is expressed as pure potentiality, only perhaps communicable, possible-impossible, between the lines or under the breath of Christian Citizenship statutes. The potentiality of redemption, which has a share in any religious charity, can only express itself in unconditional terms. It does not name a redeemed soul or a method or criteria of selection; it merely states that anyone—unconditionally anyone—*can be* recognized, is recognizable due to the image of God within. This 'anyone' is nothing but another word for 'neighbor.'

52. Riis, "The Battle With the Slum," in LC, Riis papers, Reel 3, p. 8.

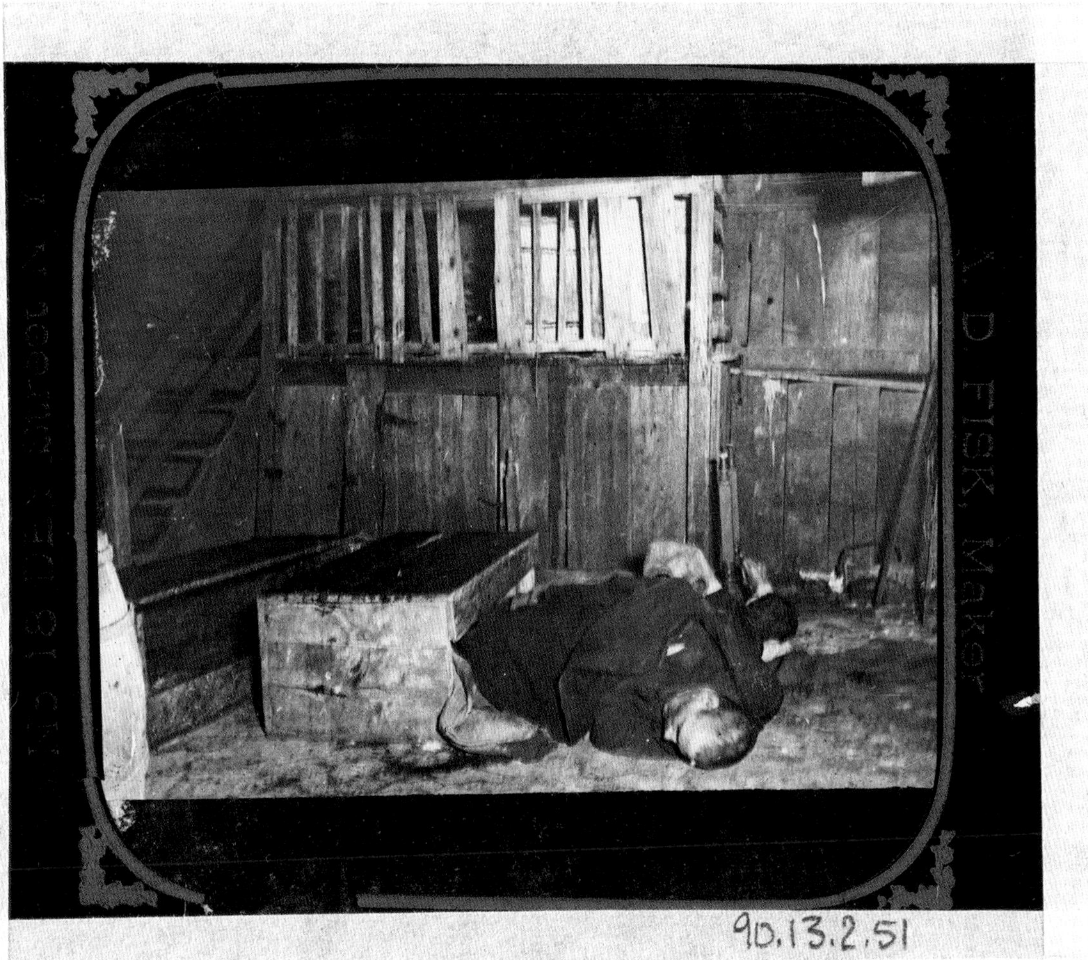

Figure 12. Jacob A. Riis, "Tramp's Nest in Baxter Street Yard, Flashlight at 2 am," [90.13.2.51] ca. 1890. MCNY.

Solidarity

The fourth proposition follows immediately from the conscientious concept of hope. A neighbor is no more a pious principle than a recognizable Other. Wealthy citizens must not separate their economic and political interests from the ethical demands posed by recognizable neighbors. Systematic disregard for this simple imperative was to Riis what lay behind the real danger that slums posed to the rest of society:

> The danger to society comes not from the poverty of the tenements, but from the ill-spent wealth that reared them, that it might earn a usurious interest from a class from which "nothing else was expected." That was the broad foundation laid down, and the edifice built upon it corresponds to the groundwork. That this is well understood on the "unsafe" side of the line that separates the rich from the poor, much better than by those who have all the advantages of discriminating education, is good cause for disquietude.[53]

If mercantile interests are not ethically restrained, that is, persuaded into prioritizing long-term targets of prosperity, they are bound to exploit all available capital, labor force, and material assets in view of maximizing immediate return for owners. Eventually, Riis feared, such unrestricted exploitation will divide the population, erode public spirit, and remove the patriotic foundation of democratic governance. "When the slum flourishes unchallenged in the cities, their wharves may, indeed, be busy, their treasure-houses filled,—wealth and want go so together,—but patriotism among their people is dead."[54] In the absence of a public spirit to bridge class divisions, a vicious and powerful foe is given free rein: public acceptance of slum tenements. This bourgeois consent, says Riis, has produced two mu-

53. Riis, *How the Other Half Lives*, 209. 54. Riis., *The Battle with the Slum*, 7.

tually contradictory reactions: one which calls for increased police or even military intervention against the rioting masses, and another, which denies any grounds for social urgency.[55] Riis's proposition of solidarity opposes both. Against the latter it maintains that the plight must be recognized as an acute social disorder; against the former it calls for civil neighborliness as the ruling principle of all commercial and political affairs, thereby to reduce class tensions, prevent rioting, and restrain the use of police force. Solidarity stakes out a new direction; out of ubiquitous political responsibility and individual civil agency grows a utopian city without slum neighborhoods:

> The millennium of municipal politics, when there shall be no slum to fight, will come when every citizen does his whole duty as a citizen, not before. As long as he "despises politics," and deputizes another to do it for him, whether that other wears the stamp of a Croker or of a Platt,—it matters little which,—we shall have the slum, and be put periodically to the trouble and the shame of draining it in the public sight. A citizen's duty is one thing that cannot be farmed out safely; and the slum is not limited by the rookeries of Mulberry or Ludlow streets. It has long roots that feed on the selfishness and dullness of Fifth Avenue quite as greedily as on the squalor of the Sixth Ward. The two are not nearly so far apart as they look.[56]

The proposition of solidarity demands action, a demand to which Riis at first responds on behalf of his audience by assuming passive responsibility for the slums: "the crime was ours," he declares in *The Battle with the Slum*, "not his,"[57] referring to a disheartened father who sent his twelve-year-old son to work, to keep the boy off the streets. The fault was "ours," he says elsewhere, not because of what we did, but because of what we have failed to do. "The half that was on top cared little for the struggles, and less for the fate of those who were

55. Riis, *How the Other Half Lives,* 207.
56. Riis, *The Battle with the Slum*, 414.
57. Ibid., 44.

underneath, so long as it was able to hold them there and keep its own seat."[58] Today, Riis says, we must recognize the other and act in solidarity with society as such: "We shall win his fight and our own together: they are one."[59] Society owns its slums, wherefore slums can only be defeated through social conduct, and thus through an alteration of society as such. Philanthropy must also address the ways of the middle and upper classes: charity must become self-reflective. During a lecture at Columbia Anniversary Chapel on Nov. 9, 1909, Riis opened his address by asking his audience: "What do you owe?" The lecture notes read:

> Citizenship: not merely a vote, you owe it to the Republic, that, in as far as it's your life, you will help us to the realization that we—all its people, go up or down together, that we are the republic—and that so long as any part of its people live in ignorance, in squalor, in miens, it does not realize its ideal of making men better become free. The subsequent question: "How can you pay the debt you owe?" was answered with a rhetorical pun and a practical proposal: "Must you go down into the slum to do it? No— if you have to go down, don't. But how can you go OVER to it? Well, for one thing, there are sixty settlements in NY.[60]

One goes down into the slums out of duty, or curiosity, but one crosses the divide out of honesty—in recognition of Christian Citizenship. The 'debt' that every citizen owes to the republic is repaid only through acts of neighborliness. These are not based on duty, but on conscience and hope. The proposition of solidarity does not therefore only target wealthy slumlords and the like.[61] It addresses itself directly to those among Riis's audiences who might take action in a burst of indignation and with little consideration for how their way of life already sustains the tenement system.

58. Riis, *How the Other Half Lives,* 1.
59. Riis, *The Battle with the Slum*, 84.
60. Riis, untitled lecture, New York Public Library, Jacob A. Riis papers, Box 6, file "Lecture Notes 1909."
61. Riis, *How the Other Half Lives*, 218.

Aesthetics

Like many other American reformists, Riis emphasized the importance of raising self-esteem, or self-respect among the tenement dwellers. American literary critic Keith Gandall has recognized a close relationship in Riis's writings between this argument for self-esteem and the importance attached to flair, fun, and color. The fifth proposition, the proposition of aesthetics, acknowledges beauty and even frivolity as factors in raising self-esteem. "Discipline has not been abandoned," Gandall observes, "but neither has it simply been dressed up and made palatable: it has been supplemented. A politics is being developed that recognizes the power of surfaces."[62] The most famous example is perhaps Riis's unorthodox idea of advertising in *The Tribune* for flowers to be redistributed in the tenements. Less noticed is the circumstance that Riis, in *How the Other Half Lives*, explicitly appreciates the sordid Italian quarters above the clean and tidy Chinatown: the latter has "little of [the Italians'] outdoor stir and life, none of its gaily-colored rags or picturesque filth and poverty."[63] Also largely unnoticed is Riis's opening speech for the William S. Seward Park on Oct. 17, 1903, which promised not only fresh air and healthy sunlight, but also "lots of fun."[64]

Although Riis at times himself subscribed to the more conventional association between 'too good a time, overindulgence and selfishness,' the positive values that he assigned to amusement and pleasure cannot be ignored. Beauty, ornament, spectacle and laughter, he said, are parts of the prosperous side of life, also for the poor, and particularly for their children. A cartoonist once portrayed a lecturing Riis hammering out the four maxims of Roosevelt, of which the second

62. Keith Gandall, *The Virtues of the Vicious: Jacob Riis, Stephen Crane, and the Spectacle of the Slum* (Oxford University Press, New York: 1997), 118.
63. Riis, *How the Other Half Lives*, 77.
64. *Formal Opening of William Seward Park (Canal Street and East Broadway) Including Pavillion, Gymnasium and Playground upon the completion of the Pavillion Saturday, Oct. 17, 1903, two o'clock pm*, in New York Public Library,, Jacob A. Riis papers, Box 6, file "Lecture Notes."

one reads : "Have All the Fun That Is Yours by Right; All That is Honestly and Decently Yours." It does not misrepresent him. Riis could suddenly exclaim: "This is what is the matter with three-fourths of the well-meant schemes of reform—that they leave the fun out. It is the yeast that makes things light and fit. A man who cannot laugh is a dangerous man anywhere. It is the optimists, the joyous souls, who make the world go round."[65] He even stood up for entirely irrational pleasures in the face of reason and sound judgment:

> We were debating, some good women who knew [Molly] and I, how best to make a merry Christmas for her, and my material mind hung upon clothes and boots and rubbers, for it was in Chicago. But the vision of her soul was a pair of red shoes! Her heart craved them; aye, brethren, and she got them. Not for all the gold in the Treasury would I have trodden it under in pork and beans, smothered it in—no, not in rubber boots, though the mud in the city by the lake be both deep and black. They were the window, those red shoes, through which her little captive soul looked out and yearned for the beauty of God's great world.[66]

Underneath the thick varnish of sentimentality, the views expressed here were not uncontroversial. Any soft-heartedness with the poor man's affection for tinsel and spangle could be conceived as misguided leniency. Relevant to note, then, are the techniques that Riis employed to make his defense for beauty a part of the mainstream progressive reform agenda: how, as Gandall might have said, he managed to politicize the ornament. What I have termed the fifth proposition of aesthetics is based on two observations. The first one detects a very banal and effective technique: Riis's lectures are often described by reviewers as being unexpectedly funny, with strings of wit-

65. "Four Maxims of Theodor Roosevelt, Who, Jacob Riis Says 'Is Wholly and Utterly Without Ambition for Himself,'" in *The World*, April 21, 1907. LC, Riis Papers, Box 16. See also Riis, "Paolo's Awakening," in *Children of the Tenements* (Macmillan, New York: 1903), 63-77.

66. Riis, *The Making of an American,* 438.

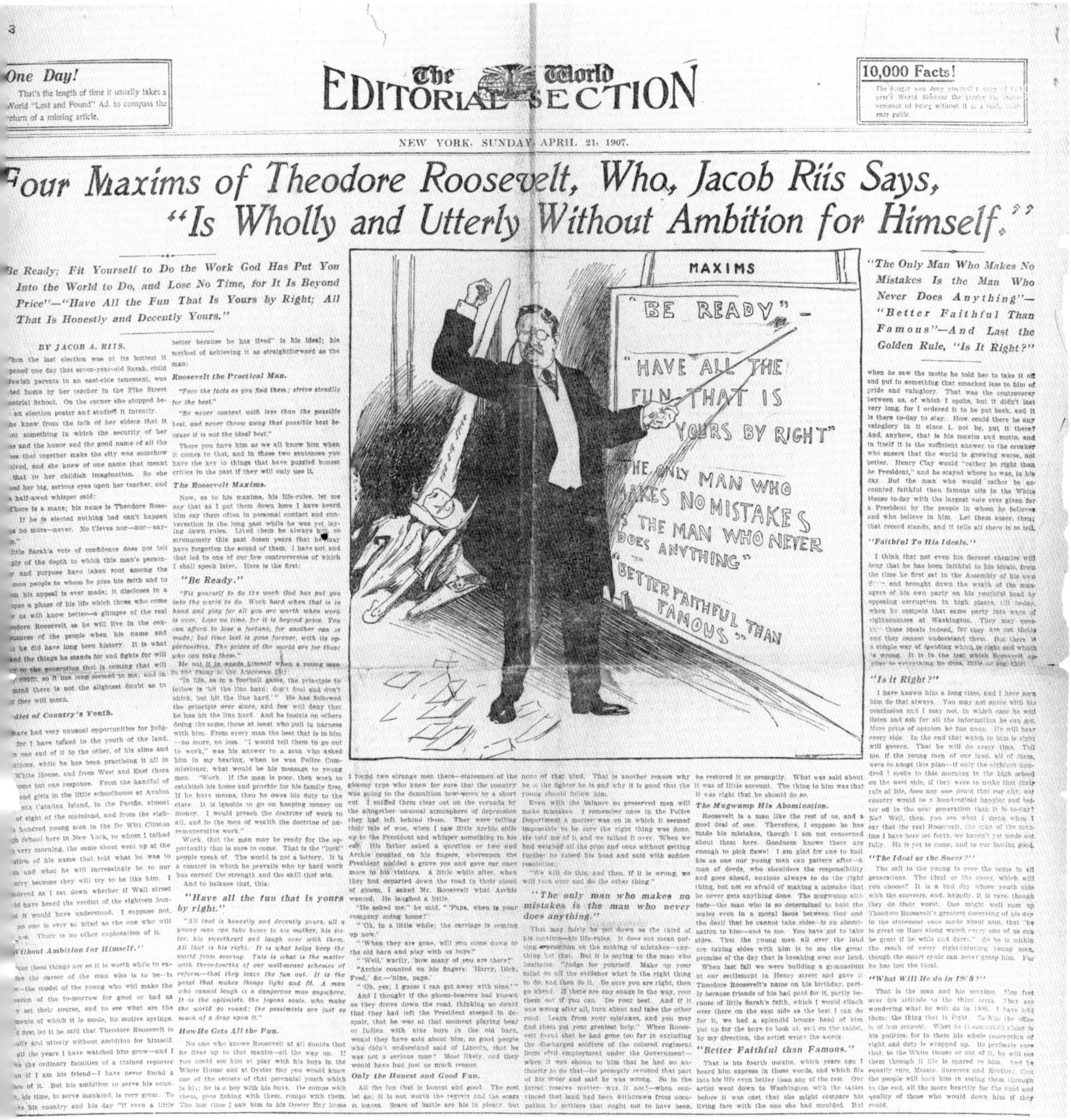

One Day!

That's the length of time it usually takes a World "Lost and Found" Ad. to compass the return of a missing article.

The World EDITORIAL SECTION

10,000 Facts!

NEW YORK, SUNDAY, APRIL 21, 1907.

Four Maxims of Theodore Roosevelt, Who, Jacob Riis Says, "Is Wholly and Utterly Without Ambition for Himself."

"Be Ready; Fit Yourself to Do the Work God Has Put You Into the World to Do, and Lose No Time, for It Is Beyond Price"—"Have All the Fun That Is Yours by Right; All That Is Honestly and Decently Yours."

BY JACOB A. RIIS.

"The Only Man Who Makes No Mistakes Is the Man Who Never Does Anything"—"Better Faithful Than Famous"—And Last the Golden Rule, "Is It Right?"

Figure 13. Anonymous cartoonist, "Jacob Riis Lecturing," from *The World*, April 21, 1907. Library of Congress.

ty and charming puns marbled in-between the horribly gruesome displays. The motley eloquence for which he was soon repudiated will be analyzed in chapter 4, but the entertaining aspect of his performance deserves mention already here. Riis's sharp alacrities were much appreciated, as were his talents for melodrama and pathos, which often provoked laughter, tears, and applause. In one sense, this frequent recourse to humor underscored his general defense of fun and beauty: the audience's high spirits made it difficult to maintain the common bar on entertainment for the poor. (On a different register, one finds that humor undermined the conventional charity protocol and opened up the discourse for new variations.)

The second observation is that Riis's defense of beauty hinged on a remarkable conceptual kinship. "The instinct of beauty," as Riis calls it, was as essential to human nature as the will to honesty, and seems furthermore to have shared its divine origins: "if any one doubt that this child of common clay have in him the instinct of beauty, of love for the ideal of which his life has no embodiment, let him put the matter to the test."[67] Obviously, the phrase "of common clay" and the homonymic "love for the ideal" point toward a divine instinct of beauty in every human being. One might even suggest that the instinct of beauty shares a conceptual position with the will to honesty. It means not that they are synonymous, but that their entirely different functions apply from the same central position. Aesthetic pleasures are critical, in more than one sense. A thief's misguided self-respect may grow strong from an affirmation of beauty, but such an affirmation is not therefore congruous with a stronger will to honesty. To affirm beauty is a necessary risk—perhaps the greatest risk of all. This is because the instinct of beauty is not a value and has no ethical compass. The pursuit of beauty may just as well lead to greater egotism and social exploitation. The instinct of beauty is morally non-discretionary; it amounts to a sheer sensuous attraction to the world. It should not be reined in, however, to service any well-meaning re-

67. Riis, *How the Other Half Lives*, 138.

form program: the red shoes show that clearly. But along with the "picturesque filth" of the Italian quarters, the red shoes also suggest something else: the structural parallelism between the instinct of beauty and the will to honesty. Philanthropy must necessarily face the risk that this implies. Any attempt to avoid confronting the risk, to curb the instinct of beauty or smother it under reason, duty or usefulness will eventually, but inevitably, ruin the family home and any honest practice of a desire to improve oneself.

The precarious position of the instinct of beauty sheds light on the concept of self-respect. Whereas the instinct of beauty and the will to honesty are both granted to every human being from birth, self-respect is built up piecemeal from experience. Self-respect is responsive to fun, spectacle, and color and it may be in accordance with the will to honesty, but only if it does not contradict one's neighborly relations. A man who prefers the joys of the saloon, or a mother who spends her household money on fancy clothes, do not represent a conscientious affirmation of beauty, but rather a selfish one, insofar as their actions negate the value of the family home. One the other hand, their actions may strengthen an isolated and egotistical self-respect. In principle, neighborly misconduct weakens the will to honesty and public conscience as well, but it does not diminish the instinct of beauty. It misguides the instinct insofar as beauty celebrates the image of oneself at the expense of others. Hence its danger: unconscientious indulgence may nurture self-respect while fostering selfishness and greed. The stereotypical prostitute, drunkard, and idler may experience self-respect when some dubious advantage is gained, but disconnected from a will to honesty self-respect rather corrupts society and must be discontinued, possibly through forced labor. Children build conscientious self-respect from the joys of play and

68. Riis, *The Battle with the Slum*, 373. "Through their play,—the meeting usually starts with a romp,—in quarters where there is not too much elbow-room, the boys learn the first lesson of respecting each others' rights." See also 233: "What the boy's play has to do with building character, Froebel has told us. Through it, he showed us, the child 'first perceives moral relations'."

from the beauty of their imagination.[68] Men and women develop true self-respect through honest labor, from their home in the republic, and with the joys, fandangle, and laughter of community life. It is imperative to secure the conditions for such development.

Two observations then, regarding the proposition of aesthetics: on the one hand it provided a performative asset during Riis's lectures, on the other it introduced an instinct of beauty that complicated the meaning of self-respect. I will later examine how Riis used aesthetics in the former sense with great refinement and risk in order to deterritorialize charity, that is, to appropriate and harness some of the chaos of the tenements for the production of truth, thereby keeping charity from closing in on itself and protecting itself against mutating forces.

To conclude this preliminary exposition of Conservative Materialism: five propositions and three values have been identified as a kind of political basis, providing a coming republic with its founding ethical structure. As a rhetorical device, this diagram proved particularly powerful. Firstly, it allowed Riis to address the same plea to all classes, and to include all social bodies in his political diagnosis without reducing the individual to a class representative. The menial laborer and his boarders, the teacher's family, the businessman and his clients, the rabbi and his congregation: all were part of the great republican body, subjects of the same neighborly brotherhood; but at the same time, each was subject to particular conditions that sized up the powers of every individual to interact affirmingly with neighbors. Secondly, and this has not been sufficiently touched upon yet, the conservative triangle was also constructed as a performative rhetorical instrument of veridiction. I will later examine how the nominal values of the conservative triangle were affected by social dynamics. Social bodies were diagnosed according to strengths and weaknesses fluctuating relative to observed interactions with various other bodies, fluctuations that Riis registered through repeated visits, conversations, statistics, photographs, interviews, etc. Such fluctuations were not merely described as social phenomena taking place 'out there' among the tenements. Given the impact- and response-dynamic of the conservative triangle, which operates also through communication, one should particularly observe how the composition of a Riis lecture or a book pursues a narrative designed to affirm the three values with the audience. The technique of veridiction rests in other words on establishing with the audience an 'adequate idea' of things presented, i.e. it pursues a formal analogy between the affirmation of values borne by his communication and the value-affirming interactions communicated. The five propositions for a better society were thus founded upon three Christian invariants (the will to honesty; the image of God; the golden rule) and three social imperatives (the instinct of beauty; solidarity; material improvements). This order successfully bridged the wide-open discursive chasm in America between religious and secular reform agendas. While it laid out the solid principles of a political program, the conservative triangle worked both as a diagnostic tool and as a performative means of imparting the program upon the general public. The diagram below (Diagram 1) outlines the relational structure of Conservative Materialism, marking the distinction between social and religious realms of assessment.

In the next chapters, I shall trace the process of mutation that resulted in this diagram, beginning with the Danish charity discourse and then moving on to the heterogeneous public spheres in New York. From a description of the Danish concerns that developed during Riis's residence in Copenhagen, I will identify the mutating agents that affected the American discourse.

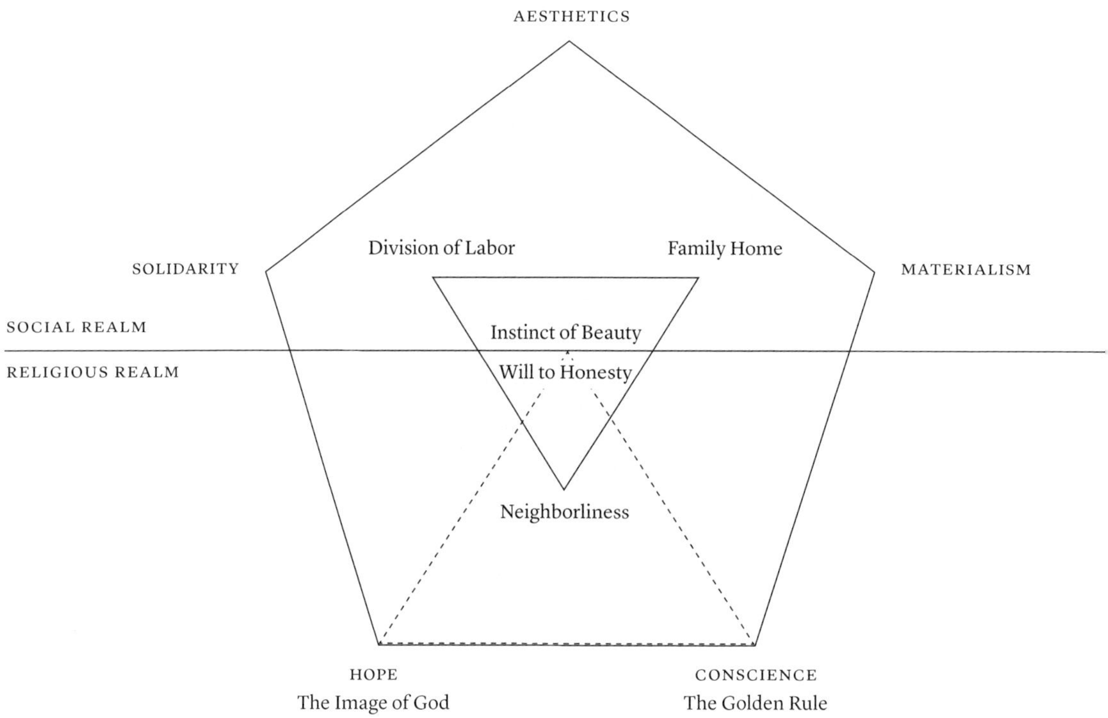

Diagram 1. The Conservative Triangle and the Five Propositions.

CHAPTER 3

Copenhagen Charity Disputes

To approach the mutation event, it is important at first to briefly remark on the strong Christian vernacular in American reform literature prior to Riis. Charles Loring Brace, author of *The Dangerous Classes in New York*, may represent common parlance: "Christ leads the Reform of the world, as well as its charity."[1] This single postulate conveys the movement's straightforward appeal to moral legitimacy, indeed its claim to superiority. Charles Parkhurst, another close associate of Riis, voiced the same evangelical appeal in a slightly alternative phrasing: "The one only guarantee of our national integrity, peace and prosperity is the power of the Gospel of Jesus Christ."[2] Anyone could then immediately recognize the missonary momentum of General Booth's charity program for The Salvation Army. "I am only making it easy where it is now difficult, and possible where it is now impossible, for men and women to find their way to the Cross of our Lord Jesus Christ."[3] While accounting for some rare exceptions among the cadre of publishing reformists, for example the Jewish moral philosopher Felix Adler,[4] the socialist Henry George, and a few others, one must conclude that Christianity, or Christian principles,

1. Charles Loring Brace, *The Dangerous Classes of New York*, 22.
2. Charles Parkhurst, *The Question of the Hour* (Anson D.F. Randolph Publishers, New York: 1886), 8.
3. General Booth, *In Darkest England and the Way Out* (Funk and Wagnalls, New York: 1891), 6.
4. Felix Adler, *Conscience – a Lecture delivered before the Society of Ethical Culture* (Lehmaier, New York: 1886), 15: "Upon the fact of morality, philosophers have founded the belief in God; but morality itself takes precedence of all beliefs. It is primal, it is sovereign, it is the central reality of the universe."

provided normative invariants to the discourse that shaped and modeled political reform propositions. This is not surprising, only worth noticing, as it marks a sharp contrast to the situation in Copenhagen. In New York, the vast majority of charity proponents and reform advocates justified their claims on the basis of Christian principles. In Copenhagen, no one did. Rhetorically, we might term these American justifications 'relational invariants': relational because they exercised argumentative power only in relation to other, similar concerns, and invariants because of their invocation of absolute and purportedly universal values. Like normatively indisputable lighthouses, they allowed trajectories of public contention to take measure of the field and plot their individual course. Apparently, Riis invented other relational invariants for the charity discourse in New York. This is probably his most significant contribution: new relational invariants that secured a lasting mutation of the American tenement discourse.

It is possible to identify three new relational invariants with Riis: the will to honesty, the golden rule, and the image of God in every man. Individually, each concept appears to be concomitant with conventional discourse, but their conceptual linkage to the triangle's dynamic pivot (more on this later) and to the propositions of hope and conscience justify Riis's political propositions in a unique way. They no longer warrant an evangelical model for social development; rather, they promise nothing less than the divine realization of man —"Christian citizenship"—in the course of successive ethical affirmations of the truth. Three new invariants, three lighthouses that redistribute the trajectories of public contention and thus create a new space for the tenement problem: a new curve, a novel concern appears with new concrete solutions. What is radically new about these invariants is that their justifying function is immanent to the actions and propositions justified. Brace, Parkhurst, and others called upon the tenets of Scripture to let its transcendental authority justify their claims 'from afar', so to speak; Riis, by contrast, claimed transcendental reality in all human interaction and justified his tenement agenda by showing that an act which affirms the triangle's values is also a realization of the divine element in man. Riis's relational invariants do not therefore invoke an otherworldly justice of infinite grace; their universal validity rather subsists immanently, *in potentia*, in every interaction, that is, as the yardstick of divine realization that measures the truth of all human attempts to better oneself and strengthen one's neighbor. It follows that Riis could not presume wide-spread recognition of these relational invariants; their justification of actions and propositions were, along with their measuring function, entirely dependent on a materially conditioned understanding of grace and a certain level of solidarity. In one sense, Riis overturns fundamental theological tenets in a manner reminiscent of Ludwig Feuerbach (whom he most likely never read). A profanization perhaps, a materialist appropriation of Christian principles for political means, but in another sense also a revitalization of the religious vernacular of charity. I will try to show that this politicized Christianity developed from a graft incised from foreign trajectories of contention, trajectories that responded to other ethical concerns than those commonly addressed by New York reformers. It was, in fact, Riis's loyalty to these foreign Danish concerns that fostered new relational invariants. Or, to put it differently, they developed in response to a certain discursive tardiness that, for sure, would have tinted any foreigner's apprehension of the tenement situation. But as a prolific police reporter and reform agitator, his unique responsiveness to the tenement situation in New York put him in a position to see things differently and to speak otherwise of what he saw.

With powers to unhinge the prevalent pious invariants in New York, Riis's new tenement problem implied a possible turn of the curve, a possible discursive mutation. To understand this situation, one has to look to both sides of the Atlantic. Notably, the Danish tenement discourse should not be considered more 'original' than the one Riis engaged with in the U.S.. The origin of transformation lies, as it were, in the writing and reading, in the speaking and listening, and in the showing and perceiving, the efficacy of which would rely on a number of various resources. It is crucial to keep in mind that the foreign graft could grow only insofar as Riis wrote about tenement problems under the particular journalistic conditions of the New York press and within the existing tenement reform movement.

Turning now to the Danish reform literature to excavate the habitat for the graft that migrated with Riis to New York, one should not expect to find any primordial versions of Riis's conservative materialism. One finds instead a complex fabric of strands twining around an endemic public concern: a certain distribution of matters qualified for dispute, a particular authorization of voices eligible to take part, certain hot spots of dissent, certain acceptable justifications of argument, a number of conventions for presenting facts and for assessing the conditions observed, and so on.

One particular matter of dispute was of course the unworthy poor. Tirelessly, Riis returns in New York to the question of the tramps and the wretched paupers who to all appearances were hopelessly mired in destitution and beyond help or influence. Among the Copenhagen reformers, this problem had been disputed in countless propositions, programs, reports, opinions, and reviewed relief applications. One may even notice an impressive inventiveness for avoiding the issue when necessary. Discussions of the unworthy poor were intense in Copenhagen. By contrast, while the phenomenon was not undisputed among American writers, it was not considered a pertinent problem. Whereas few Danish commentators failed to brood over it, most American writers assumed the category without much consternation. This is not a sign of indifference. It merely reveals a different distribution of public concerns. To us, it may serve to illustrate how Riis pursued Danish problems in an American context, eventually challenging its structural conditions. Succeeding eventually to modify its problems, its justifications, and its facts, Riis slowly mutated the American discursive charity environment.

Duty and Responsibility

Considering the clerical vocation of two of Copenhagen's most vocal charity reformers, the reverend Vilhelm Munck and the reverend Johan Christopher Holck, it is remarkable how consistently their pamphlets, books, and articles avoid Christian justification. For example, rev. Holck opened his book *Om Godgjørenhed og frivilligt Fattigvæsen i Kjøbenhavn* with an exclusively political motivation for renewed charity efforts.

> With the increase of freedom and independence that since 1848 have influenced all of our current affairs follow also quite naturally an increase of citizens' duties. Prior to the free constitution, our subjugation to absolutist monarchy made us accustomed to full custody by the government—so much so that it only occurred to a few among us to challenge its ways. No one thought of taking a hand and starting anything up by themselves, nor were there any place for such private initiatives. We have witnessed major changes in these matters since 1848: the idea that every citizen has a duty to spend time and efforts in the service of society as a whole, so long as it does not interfere with private affairs or professional life, has increasingly entered the consciousness of the people.[5]

These extended private duties that Holck refers to were concomitant with the emergence of new social structures and economic developments in Copenhagen. Monarchic rule was only gradually and partially dismantled in Denmark after the government turnover. Municipal public welfare was still in the hands of monarchically endorsed institutions, offering weak public alternatives to the guilds and to the powerful new voluntary organizations. But as the old relief programs

5. Johan Christopher Holck, *Om Godgjørenhed og frivilligt Fattigvæsen i Kjøbenhavn*, (Thanning & Appel, Copenhagen: 1869), 1. All English translations from Johan Christopher Holck, Vilhelm Munck, Frederik Krebs, and F.F. Ulrik are my own.

began to disintegrate with the changes associated with the Act of Free Commerce in 1862, these already neglected municipal institutions found themselves acutely overburdened and understaffed. Meanwhile, the economic, political, and social changes that swept over Copenhagen conjured up a new and increasingly important figure. The private citizen approached charity on entirely different terms than his predecessors.[6] Who was this new figure? A small business proprietor perhaps, a civil or public servant, a bank clerk or an insurance agent, a medical doctor, a lawyer, an artisan or a teacher; some of these citizens owned real estate and were eligible to elected offices. Most were married, preferably with children, and lived in a flat or a small house in the city, took to the countryside in the summertime, but were not necessarily born to wealth. This was the segment that quickly got accustomed to omnibuses, cafés, and the new urban public spirit. (Søren Kierkegaard's "Equilibrium Between the Aesthetical and the Ethical in the Development of Personality"[7] contains an early, but in many ways apposite description of this new figure.) It accumulated political influence in private networks, associations, councils, commissions, and eventually in parliament. It organized social networks strictly according to gender, age, rank, education, and property. From within these networks, men and women alike began to recognize a common "duty to spend time and efforts in the service of society as a whole." From the self-assumed tasks and responsibilities of these men and women rose private charity in Copenhagen.

Civic responsibility conflicted with the routines and practices established by municipal institutions and guild charities alike. One might think that these private citizens would lend themselves to already existing private associations, but civic charity issued new demands, motives, and ambitions that went beyond the time-honored charity commission. The meaning of charity transformed: whereas guild associations cared for members and their families, civic philanthropists labored as much for peer recognition as for a tar-

6. Karin Lützen, *Byen tæmmes*, 29-77.

7. Søren Kierkegaard, *Either/Or: A Fragment of Life* (Penguin, London: 1992), 475-590.

geted improvement of society. Although peer esteem demanded a certain amount of commitment and voluntary labor, the efforts spent must not, as Holck dutifully notes above, interfere with personal or professional business obligations. Furthermore, remuneration in esteem demanded visible results and measurable improvements. Whereas sovereign charity was a governmental act of mercy, and associated assistance had focused mainly on member care, the new charities rested on a frail private altruism buttressed predominantly by peer esteem. This self-centered system freed the helpers to choose any target group they preferred for benevolent support.

With this turn appears the significance of one of the most intensely debated issues of the 1860s: to what extent and how responsibility for the poor should be divided between public and private institutions. A common proposition maintained that the line of division should be drawn between the worthy and the unworthy poor. Reverend Munck presented this view more clearly than anyone else:

> A division between private and public relief must be made, so that each institution will care only for the poor that properly concerns them. [...] Those among the poor who can and will be raised may find sufficient support and relief from the private charities whereas municipal poverty aid will in time only deal with those who wish not to be raised and therefore cannot be raised.[8]

A consenting contributor to the debate, Frederik Krebs—medical doctor by profession and editor of the social reform journal *Samfundet*—added a succinct statement: "Public poor relief should merely receive those whom private charities abandon or reject."[9] This widespread distinction was, however, coextensive with a curious paradox.

The paradox derived from the moral constitution of the private citizen as a public figure, a paradox perhaps most poignantly noticed by Krebs. On the one hand, the private citizen was economically and

8. Vilhelm Munck, *Om Fattigdommen i Kjøbenhavn* (Gyldendal, Copenhagen: 1868), 79.

9. Frederik Krebs, "Den officielle og private Fattighjælp i Danmark," in *Samfundet: et Maandestidsskrift*, Vol. II, 1869, 194.

socially buoyant by dint of intense networking activities in hierarchical environments, wherefore this public figure was also very dependent on rigorous code and protocol. On the other hand, the private citizen must also at any time be able to transcend the economic and social codes to embrace the intuitive and emotional side of life. This difficulty often led to complex negotiations between 'charm' and 'reason,' occasionally resulting in a frustrating pursuit to have it both ways. For the private philanthropist in particular, these negotiations could at times raise a most embarrassing predicament. On the one hand, and for reasons of peer recognition, he or she must demand measurable results for captial and efforts invested in the poor, but on the other, charity must by its nature be a gesture of love and compassion and thus be raised above such expectations. Krebs, who generally favors private initiatives over public ones, deplores municipal organizations that merely "open their purses while closing the hearts,"[10] implying that private charity, by contrast, might open both. So on the one hand, the open purse must yield results—or the poor will be transferred from private custody to public institutions, which is a failure among peers—but on the other, these desired results are possible only with an open heart which does not recognize such conditional terms. The civic philanthropist must be attentive to progress while ignoring it at the same time. Krebs, perhaps inspired by Kierkegaard's ethical person, tried to solve the paradox by calling for the inner duty that is everyone's right to claim. Municipal assistance, he contended,

> has no right to relieve society, that is, the community of responsible individuals, from one of its main duties: to care *immediately and without middle men* for the poor in their midst. On the other hand, these private persons cannot unburden themselves of their duty without irreparable damage. A municipal relief discharging them of their duties works to dissolve society.[11]

10. Ibid., 178.

11. Ibid., 179. Author's italics.

Duty, as we see here, helps to bridle the paradox. It ties peer recognition closer to the individual's earnest willingness to act philanthropically, and it lessens somewhat the emphasis on measurable results. Duty is personal but must nonetheless be publically recognized; it must be acknowledged among private citizens and be expected from its class. It is crucial not to revoke anyone else's right (or opportunity) to perform one's duty; on the other hand, duty cannot be enforced upon someone who does not assume it—a significant drop in social status follows instead. Although private duty is certainly recognized, measured, and encouraged in the social milieu, it must always be assumed personally and uncompelled—as intimately as one's heart's devotion dictates, yet outwardly manifested in voluntary actions and face-to-face engagements. The paradox will not disappear. But the implication is that duty will make it manageable and serve to attract patrons to the cause. Above all else, Krebs maintains, duty must remain informal: charity must not be soiled by formal institutions.

From this perspective, it makes sense to be suspicious of charity associations. Any personal sense of duty quickly evaporates with the formalities, standards, and policies that govern formal associations. However, Krebs understood that industrial mass poverty is much too powerful an adversary for anything but organized charity. He was therefore forced to limit the scope of his civic philanthropy to advice, guidance, teaching, and occasional alms. He understood that chances of success would be limited only to the most worthy poor. Subjects who, by contrast, pursued a way of life that continued their present destitution, had to be transferred to the heartless municipal aid system.[12] They would be transferred not in view of restoring their will, as one finds it in Vilhelm Munck's writings, but rather in order to raise a sense of responsibility for themselves. Krebs attributed the general failure of the municipal aid system to its numbing form of compassion and demeaning mercy, which rather weaken the recipients' sense of responsibility:

12. Ibid., 170; 181; 193.

> A municipal aid system that is slipshod and lenient can only do damage. [...] The feeling of responsibility that everyone —even the day laborer—senses as he is about to start a family, is severely weakened. [...] Applying for municipal aid causes neither grief nor humiliation. It is increasingly common to think of it as a pension fund to be used for the quickest possible benefit and to that objective appear as weak and fragile as possible. The spendthrift poor are too quick to reason like so: when I cannot provide for my family, the city shall.[13]

The unworthy poor who think that society owes them a living are unreachable for the private citizen.[14] And municipal aid can exclusively be of service in the form of forced labor, which is the only way to discontinue the spreading of pauperism from the almshouses. The workhouse may, in exceptional cases, help an unworthy poor regain some of his lost responsibility, but only if he willfully commits himself to changing his ways. It is curious to find in Krebs's argument a controversial notion of will. "Should they *desire* assistance proper, they must find it at the labor house, where several might be rescued, upon whom milder means did not avail."[15] In Krebs's view, the poor are capable of choosing to will their improvement. The public aid system must then be sensitive to a burgeoning will when it appears among hardened inmates. With such terse and sparse acknowledgements of the municipal system, one catches a glimpse of a few other important ambiguities regarding the unworthy poor. First, it seems impossible to gain absolute, or even sufficient certainty about the state of someone else's will to improve. There is always a chance that a hopeless case may in fact awaken and desire rescue. Second, there is constant vacillation regarding forced labor as a remedy for those who are lacking ambition and responsibility. Views in favor of the labor house are never unambiguously substantiated but hold sway

13. Ibid., 170.
14. Ibid., 197.
15. Ibid., 198, author's italics.

nonetheless against pervasive arguments that find it socially counterproductive and detrimental to the market forces. Third, the question of the social production of pauperism is never resolved. Its contagious nature is neither disputed nor clearly understood. All of these issues were being dealt with from a different perspective by another of the city's vocal reformers.

Will vs. Responsibility

Vilhelm Munck agreed with Krebs on worthiness as the most adequate parameter for dividing aid responsibilities between public and private organizations. But unlike Krebs, Munck set out to discover the causes of poverty in order to fight it prophylactically. Voicing mainstream conservative views regarding core values such as home, family, and labor rights, he also introduced some rather unique materialistic suggestions for how to maintain and strengthen these values. For example, the first pages of his book *Om de fattiges Vilkaar paa Christianshavn* warns against the moral detriment caused by materially inferior dwellings:

> The ultimate preventative means against poverty we firmly believe to be the possession of a decent friendly home [...]. Put any man or woman who loves order and cleanliness in an apartment where the light is dim at high noon, where the air is malodorous, where the fireplace gives away smoke instead of heat, where the ceiling and the floors compete in terms of blemishes and dirt, where the floor is littered with holes, and where vermin throng in all cracks and crevices; how long would it take to forget tidiness and order? Is it strange, under such circumstances, if the husband rather seeks out the bar than the home, if the wife becomes unthorough and inattentive and the children sickly and ailing?[16]

16. Vilhelm Munck, *Om de fattiges Vilkaar på Christianshavn* (Gyldendals, København: 1867), 8.

Munck's conception of the family home as a hub of social cohesion is later on identified as the place from where a tenable political structure may emerge. It is a design of argument that effectively suspends Krebs's dual concepts of responsibility and duty. Not only is human character perceived by Munck as being malleable by its physical surroundings, it also responds back to its milieu according to perceived advantages, risks, and opportunities; a wealth of social factors beyond responsibility and duty—including certain unfortunate habits amongst the poor themselves—concert to advance the conditions for a growing proletariat. "That the poor are often involved in bringing about their own misery does not mean that no other individuals and social conditions lend a hand."[17] Munck's multiplicity of circumstances and factors, acting upon the poor from within as well as from outside the tenement quarters, posed a challenge to the conventional, simple notion of unworthiness, commonly associated with a mental state of anti-social self-deprivation. But while recognizing a complex multiplicity of causes—thereby involving all of civil society in the fight against poverty—Munck nonetheless proposed a clear and distinct concept of worthiness from which to organize the division of aid. It is based on the will to improve oneself rather than on a responsibility to care for oneself, and it is a will that one cannot choose to have or to have not, as in Krebs. Munck's concept of will is rather one that defines human spirit. The unworthy poor are "those who *do not want to* raise themselves and therefore cannot be raised."[18] Munck's will to improve has a share in shaping a very different argument from the one Krebs had constructed with a focus on responsibility.

Firstly, Munck's will is not only a key element in the assessment of the poor. Their will and the multiplicity of forces acting upon it also make him look back on the charity institutions to assess their initiatives and responsibilities. How do they diagnose will? How, if at all, is it nurtured? Munck's analysis accentuates a passive civic responsibility, the failure of which Munck's readers seem to have willingly acknowledged.

17. Ibid., 37.

18. Ibid., 79.

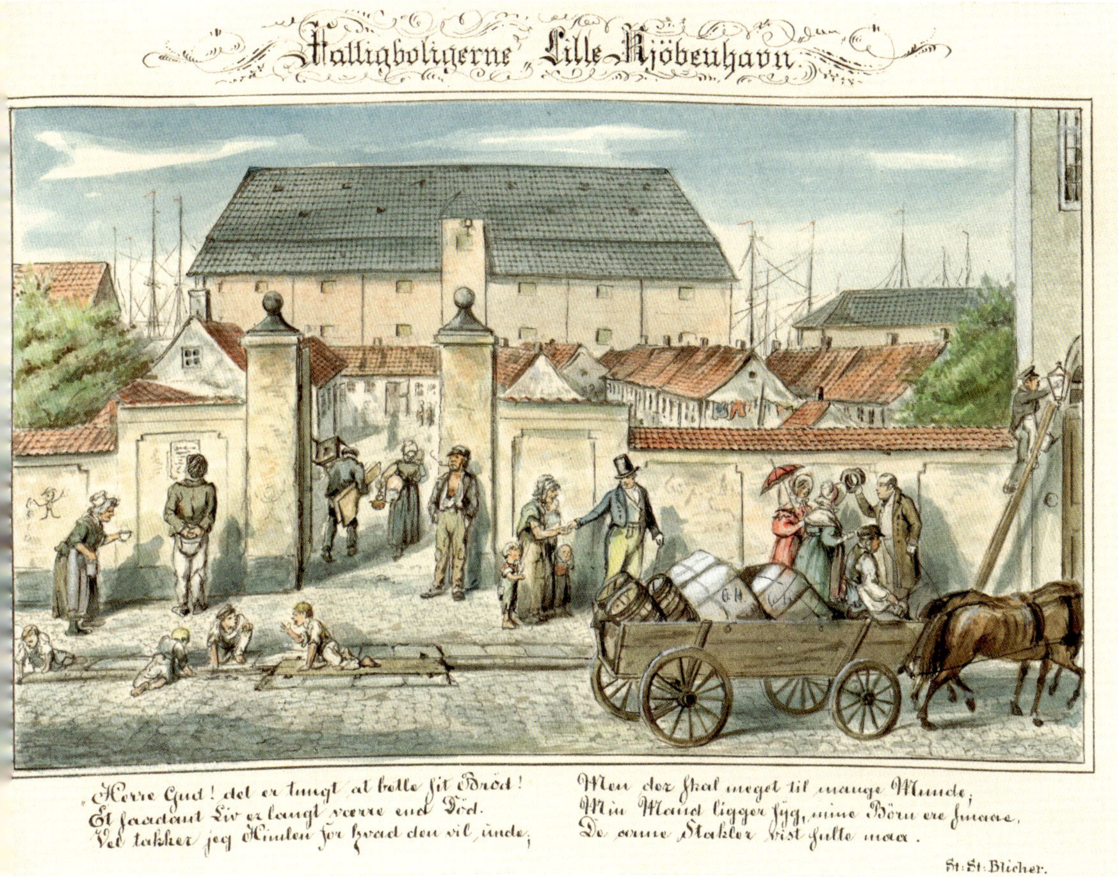

Figure 14. P.C. Klæstrup, "Fattigboligerne i Lille Kjøbenhavn" in *Det forsvundne Kjøbenhavn*, 1879. The Danish Royal Library, Collection of Prints and Photographs.

> I would refrain from blaming the society of Copenhagen for causing the growth of poverty among us. It has at present befallen us, most likely against our will, and we must deal with the state of affairs as given. But, to continue the previous metaphor, as innocent as village citizens are of a river's swelling after heavy rainfall in the mountains, as guilty are those who stand idly by with arms crossed, trusting the old failing dams that allow the stream to spread its destruction far and wide. [...] If we have none or very little guilt for nurturing the conditions formative to the proletariat, at least we bear great responsibility for having allowed the same conditions to prosper undisturbed and unchallenged. We have kept the old ramparts, although we should have known that new and stronger ones were needed.[19]

Secondly, by emphasizing the poor man's will, the author is compelled to create new concepts and new relational invariants, such as learning to live and universal self-esteem. Like Krebs, Munck often speaks about augmenting self-esteem and self-respect among the poor. But for Munck, self-esteem (which is coextensive with the will to improve[20]) is not something that directly results from agreeable social experiences. Munck considers self-esteem an original resource inside the human being, one which may be corrupted or developed according to experience. "A sad truth is concealed in the fact that many of the poor have lost the self-esteem that actually exists originally within every human being and is the root of all ambition and industriousness."[21] Self-esteem is a fundamental category for the social nature of human beings, much like the will to honesty is in Riis. It begs to be noticed, however, that while the assessment of self-esteem in Munck's theory depends solely upon observed behavior in a particular social structure, the will to honesty is in Riis formally deduced from another relative invariant, the image of God.

19. Ibid., 41.
20. Munck describes the two tasks of "increasing [the worker's] self-esteem and encouraging him to want to stand on his own feet" as identical ones. Ibid., 63.
21. Ibid.

The absence of religious invariants in Munck's writings marks an important distinction with respect to Riis. But this absence does not imply some naïve materialism. Munck is certainly attentive to how material standards are needed to sustain and develop the poor's self-esteem, but he also warns against an "abundance of material assistance," which he considers a "cause for the misery."[22] Thoughtless material benefactions often do as little good as mere moral preaching,[23] he contends, and may in fact partake in the corruption of a man's original self-esteem. Endowments, alms, donations, and allowances offered from disinterested or uninformed philanthropists—be they private or public—serve only to increase pauperism, or rather, to escalate the contagious epidemic of depletion. Munck sees tenement poverty as an urban communicative disorder in alarming stages of advancement, to be effectively battled only with personal contact and socio-clinical institutions. Mere improvements in housing standards, free bread rations or monthly allowances are not the way to contain the growing epidemic. It would instead be necessary, first of all, that the members of the powerful bourgeoisie regain *their* will to improve. Their personal engagement must be invested collectively in what would be an educational reform process, one that is necessary to foster a resilient help to self-help. The task of the affluent is "to help the poor recognize the advantages of modesty and thrift through persistent personal contact."[24] Effective aid institutions, always working in tandem with the personal touch, are those which are predominantly prophylactic and pedagogical. In the absence of religious invariants, Munck offers the invariant of learning; to learn to live among the multifarious urban dangers and there to nurture one's self-esteem: this ability is of course limited among many of the rural immigrants. The crucial distinction to be made in terms of will sequesters those who may be taught from those who may not.

The first stage of recommended treatment is to clinically divide and physically sequester the poor according to their state of self-

22. Ibid., 61.

23. Munck, *Om Fattigdommen i Kjøbenhavn*, 86.

24. Munck, *Om de Fattiges Vilkaar på Christianshavn*, 118. See also *Om Fattigdommen i Kjøbenhavn*, 41-43 for discussions about civil security.

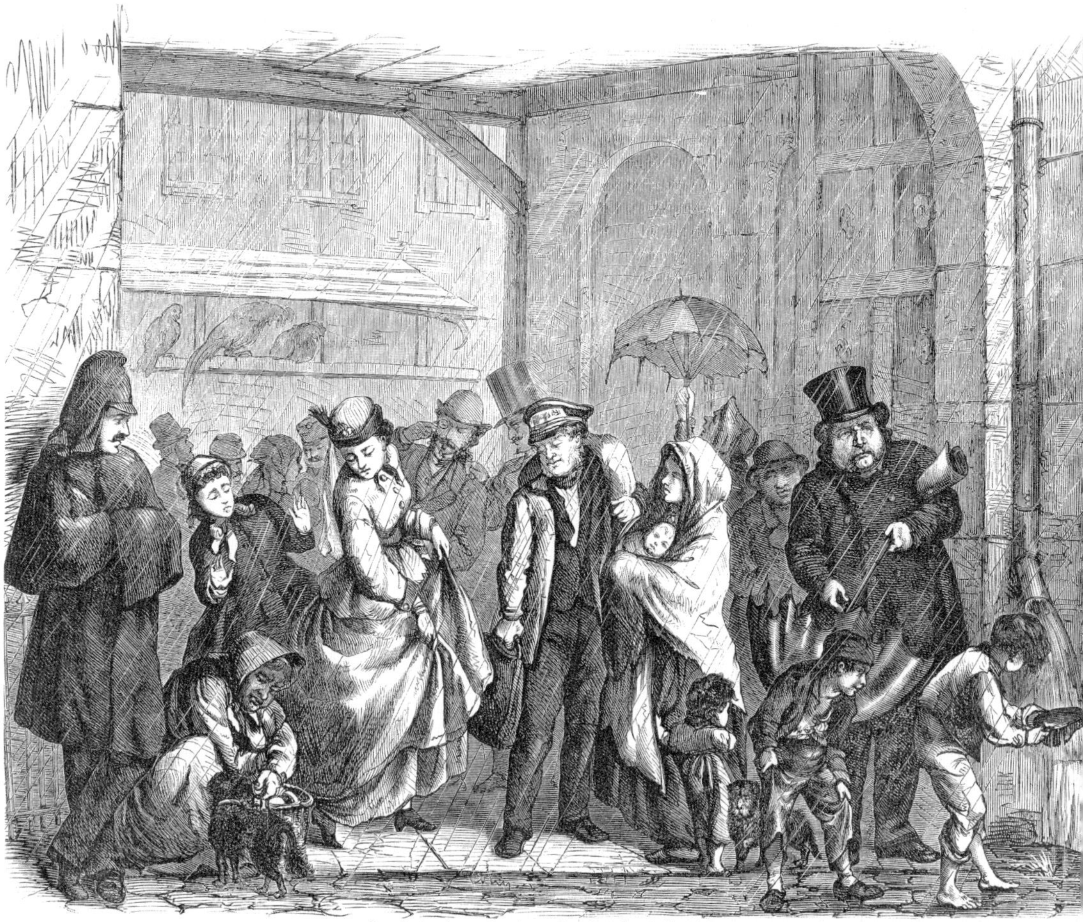

Figure 15. Knud Gamborg, "I en port under en regnbye," *Illustreret Tidende*, 374, 25/11, 1866. The Danish Royal Library, Collection of Prints and Photographs.

esteem and then to make sure that the unworthy do not come in contact with the worthy. Subsequent efforts follow a differentiated reform program that sweeps the entire city. It aims to remove any infectious elements from the poor neighborhoods such as overpriced and dangerous housing, unsanitary water and sewage systems, underpaid and insecure labor conditions, usury, uncontrolled flows of immigration, and mind-numbing entertainment. By promoting cooperative providers of daily goods and low-dividend model tenement corporations, small-scale savings banks and workers' pension funds, Munck seeks to install a heavily regulated capitalism in the tenements, a protected mercantile seedbed, capable of cultivating the many fragile, small-scale economic agents and entrepreneurial talents without crushing them. Self-esteem must be nurtured slowly by personal, commercial, and social interests. The goal is to design a private institutional structure that distributes personal contact across social divides while initiating economic institutions that are market driven and self-sustaining. Both will together offer the poor real growth opportunities. Still, the poor must be taught how to use these institutions. An example is workers' savings banks, which are both structurally and individually preferable to pawning in times of scarcity or loaning at usury rates. Still, many poor are suspicious about banks and need help to approach the institution. Likewise, health insurance associations are meant to increase workers' independence from charity organizations and to reduce financial vulnerability in case of sickness or accidents. Without teaching, however, their clientele are likely to stay with the already familiar but less beneficial options. To Munck, the most effective prophylactic is found in model tenements, such as the ones described in chapter 1. Replacing not only the existing inferior houses, but also their owners and their imposed tenant-immobility with cheap, hygienic, bright homes in sufficient numbers and with viable self-management is "one of the most powerful means for raising thrift, industriousness and self-esteem among the poor."[25] Good homes produce social virtues. But

25. Munck, *Om Fattigdommen i Kjøbenhavn*, 48.

a good family home is something more than an affordable and functional apartment.

Contrary to Riis's endorsement of single women on the labor market, Munck voices skepticism.[26] The economic freedom that young women enjoy from wage labor and self-employment, paired with a leisurely single lifestyle amidst many amusement venues, is altogether detrimental, he says, to the family structure. Assuming that girls are more susceptible than boys to the influences of inadequate homes, and having registered an increasing number of such corrupting tenement dwellings, Munck predicts a long-term decline in family culture. The entertainment industry in particular is responsible for expensive habits and egotistical priorities which work for the dissolution of family structures. Munck suggests that household servant positions are preferable to factory labor for young women, mainly because domestic life protects them from alluring dancehalls while also teaching them the necessity of household economics. A clear division of labor is said to inoculate the working family against the threats of disintegration and poverty.

Munck's educational program seeks to prevent the corruption of will, or self-esteem, among the poor, thereby to secure their potential for a full civic life. In Riis, one may recognize a legacy from this pedagogical scheme, for example in the support of neighborhood settlements.

Unlike Krebs, however, Munck hesitates with regard to the hopeless. For those among the poor who "exaggerate their weakness to avoid making an effort, it would be improper to offer the least of material assistance; much rather, constant encouragement and serious correction are needed. Here, we proceed with the greatest caution, searching and experimenting, always ready to increase the type of assistance that works, and stop when no progress is detected."[27] On the one hand, he suggests "severe and forceful treatment, as nothing else has any effect on them."[28] On the other, he at one point

26. Ibid., 26-29.
27. Munck, *Om de Fattiges villkaar på Christianhavn*, 73.
28. Munck, *Om Fattigdommen i Kjøbenhavn*, 78.

corrects himself with regard to a previously endorsed case of withdrawn assistance to an unworthy pauper, now recommending restraint, yet "only as material aid is concerned."[29] Possibly, Munck suggests that aid in the form of advice and personal contact should still be available.

To the extent that some sort of aid is considered beneficial for the unworthy poor, there is hope also for the hopeless. In one particular passage, Munck is curiously ambiguous: "Among the [worthy] thrives a sense of both honor and hope, among the [unworthy] these are almost entirely extinct."[30] 'Almost' is hardly necessary for the communicated meaning, and no indication is given elsewhere of what the allusion to lingering traces of honor and hope might amount to. Munck adds 'almost' although it complicates the picture and weakens the argument. One possible explanation could be that self-esteem must not die, as it would be the demise of what makes us human. Alas, such a proposition is never articulated, however consonant it would be with Munck's general argument. Hence, the question of how to deal with a fully broken self-esteem is not addressed, merely touched upon, which is itself an indication of the powers at stake.

Forced Labor and the Diagnosis of Will

Munck's colleague and friend, Johan Christopher Holck was more explicit about this issue. Holck shared Munck's conceptualization of will, labor division, and home, and he too distinguished unworthiness in terms of the will to improve. "It is imperative," he wrote, "that distinctions are made between those needy subjects who do not want to help themselves and are thus beyond rescue, and those who may be elevated, as these both can and will help themselves."[31] Holck moreover agreed that private charity should care only for the worthy, and that material standards were conditional for any effective moral instruction. And although Holck on rare occasions called upon "a prop-

29. Munck. *Om de Fattiges villkaar på Christianhavn*, 90.
30. Ibid., 15.
31. Holck, *Om Godgjørenhed og frivilligt Fattigvæsen i Kjøbenhavn*, 8.

er religiosity, living Christianity, and true enlightenment,"[32] he too avoided any systematic use of religious invariants. He did, however, elaborate on two issues that Munck left largely unexplored, namely the use of forced labor as a possible rehabilitation treatment for the unworthy and the problem of how to diagnose will. Quite unequivocally, Holck recommended forced labor where the will to improve had sufficiently eroded.

> Should not all be done to help the worthy to stand on his own feet, whereas for the unworthy there is nothing other or better to do, than to force him to work for his support? All those who cannot be helped, but have sunken so deeply into idleness that they *no longer value being rescued from the filth, and make no efforts to raise from it*, should be left to public assistance. The public should preferably deal exclusively with such destitutes, as it may thus accomplish some serious good, that is, keeping the lower population on a short leash, care to educate their ill-reared children, and thus put a stop to the growth of the proletariat.[33]

The labor houses are not meant to restore the will of the unworthy but, conversely, 1) to deter the poor from seeking their assistance, primarily by forcing inmates to earn their own living in utmost austerity, and 2) more importantly, to keep those submitted from contaminating their children and the rest of society with their anti-social ways. The pedagogical prospect is even less pronounced here than it is with Munck's ambivalent calls for experimentation, or even with Krebs's unsubstantiated hopes: Holck speaks of "lazy, indifferent, obstinate, and debauched persons who may not be helped in other ways but through forced labor,"[34] suggesting little beyond a mere quarantine.

Labor houses were, in his view, only really effective as deterrents. Holck belonged to those reformists who advocated hard enough con-

32. Ibid., 79.
33. Ibid., 11. Author's italics.
34. ibid., 60.

ditions in the labor houses to dissuade anyone from seeking their assistance, thereby forcing the last remnants of ambition out of every idle pauper. As a consequence, he paid close attention to establishing viable criteria for assessing private charity applications. Formulating these made him reflect upon a method for diagnosing the will to improve.

> When everyone cannot be helped, one should be somewhat exacting when selecting those to admit, in order not to accidentally expose oneself to helping the unworthy, that is, those who could, or rather should be able to help themselves. One should make it known to all, both to donors and receivers, that help is only extended where help is due, where there is a sincere will to help oneself and where this will is clearly visible. They all say they want to help themselves, but that is not often the truth. The point is, they are happy to help themselves when it is easy, but will not gather all their strength for a sincere and honest effort.[35]

What to look for when diagnosing the poor are not actual deficiencies in the domestic environment such as scarcity of clothes or want of food. Instead, one should look for signs of a battle against deficiency, for example documents from insurance associations, account statements from savings banks, school reports or visible evidence of cleanliness and wholesome cooking. For Munck, we remember, these signs would represent livelihood skills that one would first have to teach the poor in order to raise their self-esteem. Contrarily for Holck, they were signs of a level of self-esteem that underpinned eligibility for assistance. For the volunteering laymen that took on the role of observers in Holck and Munck's relief organization, *Christianshavns Understøttelsesforening*, the task of entering the homes of the poor to investigate for signs of a desire to improve and general self-esteem

35. Ibid., 43.

was a difficult one—enough, reportedly, for many to quit and look for alternative charity duties.[36]

Whereas concordance between formal protocol and actual appearance was essential for a just decision, observers often found signs that were difficult to decipher or even paradoxical. Critical newspaper articles picked up on the situation. "It is a dangerous thing to judge poverty by external signs and from that decide upon someone's right to aid."[37] Thus opened a front-page item in the daily *Dagens Nyheder* of May 1869, which continued:

> These wretched dwellings, this scant and bad food, these ragged clothes, skinny physiognomies and pitiable faces, they are all uncertain indicators. All of them may testify to poverty, but they leave us none the wiser about its character. Neither can a lesser or a greater sense of orderliness and cleanliness—though trusted as unfailing signs—provide the yardstick. Many men are despicably sordid to behold, but work unceasingly and may possess a personal honor that is second to none. Rather, if what one seeks are segregating markers, one must look to a man's character; one must weigh his sense of honor and respectability, notice his diligence and assiduity, for only then is an idea conveyed of his worth as a human, of his value for society, and qualification for aid.

36. Munck even dared a humorous anecdote about the difficulties faced by a well-meaning volunteer: "A very corpulent Lady, in most becoming attire, married to a colonel, endeavored with the best of intentions to observe a very poor family. Having once, with some trouble, climbed the narrow stairways to the loft where the family lived, the place she found was so small (this was in the crinoline times) that her first achievement was to knock over a little table and whilst twisting around in shock over the destruction she swept down a child who promptly began to howl at the top of his lungs, what terrified the Lady colonel so much—unfamiliar as she was with such insufficient premises—that she immediately gave up observation. Thus she followed several others whose nerves could not muster the poor at close proximity." *Fængelsepræsten Pastor Vilhelm Muncks Optegnelser* (August Bangs Forlag, Copenhagen: 1972), 108.

37. "Fattigdommen i Kjøbenhavn," *Dagens Nyheder*, May 11, 1869, 1.

Such highbrow newspaper moralism would not be left unanswered. In defense of his inspectors, Holck replied that observations aimed to do just that: to observe as a means to *know* the conditions of the poor, not merely to apprehend them. In ways reminiscent of Krebs, he argues that an observer must regularly make his rounds and establish "a close and steady relationship" with the poor, even "be known by them as their true friend."[38] Yet Holck was aware of the problems raised by the newspaper and knew well how easily an observer may be manipulated or mistaken by the slum's semiotic incongruity.[39]

Observation was, however, as necessary as it was potentially misleading. On the one hand, it would be imperative to observe the poor, to perceive their environments and habits, and to register the structure of a family, but on the other hand, the accumulated visual impressions were often deceptive or ambiguous and could but provide a mere supplement to verbal testimonies and numerical facts. What the local bartender or an employer had to say, what records of income and expenses might reveal: such statements would more unequivocally serve to determine the status of worthiness and would therefore decisively frame any visual observations. But visual impressions must nonetheless be obtained. "By visiting the poor and comparing one with the other," the charity observers will eventually learn, according to Holck, how to judge properly where aid should be given and where not.[40] Visual observations were not then entirely reducible to signs, or to determinations by category, but should also be assessed intuitively through sensuous comparison with other observations. A visual paradigmatic grammar emerged parallel to the coded signs; a way of seeing was taught and developed, amounting to a situated knowledge that, unfortunately, has left all too few historical traces.

38. Holck, *Om Godgjørenhed og frivilligt Fattigvæsen i Kjøbenhavn*, 26.

39. I have elsewhere translated a lengthy passage from Holck that instructs in how to read the signs of a pauper's home. See exhibition catalogue *Jacob A. Riis*, ed. Dag Petersson, (Det Kongelige Bibliotek: Copenhagen, 2008), 146-49.

40. Holck, *Om Godgjørenhed og frivilligt Fattigvæsen i Kjøbenhavn*, 36.

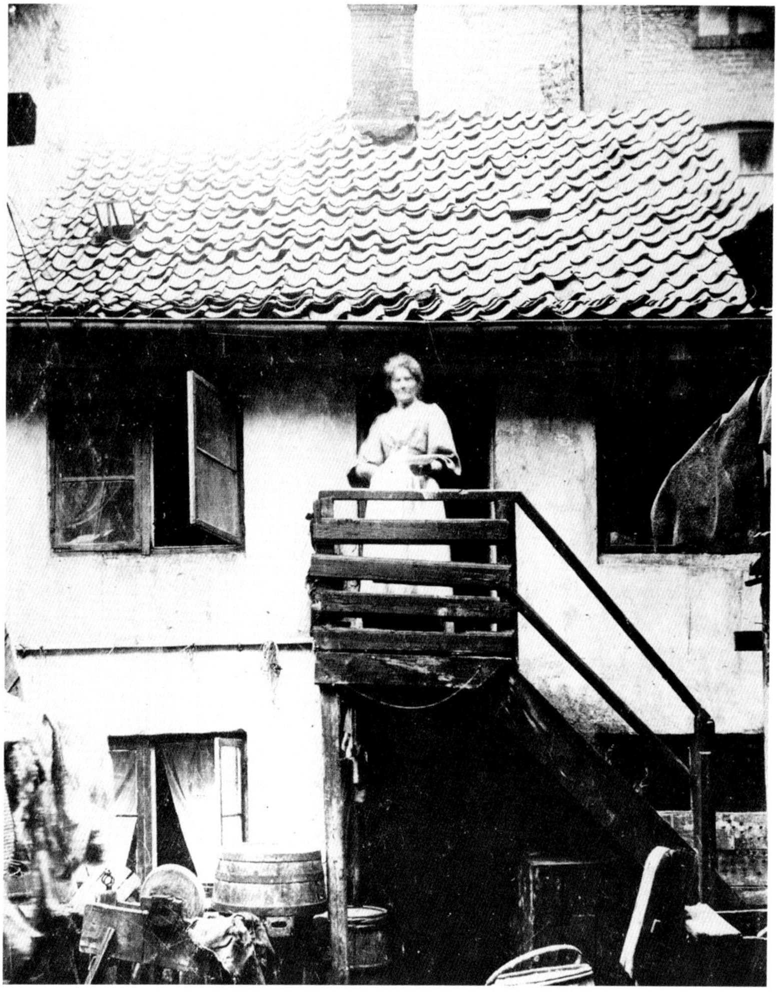

Figure 16. Anonymous photographer, "Dronningensgade 23, Baghus," n.d. The Danish Royal Library, Collection of Prints and Photographs.

Observers kept careful records of their visitations. These documents provide rare insight into the procedures of visual assessment. On Dec. 13, 1866, Frederikke Pedersen, 68 years old, was interrupted during coffee by a visit from Mrs. Roed, who upon witnessing such extravagance found no reason to recommend her for continued assistance. Similar sightings of affluence were common, and easily categorized in formal assessment reports. More interesting, therefore, is the case of Bengta Petersen, a 57-year-old widow, found eligible for support by her observer, a certain Mrs. Wegener, on the following account: "4 years in the present apt. Occupation: washing and cleaning, a little. Rent: 4 Rdl per month (from 2 male boarders 3 sk. each week) poor. Husband's disease and death in addition to her weakness have caused decline. Observ. Small monetary aid soon." Surprisingly, Mrs. Wegener's recommendation was rejected by the board with the motivation that "the applicant seems dubious as she lives in the same room with two working men."[41] Mrs. Wegener's 'erroneous' judgment was likely due to insufficient visual reading competences. From a strictly discursive perspective, Mrs. Petersen's decision to take on male boarders was neither uncommon nor necessarily immoral but rather evidence of sound economic judgment. The suspicions of illicit or dubious conduct raised by the charity board seem to have originated either from previous observations or other sources, for Mrs. Wegener's report does not inform of the single room and the fact that the boarders are working men. These and possibly other circumstances too should apparently have been observed by Mrs. Wegener and resulted in an alternative recommendation.

Institutional access into poor people's homes had previously only been granted to priests, midwives, undertakers, the police, and medical doctors. The observers represented a new authority, to which the poor subjected primarily in view of some advantage: perhaps a job, a contact with the upper classes, perhaps material aid (money allow-

41. Visitors' Protocols, filed under *Journaler 1866-1877*; Christianshavns Understøttelsesforening (2-67-22). Provincial Archives of Zealand, Copenhagen.

AQUARIUM. 22

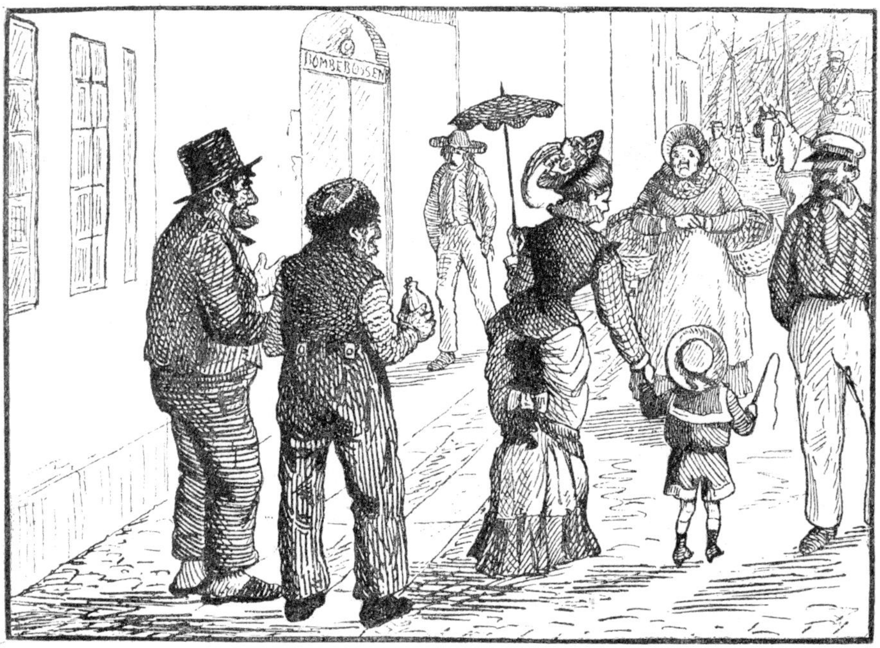

(Ulke.)

Figure 17. Vilhelm Pacht, "Aquarium: 24 humoristiske tegninger," 1876. The Danish Royal Library, Collection of Prints and Photographs.

ances, coal or bread). Regardless of which, most observed subjects played their part in the performance as best they could. Some resisted, others may have compared visits and developed tactics to increase their chances of obtaining the desired advantages. Although an observation was formally performed like a hearing of catechesis or a sick visit, the untried institutional authority of charity associations also made the visit difficult for the observer. Her appearance—for the observer was often a woman—at home with the poor was as new and unprecedented to her as it was to the ones being visited. "Many observers whom we have particular reason to pride ourselves of, were from the beginning worried and in doubt of their capabilities regarding the job," wrote one of the association's founders, well aware of the awkward and sometimes comical figure these women presented.[42]

One should note, however, that the new authority proved quickly to be both operative and highly effective: assessments reported actually divided the poor population and sent some to the labor houses and others back home with an allowance or a coal ration. The performative power of these practices, which were constantly subjected to public debate and scrutiny, and whose self-declared legitimacy called for much defense and explanation, this rising power was perhaps of greater significance than the debates were able to express. In many ways the fervent discussions about social diagnosis were subordinate to the more or less randomly performed ones: these exercised assessments shaped the apprehension of an urban sickness and staked out its course of development.

How to Mend a Broken Will

One sole philanthropist recognized with acute concern the political vacuum surrounding the arbitrariness of charity assessment. F.F. Ulrik was a medical doctor practicing in the poor neighborhoods

42. Holck, *Om Godgjørenhed og frivilligt Fattigvæsen i Kjøbenhavn*, 37.

of Christianshavn. His pamphlet from 1869, *Ved hvilke Midler bør Fattigdommen modarbejdes?* was a singular virulent protest against an official report, published one year earlier by a public committee which he originally had been a member of. Ulrik argued forcefully against the common notion that public and private assistance should be divided along the distinction between the worthy and the unworthy poor. In a brief preface he even declared that, "voluntary poverty relief is as such inadvisable since it, while partaking in the damaging effects upon the self-esteem and the general attitudes of the poor, is far inferior to a well structured public relief system, both with regard to the institution and in consideration of the frail altruism of the volunteers."[43] In most respects, Ulrik represents a view that is contrary to Krebs and Holck, yet he discovered from this perspective a new conceptual relationship between will and labor.

Ulrik argues that assistance in times of need is a social right, and that no one can be dishonored for claiming it. Whereas Holck broods over paradoxes of auditing (e.g. that the worthy must display a will to improve while the surest sign of worthiness is to suffer in silence[44]), Ulrik maintains that any alimony bestowed upon such proud unfortunates will be sure to produce beggars. Political rights actually owned and feelings of pride genuinely held will sooner corrode from the meddling of private observers than be strengthened by amateur aid associations. His proposals for alleviating the situation are reminiscent of Munck's, but he addresses them exclusively to public organizations and institutions with municipal backing. Ulrik proposes small savings banks and protected businesses for unskilled laborers (for instance, coffee cleansing); he suggests associated low-interest pawn shops and workers' health- and life-insurance associations, and also, of course, model tenements (self-owned or financed with 5% shares). Ulrik too envisions a government-regulated 'slow'

43. F.F. Ulrik, *Hved hvilke Midler bør Fattigdommen bekjæmpes?* (Gyldendals, Kjøbenhavn: 1869), np.

44. Holck, *Om Godgjørenhed og frivilligt Fattigvæsen i Kjøbenhavn* 47-48.

capitalism where the poor could school their economic engagement according to abilities.

But he also suggests a new, remarkable way of diagnosing poverty. "Labor in well-equipped workhouses under proper discipline is to be employed as the yardstick of true misery and need."[45] Curiously, 'need' is not here understood as a negation of affluence, but rather as a psychological variable relative to a person's self-esteem or will to improve. An individual's true level of need can be determined by observing him at labor.

> The best indicator of an able-bodied poor man's need is his labor in the workhouse. For here, insofar as he has a claim to support his family, he must also subject to the necessary rules and regulations that are prerequisites for the maintenance of such an institution and for the welfare of the moral and physical conditions of the detainees.[46]

In other words, social behavior under rules and regulations within the structure of a large closed institution offers a direct measure of an individual's need relative to his self-esteem. The measurement is given as the subject finds a natural place for himself somewhere in the artificial structure of rules and opportunities. This place is where an economic balance begins to work and concurrently where self-esteem may begin to grow. Ulrik argues that the general economic relationship between self-esteem and labor must be the operative hinge in the process of administering effective assistance: "No other form of relief sustains the recipient's self-esteem like this one does, for it evokes the feeling that work is payment for assistance received. No other help may better motivate him to reassume the business of self-support."[47]

But Ulrik goes further and considers also the so-called unworthy. For them he pictures alms houses of great austerity with separate

45. Ulrik, *Hved hvilke Midler bør Fattigdommen bekjæmpes?*, 33.

46. Ibid., 29.

47. Ibid.

sleeping quarters for men and women, and without any possibility of permanent residence. "Admit but shelter for the night, each sex in their own lodgings, under proper supervision for the sake of order and cleanliness, and the provisional nature will press upon anyone enough that only a few would not strain every nerve to regain proper housing. While alternative modes of assistance rather dim their prudence, this would urge it on."[48] More attractive arrangements would then be made available in exchange for signs of submission to house economy. Ulrik envisions how the unworthy will begin to associate actual need with the real expense of their labor. The sense of honest labor rewarded may then return to the worker and nourish the individual's self-esteem. There was hope, perhaps not for everyone, but for anyone of the most downtrodden. Although a seemingly extinct self-esteem could always possibly be awakened, there would always also be some who would fall by the wayside. The implication is that one cannot know in advance who will rise and who will not. One cannot know at which point, or under what circumstances, or for what reasons a person will abandon sloth and egotism and actually desire to be part of social structure. Hope, therefore, is based on pure potentiality, on what may come perhaps, rather than on religious faith.

This marks an important difference with respect to Riis. Or better yet, all of the proposals above are markedly different from Riis's. None of the Danish charity positions examined here resemble his conservative materialism. But the argument that I am trying to raise is not based on likeness but on difference. What migrated with Riis from Copenhagen were a certain number of structurally resilient problems, problems whose pertinence and possible solutions articulate themselves through differing opinions, ideals, and programs. I do not suggest that Riis synthesized those diverging views. Such an argument would require evidence of Riis having studied these texts, or been familiar with their argument and form. My argument,

48. ibid., 27.

by contrast, does not imply that he was, and I am convinced he was not. The texts I have elaborated upon did not provide any ideological or theoretical points of departure for Riis's work. They are presented here much rather like fossils of an extinct discursive ecology—deposits from a once living way of thinking, talking, writing about, and looking upon urban poverty—one which Riis was exposed to, indeed a part of. It is neither possible nor necessary for us to draw a complete picture of this living discourse. But it is of importance to have made it clear that *problems* were intensely debated pertaining to a) the causes of poverty growth and its effective remedies; b) the distinction between the worthy and the unworthy poor; c) labor houses as moral restoration facilities; d) techniques for poverty diagnostics; e) the psychology of self-respect and the will to improve; f) whether family life is an earned right or a precondition for hope; g) whether skills in urban livelihood should be taught or demanded; h) the role of commerce and thrift vs. assistance; i) bad housing and its effects and causes; j) the proper distribution of public and private initiatives. Safe to say, Copenhagen and New York differed significantly with respect to the intensity with which these public concerns were disputed between 1860 and 1880. All of those listed here were stirring less controversy in America. Jacob Riis showed not only an extraordinary interest in them, he went against the tide in New York and made them publically significant. In his early news reporter writings, they tend to appear guardedly and piecemeal, one at the time; later, more extensive work show signs of combining them into greater complexes, evoking new relative invariants that further raise the bar of his claims.

Regarding the actual migration itself, my concern is less with the 'host' of the transport, the person Jacob A. Riis, than with the conditions for migrant problems to take root in New York. And more than just taking root—I am interested in how the conventional American ways of thinking, talking, writing about, and looking at mass urban poverty could mutate with Riis and form a new curve, pursue a new 'statement', with new capacities to conduct political agitation. Which were the processes that facilitated mutation? In the next chapter I shall seek for parts of an answer in the rhetorical styles that parcelled the American representations of tenement poverty. Riis's humor and particular diction seem to have probed the existing charity discourse for places to graft a new set of concerns. This probing may provide answers to how the diagram was grounded and able to prosper, but it does not explain the event of mutation itself, which will be explored in a later chapter.

CHAPTER 4

Probes of Jokes and Bricolage Writing

A developed sense of humor distinguishes *How the Other Half Lives* from other charity monographs published around the same time. Volumes like Charles Loring Brace's *The Dangerous Classes of New York* (1872), Felix Adler's *The Moral Instruction of Children* (1893), Henry George's *Progress and Poverty* (1879), Josiah Strong's *Our Country* (1885) or *In Darkest England and The Way Out* by General Booth (1890) are anything but funny. They occasionally explore wit and eloquence, but they are entirely devoid of railleries, satire, jokes, or even simple puns. The same is true of charity publications in smaller formats, i.e. magazine articles, booklets, pamphlets, or newspaper reports. Reformers preferring these media, e.g. Charles Parkhurst, Josephine Shaw Lowell, Washington Gladden, Elisha Harris or Stephen Smith likewise reveal no talent for farce or comedy.

A similar appraisal can be made of the generic literary style of charity: overall, the genre was stylistically uniform and, it appears, perceived as quite wearisome. In spite of its dependence on persuasive impact, the collective body of writers never experimented with composition or rhetoric. Instead, the genre remained between the binary poles of classical charm and modern objectivity, which, when overlaid with appeals to public sentiment, produced a crossbreed between the affected and the academic. Conventional charity rhetorics differed primarily in terms of sentimental pathos. By contrast, Riis's capricious style, his helter-skelter jumble of objects and methods, his odd habit of switching effortlessly from statistics to anecdote, from interview to irony, from tear-jerk to fury, even within a singular passage—this bricolage writing introduced a new choleric voice to the city's charity chorus.

This does not mean that all popular writings on urban poverty and tenement life were boring, earnest, and unexciting. A plethora of skid row adventures, tenement novels, and short stories from the slums offered a rich palette of low-life drama and excitement, targeted particularly to the more sensitive souls of the bourgeoisie. For the more callous audiences, a daring and explicit tenement literature had developed, one that excelled in thrilling peeks and spectacular descriptions, and which explored every possible chance to amuse with witty tropes and provocative formulations. These latter works catered to the male, curious bourgeoisie with a range of stylistic tastes, from the facetiously epigrammatic to the explicitly sordid. The genre is sometimes referred to as "Sunshine and Shadow" after Matthew Hale Smith's 1868 tome *Sunshine and Shadow in New York*. Earlier similar publications are easy to find, for instance George G. Foster's *New York By Gaslight and Other Urban Sketches* from 1856. Foster had previously published two similar, if somewhat more fictional books, *New York in Slices* (1849) and *Celio: or New York Above-ground and Under-ground* (1850). Later important genre contributions include James MacCabe's *New York by Sunlight and Gaslight* (1882), and Riis's contemporary, Helen Campbell who, like Riis, wrote for *The Tribune* and had her *Darkness and Daylight, or Lights and Shadows of New York Life* published both as a single volume and as a feuilleton between 1892 and 1900. Smith later co-edited *Wonders of a Great City: or, the Sights, Secrets and Sins of New York* together with Henry L. Williams and Ralph Bayard: a far more daring review was this one relative to Smith's earlier work, comparable to Heinrich Oskar von Karlstein's *Gotham and the Gothamites, or the Gay Girls of New York* (1886) or Howe and Hummel's *In Danger, or Life in New York* (1888). Such titles exemplify a bold and explicit address that went deep and straight into the horrors of slum life. But none of these works supported any particular charity program or even social reform in general, nor did they explore the characteristic jump-cut bricolage style that would become Riis's trademark.

Audaciously amusing slum stories were not, of course, exclusively available through books. Respectable Sunday magazines such as *Harper's Weekly, Frank Leslie's Sunday Magazine* (along with less reputable papers such as *The National Police Gazette* and *The World*) regularly brought a slice of the curious slum to the middle class in the form of cartoons, causeries, and illustrated features. From the witticisms of *Harper's* and *Frank Leslie's* to the sideshow absurdities of *The Police Gazette*, the poor were regularly portrayed as funny, stupid, and ridiculous, but often also as victimized, sympathetic, and tragic. If the dangers of the slums ever surfaced in entertaining print venues, the violence depicted was exclusively exercised upon a fellow tenement dweller or a citizen of questionable repute (cf. fig. 38). One example of the milder type of cartoons, published in *Harper's Weekly*, shows a tramp in a tattered coat appearing before a judge. Underneath is a caption, "No Parvenu about him", and the following dialogue:

> POLICE JUDGE: "It seems, Gabe, that you have been here a good many times before—*in short,* that you are an old-timer!
> UNCLE GABE: "Yes Jedge, I is. I been here befo', an' I ain't gwine ter put myself *down on de lebbul* wid dese mushroom niggers an' loafers dat come here fo' de fust time."

A more direct and cynical kind of humor can be found in the New York edition of *The National Police Gazette*, on a popular page called "City Side-shows." With a few crude drawings, this regular page recounted 6-10 burlesque anecdotes from the tenements. A tramp found rat-bitten and dying in a cellar (Nov 15, 1884); a troupe of Italians attempting to marry off a twelve-year-old girl at the Alderman's office (Oct 18, 1884); a gentleman discovering being pickpocketed of his gold watch (November 8, 1884)—each week produced a new series of cruel and sentimental sketches upon a monochrome backdrop of prejudice and bigotry. There is scarcely a twist to these stories: like short vaudeville acts, they present an absurd scene for as long as curiosity lasts.

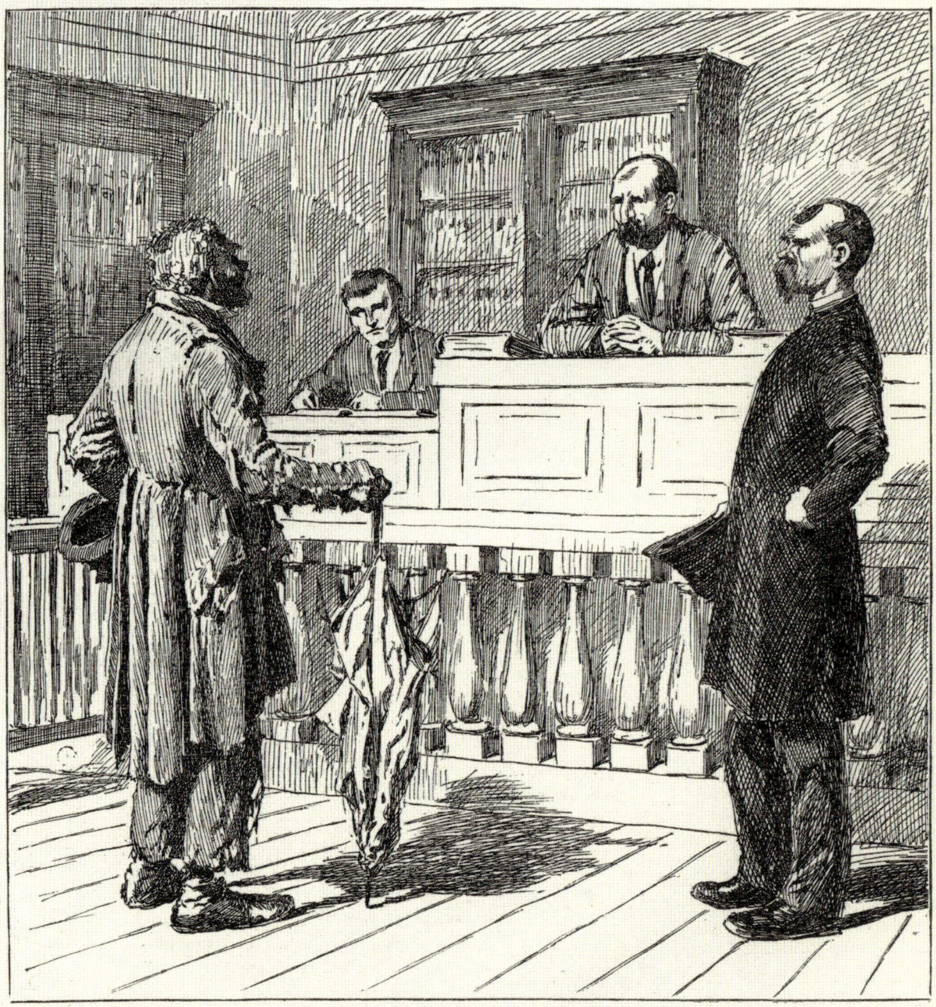

NO PARVENU ABOUT HIM.

POLICE JUDGE. "It seems, Gabe, that you have been here a good many times before—*in short*, that you are an old-timer!"

UNCLE GABE. "Yes, Jedge, I is. I been here befo', an' I ain't gwine ter put myself *down on de lebbul* wid dese mushroom niggers an' loafers dat come here fo' de fust time."

Figure 18. Anonymous cartoonist, "No Parvenu About Him," Harper's Weekly, Dec. 21, 1889, 1015.

Figure 19. "City Side-shows," National Police Gazette, Nov. 29, 1884.

CITY SIDE-SHOWS.

What One Sees in the Wings of the Great Metropolitan Human Comedy.

IN A NEW YORK JUNK-SHOP.

Among the odd places in a large city like New York few are queerer than the junk-shops. In the first instance pieces of old rope, bits of chains, parts of cable and other marine odds and ends make up the stock in trade. On the other side of the Atlantic they are still called "marine shops." In every city most of the junk-shops are situated near the wharfs, and furnish a convenient market for the ropes, chains and irons filched by moneyless sailors or "dock-rats." The police find it difficult to detect a theft of this kind, for often the thief has confederates among the subordinate officers of the ship.

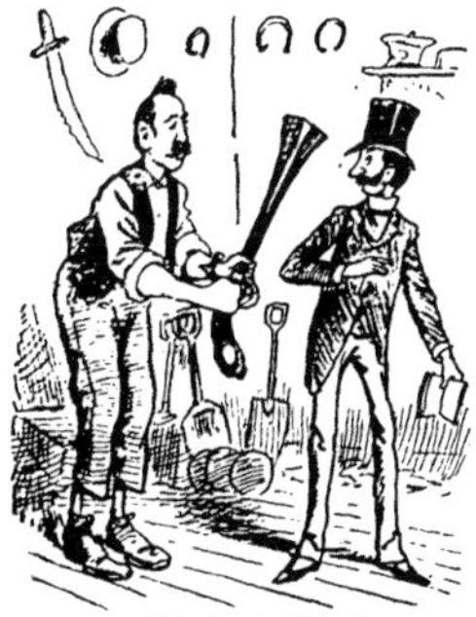

Julius Cæsar's pistol.

From dealing in junk or ropes in the first instance the junk-shop has now developed into an important and in some cases exceedingly profitable concern, and deals in all sorts of second-hand commodities. The law prohibits junk-dealers from handling new and unused merchandise. Some shops deal exclusively in rags, others in old metals, and others in old paper. But most of them deal in all sorts of wares. One of the representative junk shops of the city is in Spring street, near Elm street. It is an old rambling wooden structure, and the brown paint has almost disappeared from its weather-beaten front. Some of the green shutters are broken and others swing creaking on their rusty hinges. On the first floor a large would be show-window, with dusty cobweb-curtained glass, contains specimens of the shop's wares. The door stands awry, and an old lager-beer sign takes the place of a pane of glass in its upper panel. The iron doorstep, once corrugated and embossed with figures, is now worn smooth. An old rusty safe, rescued from some fire, stands a lone sentinel on the pavement. A rugged looking door opens on the pavement and discloses a mass of chains and irons on the dark, musty cellar below. The lintels of the doorway are pierced with awls, nails and all sorts of pointed instruments. With difficulty one deciphers the sign above the door. The first object that attracts the attention as one enters the shop is a large sword hanging from the ceiling. This is the "Only Original Sword of Bunker Hill," or so says the salesman. Near it are a brace of daggers—one of them dented as if it had done bloody work in its time. A little further on rests upon a shelf a military officer's cap, keeping company with a slouch hat on one side and a clerical looking hat on the other.

Just as a reporter was admiring the military hat and wondering what man had worn it, the salesman, drawing from its hiding-place a large horse-pistol, said:

"Here is one of the greatest rarities in the shop. This pistol was used by Julius Cæsar at the battle of Pharsalia."

"But pistols were not invented at that time."

"Just so—hence this pistol's rarity."

From different parts of the ceiling lamps of all sorts are hanging. Here is a dinner-bell and there is a

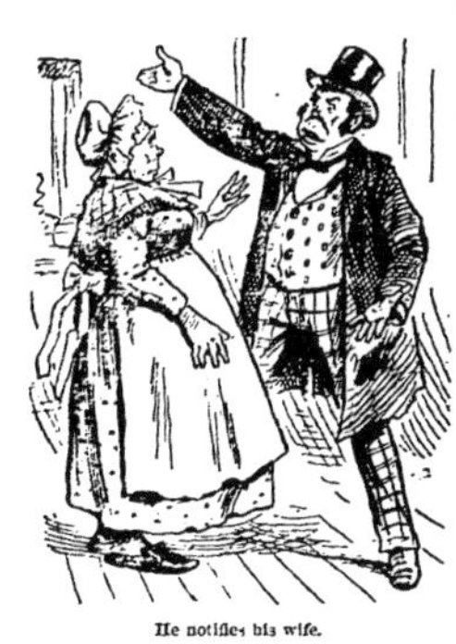

He notifies his wife.

hungry-looking meat-ax. A trombone in the corner stands in a tipsy, top-heavy attitude. On one side of the door a group of crowbars is huddled together, and on the other side a family of spades and shovels is assembled. A sign hangs from the ceiling: "Beware of the Dog. No Smoking." For good luck, horseshoes in great numbers are fastened over the doorways. Immediately above the trombone, and not far from a bevy of beer-bottles, an old family Bible lies on a shelf. A leaf of the family record is still remaining, although the names are faded and illegible. On the same shelf near to some suspicious-looking demijohns lies a curious volume, curious only by being in such strange company. The book is entitled "Key to Heaven." In the junk-shops missals and prayer-books are mixed up with dime novels and vilely illustrated newspapers in one common heap.

THEY WORKED THE CANDIDATE.

"Patrick Lefoe," said Justice Duffy, at the Tombs, "how did you come to get drunk?"

"I'm a candidate for office, sir," was his answer.

"For what position?"

"Alderman. I was nominated by the People's party. I asked for five minutes' delay before I gave my word of acceptance. I ran home to my wife. 'Kate,' says I, 'if I get to be an Alderman it will be the making of me. We can afford to live on Fifth avenue. Now, answer me truthfully, was there any one in your family ever arrested for stealing? If so, let me know right away, or it will be out in the papers and we will be disgraced. But if you say not, I will go ahead and be elected.' She said 'no,' and I ran back to the hall, and accepted the nomination, and then——"

"Well?"

"I threw a twenty-dollar on the counter in the bar-room, and said: 'Refuse no one a drink.' I started to go out when I was accosted by a committee of young men, who asked me to purchase tickets for a benefit. They claimed to represent 500 voters, and I purchased $10 worth of tickets. Then committees from four pleasure clubs, representing each 100 voters, asked me to buy tickets for their annual ball, and I took $10 worth from each. Next came a big fellow who seized me by the shoulder and said: 'I want to talk with you. I'm the man who runs this district, and you can't be elected unless you are solid with me. You want to fix me, to get the boys in your favor; say $200, that will do now until I see you again.' I then sneaked into the yard, up the stairs to the roof, then climbed over several buildings and made my way on the street and went home."

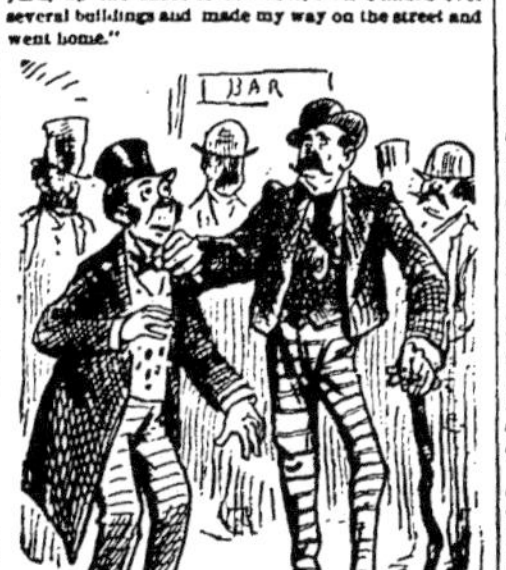

The big fellow who wanted to talk with him.

"You haven't explained to me yet how you came to be arrested?"

"Well, hold on: I'm coming to it now. No sooner did I get home when a brass band appeared before my door and serenaded me. I went on the stoop and made a speech, after which I went with them to a saloon and put up the drinks again. This time I began to drink and I got pretty full. A man, whom I am now informed is a swindler, came up to me and said: 'I hear you want to be elected. Here's a chance for you. A woman with three children will be dispossessed Monday and if you do the right thing the district will go wild over you.' I gave him $25 and then I was informed of the man's character. I became so disgusted that I drank more and this morning I awoke to find myself in a station-house."

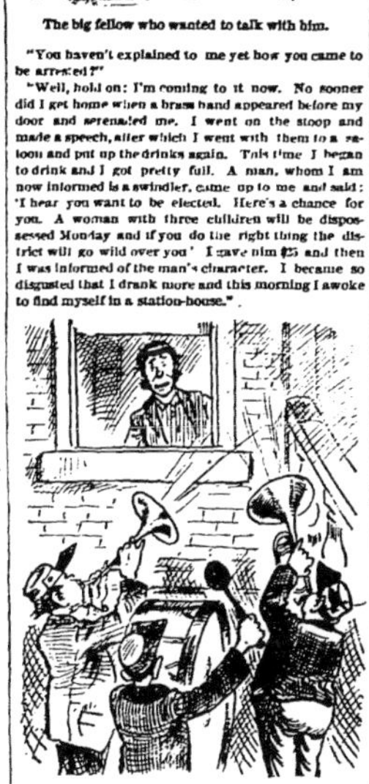

He is serenaded.

He was discharged, and as he went out he was heard muttering: "I'm sick already of the whole business."

LEVIED ON THE BUTTER-DISH.

Jacob Hanterman ran up a bill of $8.90 at Charles Khuen's drug store, 401 North Third avenue. Khuen dunned him unavailingly. On Friday morning he waited an hour in Hanterman's dining-room, at 88 East One Hundred and Eighth street, to see Hanterman. Hanterman did not come.

A silver butter dish on a sideboard gave Khuen an inspiration. He picked up the butter-dish and scribbled this note to Mr. and Mrs. Hanterman:

"I had to help myself. I take this butter-dish as security, and I promise to return it immediately on payment of bill."

The druggist went home. He was at the Harlem Court next day on a summons sworn out by Hanterman.

"Mr. Khuen," said Justice Gorman, "return the butter-dish to Mr. Hanterman, and you, Mr. Hanterman, pay the debt you owe Mr. Khuen."

The druggist promised to return the butter-dish, Mr. Hanterman said he would settle his bill, and the Justice dismissed the case. Then complainant and defendant went out of court.

Ten minutes later the druggist hurriedly presented

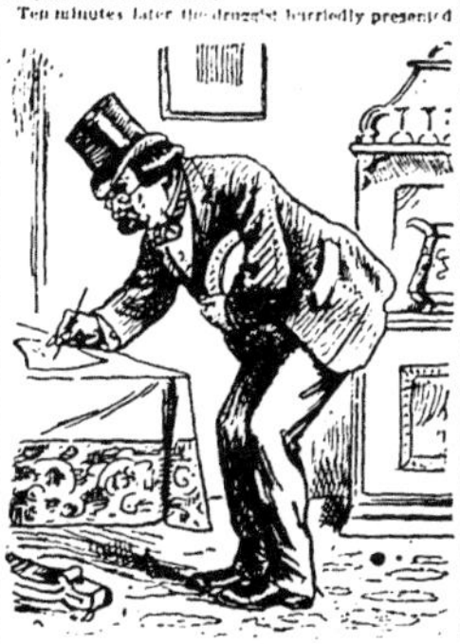

He levies on the butter-dish.

himself to Justice Gorman, holding aloft the butter-dish.

"Mr. Hanterman refuses to accept it," he said.

"All right," replied the Justice. "Keep it."

The druggist smiled and took the butter-dish home.

A RAT-BITTEN SPECIMEN TRAMP.

Thomas Mersen, who lay in a hammock in the Liberty Street police station the other night, was about as miserable a looking specimen of humanity as could possibly be looked upon. The police discovered him the previous night apparently dead, lying on the sidewalk in Canal street. When brought to the station-house he was helpless and unable to give any account of himself. He was offered food, which he refused to take, saying that he preferred to be left alone to die. A Bellevue Hospital ambulance was sent for, but the doctor would not permit him to be carried to the hospital, because it was the duty of the authorities in Philadelphia, whence he came, to take him in charge for treatment. The Emigration Commissioners refused to extend any aid, as the man has been more than a year in the country.

"I can do nothing with the unfortunate fellow," said Capt. Bergbold, of the Twenty-seventh precinct. "Still he is a man, and 'tis too bad that he should be left to die of hunger. There is no provision made here for the purchase of food in a case of this kind, but I had refreshments provided for him at my own expense a few times and he refused to eat. It is the most awful case of destitution I have ever seen. He is so filthy that you can't go near him. Just try."

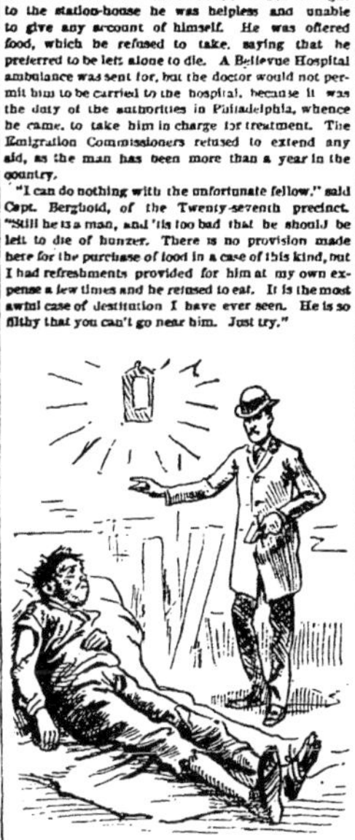

A woful end to a wasted life.

The reporter went to the cellar in the corner of which was a dark, shapeless mass. The dying man turned a few times when he heard the strange voice and moaned piteously. His right hand was crippled and broken. His face was swollen so much that it looked like a gutta-percha ball. His clothes were ragged and dirty, and looked as if rats or other animals had been striving to make a meal out of them. He had no stockings on, and the wretched covering that did duty for boots was broken in many places.

"Hi'm an Englishman," said he, "an' may jest as well say hi'm dyin'. Hi dean't mean hi'm at my old trade," he continued, with a sickly smile, "when I tell you hi'm dyin', because hi happen to be a dyer by trade; but hi'm dyin' in real earnest from—hi don't know what. The last place hi worked was at Samuel Wilson's dye works, Manayunk, Philadelphia. Hi got my hand broken there by the machinery and tramped to New York, where hi could get nothin' to do, as I hain't fit for much now. Hi peddled about for some months and fell down last night in the street from weakness. The police then brought me here."

"How old are you?" asked the reporter.

"Hi'm twenty-four."

"Why, you look forty-four, man!"

"Do I? Ah, well; jest you wait till ye have weathered the times like me, h'an' I bet ye'll look no better if ye be alive at all."

ELECTION DAY.

[Subject of Illustration.]

Our last page illustration represents the various incidents which contribute to the humor of an Election Day in New York. The challenge of a vote, the Chinaman who can't understand the fact that he is an exception to the general rule, the distribution of the "soap" and the bulletining of the returns, make up the graphic picture.

A TRIPLE TRAGEDY.

A Discarded Husband Mortally Wounds His Wife and Female Friend and Commits Suicide.

[Subject of Illustration.]

Richard J. Waddy, who was a stove-molder in the Great Western foundry, Leavenworth, Kan., became intimate, some years ago, with a woman whom he subsequently married. Afterward they had trouble and separated. She went to Kansas City, and there caused his arrest. She there became intimate with a woman named Mollie Logue, and Waddy advised her not to go with her. She visited Leavenworth on Oct. 19, in company with Miss Logue, and Waddy followed them about the streets for about three hours, when they went to Mrs. Webster's home on Miami street. Mrs. Waddy was seated at a table, writing something for an old lady named Cook, who was in the room, when Waddy entered, saying:

"What are you doing there?"

"I am writing," she replied.

He pulled out a 38-caliber bull-dog, saying:

"I have something here for you."

His wife jumped up and started to run, when he caught her by the dress and fired. The ball struck her in the spine, a little below the shoulder-blade. Mollie Logue, who was in the room, jumped and started to run, when Waddy fired at her, saying:

"And you, too."

Mrs. Waddy fell, and Miss Logue, who had been struck in the back, a little to the right of the spine, wheeled around and started back toward Waddy, when he fired at her again, the ball entering the right breast, making a fearful wound. She staggered, and as she was falling he fired at her again, this shot wounding his victim in both hands. He then, while she was falling, placed the muzzle of the revolver to his right temple and fired, tearing away a large portion of the skull, and fell dead almost instantly. Both women are yet alive, but physicians think there is no hope of their recovery. When the news spread large crowds congregated about the premises, and it was with difficulty the police could make room enough for the surgeons to attend to the wounded. The man is said to have a wife and family in Troy, N. Y. He was about fifty-five years of age and was considered by the iron-molders to have more than ordinary intelligence. When Waddy's body was searched the revolver was found, and a two-edged knife about a foot long, both edges sharp as a razor.

In Waddy's pockets were found several letters, which show that the tragedy was premeditated. "Sunday, Oct. 19," he wrote, "will end the career of a deceitful and adulterous woman, who ruined the happiness of myself and of her first husband, Edward B. Manchester." The wife's flight a few weeks ago seems to have preyed upon Waddy's mind. He thought Mollie Logue induced her to leave the city. "I came to my dinner on the 1st of September last," he said in one of his letters, "to find the house empty, trunks gone, articles of furniture taken and given away to her particular friends, and everything done to make me as desolate as they possibly could."

WHERE THE PRIZES GO!

A Fortune at a Stroke--The Whole of the First Capital to One Person.

NEW ORLEANS, Oct. 15, 1884.

The undersigned certifies that he held for collection for account of a depositor in the Louisiana National Bank, whole ticket No. 78,455, in the Louisiana State Lottery, which drew the First Capital Prize of SEVENTY FIVE THOUSAND DOLLARS, on Tuesday, Oct. 14, 1884, said ticket having cost the sum of five dollars, and that the amount was promptly paid by a check on the New Orleans National Bank, on presentation of the ticket at the office of the Company.

E. B. LHOSTE,
Exchange and Discount Clerk,
Louisiana National Bank, New Orleans, La.

NEW ORLEANS, Oct. 17, 1884.

The undersigned certifies that he held for collection for account of Harry Smith, Justice of the Peace, and William M. Kennedy, Planter, Greenville, Miss., through Bank of Greenville, one-fifth each of ticket No. 77,956, in the Louisiana State Lottery, which drew the Second Capital Prize of TWENTY FIVE THOUSAND DOLLARS, on Tuesday, Oct. 14, 1884, said tickets having cost the sum of one dollar each, and that the amount was promptly paid by a check on the New Orleans National Bank, on presentation of the tickets at the office of the Company.

W. A. POLLOCK & CO.,
50 Union street, New Orleans, La.

NEW ORLEANS, Oct. 20, 1884.

The undersigned certifies that he held for collection for account of A. C. Bennett, 210 Sedgwick street, Chicago, Ill., one-fifth ticket No. 77,956, in the Louisiana State Lottery, which drew the Second Capital Prize of TWENTY-FIVE THOUSAND DOLLARS, on Tuesday, Oct. 14, 1884, said ticket having cost the sum of one dollar, and that the amount was promptly paid by a check on the New Orleans National Bank, on presentation of the ticket at the office of the Company.

F. R. OSBURN, Agent,
Southern Express Co., New Orleans, La.

NEW ORLEANS, Oct. 21, 1884.

The undersigned certifies that he held for collection for account of W. C. Briggs, Chicago, Ill., one-fifth ticket No. 77,956 in the Louisiana State Lottery, which drew the Second Capital Prize of TWENTY FIVE THOUSAND DOLLARS, on Tuesday, Oct. 14, 1884, said ticket having cost the sum of one dollar, and that the amount was promptly paid by a check on the New Orleans National Bank, on presentation of the ticket at the office of the Company.

B. W. CASON, Agent,
Pacific Express Co., New Orleans, La.
—*Texas Siftings.*

THE WHIRL OF SPORT.

[Subject of Illustration.]

Our sporting page of illustration this week represents as its principal feature the encounter between Jack Dempsey and Tom Henry, which recently took place at the Eighth Street theatre. Among the attendants, whose portraits will easily be recognized, were Capt. Brogan in full uniform, time-keepers Mike McDonald and William E. Harding, and referee Al. Smith.

The other illustrations depict the night parade of the "Mets," Al. Smith's famous visit to and challenge of the Republican National Committee with a $20,000 bet, and the triumphal reception in Pittsburg of Dominick McCaffrey.

Feature columnists would on rare occasions also poke fun at philanthropists of the lower bourgeoisie. In February 1888, *Lippincott's Monthly Magazine* brought a story by Charlotte Adams, a middle-class woman, who had gone undercover in a working-woman's boarding-house "to 'see life'" and "to do something of which I know my Philistine acquaintances will disapprove."[1] Her humor is sharp, clever, and laconic, targeting fellow inmates as well as old friends. The style is jerky, unadorned, and anxious to quickly deliver the next witty remark. Here is a sample:

> As one woman they rose against me, although I am sure no human being could have been more inoffensive. They dubbed me 'Shoddy'! That particular epithet, as far as I know, had never been applied to me before. I had, on the contrary, been sniffed at, in circles of wealth, for being 'literary'. I thought it rather amusing that I should have had to go to a working-woman's house in order to win my social spurs. As time went on, the impression strengthened that I was an interloper and a bloated aristocrat. Goodness knows what there was to bloat on, with only bread and tea and stewed prunes for luncheon! [...] There was sweet little Lily, the youngest of the flock and everybody's pet, who turned out to be a professional sneak-thief; there was the tearful young widow who 'jumped' her board; there was the proud and haughty dame who returned at two o'clock in the morning in hiccoughly condition and roused the house by ringing the bell until she was admitted, when she calmly remarked that she had been out for pickles. This part of her story was true, for her progress up-stairs was accented by the dull thud of salted cucumbers, and the early risers among the boarders nearly broke their necks over these slippery forms the next morning. This tale, my dear young readers, is designed to show the folly of early rising. [...] There is one public nuisance

1. Charlotte Adams, "Life at a Working-Woman's Home" in *Lippincott's Monthly Magazine*, Feb 1888, 235-240.

> against which the American shop-girl protests, and with reason, and that is the American female philanthropist. What pleasure the shop-girl takes in snubbing her would-be patroness! and, oh, how strongly my sympathies are with her![2]

A far more common form of satire were the facetiously eloquent flaneuring causeries that took readers through the lower wards. On April 19, 1890, "Of a Friday in the Jewish Quarter in New York" was published in *Harper's Weekly* family magazine:

> The woman is past fifty, and wears a scratch—the ugliest of all known wigs. It is a mere shred, a mangy whisp of false hair, with an uncommonly bad artificial part to it. It is not more than a three-finger-breadth of a wig, and she carries it awry, and her own hair, with gray streakage through it, would be so much more becoming. She wears her scratch, which hangs over one temple, because she is an orthodox Jewess. Probably she is a Polish woman. She has been taught by a cruel tradition that it is unbecoming for a married woman to wear her own hair, and so she makes that greatest of all sacrifices when she dons a scrawny wig, and tries to make herself hideous. The poor soul does not know that she follows the fashion of the Japanese married woman, who for precisely the same reasons blackens her snow-white teeth.[3]

The piece abides by an important rule of the genre: to inform the reader that the poor ignorant woman is the victim of a cruel structure. Another example, which ridicules the "wash-tub Amazons" bickering at the busy tenement house water tap, illustrates the same principle: "each and every one of them wants to fill her tub at the same time, while only one of them can be accommodated by the feeble stream of water that flows in the average tenement-house above the second floor. [...] It must be drawn before seven o'clock in the morning, at which hour the great manufacturing establishments commence their

2. Ibid.

3. "Of a Friday in the Jewish Quarter in New York" in *Harper's Weekly*, April 19, 1890, 34: 1739, 306.

daily drain upon the inefficient water mains of the city."[4] In other words, an infrastructural shortcoming causes this particular inconvenience, which, of course, excuses the quarreling women and their ridiculous-looking behavior. This commonplace trope appears to have functioned as a form of forgiving safety valve, which protected the narrator from appearing overtly condescending and morally judgmental. Ridiculing the poor and their behavior was no breach of protocol as long as the writer also showed knowledge of and sympathy with their situation. However, this rule applies only to the worthy poor, insofar as they muster some thrift against the structural adversities. As the cartoon from *Harper's Weekly* suggests, the unworthy need no such consideration.

Riis was often noticed for his sense of humor. Many reviewers commented on his alacrities and particularly on how they fitted with his otherwise mindful message. "Sprightly Humor enlivens a Thoughtful Address on Reforming Street Savage," read a headline in 1905 after a lecture in San Francisco.[5] Fifteen years earlier, the *New York Tribune* reviewed *How the Other Half Lives* with similar emphasis on its entertaining aspect: "To the reader who seeks only amusement the volume will furnish all that is required, but the reader must be something worse than a cynic who can lay it down without serious reflection."[6] But Riis's tenement jokes were not only different from conventional parodies—they also served a different purpose. Whereas ordinary newspaper quips preserved and enforced bourgeois preconceptions, Riis's jokes rather seduced the audience, undermining common conventions and opinion, probing, as it were, for opportunities to install unfamiliar problems and connections. It is a fine distinction to make, but an important one.

Unlike the generic tenement joke, Riis made no distinction between funny appearance and redeeming social structure. In Riis's work, the poor do not merely look stupid, the poor *are* as stupid as the slums have

4. "Wash Day in the Tenements", in *Harper's Weekly*, Dec 21, 1889, 33: 1722, 1014.
5. "Plea for Boy of the Slums" in *San Francisco Call*, Jan 10, 1905, LC, Riis Papers, box 16.
6. "The Seamy Side: Great Social Problems Illustrated" in *New York Tribune*, Nov 25, 1890, 8.

made them, and that brings a sinister quality to his raillery.[7] For example, Riis's joke about water shortage in the tenements is distinctly different from the one in *Harper's Weekly*. It is ironic: "the water does not rise in summer to the second story, while the beer flows unchecked to the all-night picnics on the roof."[8] Riis's tenants are not victimized by structure and the root cause of their ordeal is not found in the factories' drainage of public water supplies. The source of their problem is what he calls "the system." What is particularly worth noting about this vague term is that the system includes the poor as a contributing cause to their own poverty. Because the poor help to impoverish themselves by sustaining the tenement system, it would be unconvincing to mock their awkward behavior and then to express empathy with their battle against the structure. Irony is more appropriate as it allows the author, after Kierkegaard, to negate the immediate phenomenon at the same time as the ironic statement negates itself. Silently presuming a certain shared preunderstanding, the ironic speaker may lean on this double cancellation to dialectically identify the phenomenon with some presupposed essence, and suggest jokingly what is meant in earnest.[9] Let's look at another example where Riis establishes accord ironically.

7. Riis, *How the Other Half Lives*, 214.

8. Ibid., 17.

9. See Søren Kierkegaard, *On the Concept of Irony* (Princeton University Press, Princeton: 1989): 248. "The ironic figure of speech cancels itself, however, inasmuch as the one who is speaking assumes that his hearers understand him, and thus, through a negation of the immediate phenomenon, the essence becomes identical with the phenomenon. If it sometimes happens that an ironic figure of speech such as this is misunderstood, this is not the fault of the one who is speaking, except insofar as he has come to grips with such a crafty fellow as irony, who likes to play tricks just as much on friends as on foes. In fact, we say of such an ironic turn of speech: Its earnestness is not in earnest. The remark is so earnest it is shocking, but the hearer in the know shares the secret lying behind it. But precisely thereby the irony is once again canceled. It is the most common form of irony to say something earnestly that is not meant in earnest. The second form of irony, to say as a jest, jestingly, something that is meant in earnest, is more rare. /fn: This most frequently happens in connection with a certain despair and thus is often found in humorists, for example, when Heine waggishly ponders which is worse, a toothache or a bad conscience, and declares himself for the first." For an illuminating and entertaining compilation of humorous passages in Kierkegaard, see *The Humor of Kiekegaard: an Anthology* ed. Thomas C. Oden (Princeton University Press, Princeton: 2004).

> The one thing you shall vainly ask for in the chief city of America is a distinctively American community. [...] They are not here. In their place has come this queer conglomerate mass of heterogeneous elements, ever striving and working like whiskey and water in one glass, and with the like result: final union and a prevailing taint of whiskey.[10]

The heuristic analogy contrasts its sinister meaning. Riis's witty identification of social and chemical processes is the rather eloquent opposite of the whiskey-tainted masses that the trope conjures up. The polarity gives to Riis's message a unique ironical edge. His wit only deepens the menace.

Irony is used with impressive variation. Examples include simple one-liners: "Blind Man's Alley takes a day off and goes to 'see' Mr. Blake."[11] But there are also complex metonymic jokes, for example about the ill-tempered Italians and New York's phlegmatic law enforcement: "When the police do not know the name of an escaped murderer, they guess at Pascale and send the name out on alarm; in nine cases out of ten it fits." As Keith Gandall and many others have observed, Riis was no stranger to exploiting racial prejudice for the sake of amusement. Two well-known passages often illustrate how stereotype is employed to salt his ironies: the first about suspenders in Jewtown, which, he says, are intensely peddled but never used; "perhaps they are hung up as bric-a-brac in its homes, or laid away and saved up as the equivalent of cash;" the second about Chinatown, which "has enlisted the telegraph for the dissemination of public intelligence, but it has got hold of the contrivance by the wrong end. As the wires serve us in newspaper making, so the Chinaman makes use of the pole for the same purpose," that is, to stick up notes and posters on it.[12] Preconceptions of illegal gambling notes in Chinatown and secret currencies in Jewtown were certainly not as amusing as were Riis's sardonic analogies. The contrast between the joke and its

10. Riis, *How the Other Half Lives*, 19.
11. Ibid., 30.
12. Gandall, *The Virtous of the Vicious*, 63, 70; See also Riis, *How the Other Half Lives*, 94, 82.

point is important to take note of as it forbids the common reduction of his humor to "a reassurance that the immigrant is more ridiculous than threatening;" Riis's jokes are precisely not "a sort of comic relief from the tragedy of his documentary report."[13]

Rather than "a break from his philanthropy," witty remarks were effective agents. Their jolly tone underscores the acuteness of the plight and the dangers brewing, and their unarticulated preconceptions helped making Riis a remarkably welcome and reliable harbinger of bad news. During his many public lectures, wit also served as a probing device that measured his audience and revealed their stance on various charity concerns. Riis did not joke on sensitive topics merely for hoarding support; like most skilled orators, he was able to pick up on the responses that he provoked in areas touched upon. Ironies were rarely heard, to say the least, during American charity lectures and responses to such radical yet indeterminable assertions could be exploited for significant advantage. Based on the audience's responses, Riis could devise agreeable ways af raising problems or suggesting uncomfortable solutions. Irony secured a palatable tone to his admonitions while, as provocations, they were crucial for wedging in conservative materialism among the already established ideologies of charity.

But where did it come from, this irony that was so foreign to American charity? Kierkegaard was of course its strongest champion and most cherished theoretician in Denmark, but among the debaters on poverty aid in Copenhagen, the most ironical one was Vilhelm Munck. Many of his texts offer frequent examples of the same kind of Janus-faced joke, whose point is to create agreement with the reader through unarticulated preconceptions that identify mere appearance as an essence of the poor: "Should one weep or laugh when a poor madam is heard asking her neighbour: 'Lend me 8 Marks to pawn my boots, for I want to see the priest and divorce my husband.'"[14] Or, another example: "A man rented a little duvet and two

13. Gandall, *The Virtous of the Vicious*, 64.

14. Munck, *Om Fattigdommen i Kjøbenhavn*, 25.

pillows for his wife's childbed at 4 Marks a month and then pawned these for 9 Marks, at an interest of 12 sk. a month. For more than six months he paid 4 Marks and 12 sk. a month for bedclothes he did not have and for 9 Marks that he did not own."[15] Formally, the railleries are comparable to Riis's although they are somewhat blunter and less threatening as menaces go. Evidence of matrimonial neglect and economic ineptitude were cause for concern, but such shortcomings were not as offensive to bourgeois sensitivities as those mustered by Riis. Their discursive function in Munck's writings was, moreover, an altogether different one. Whereas Riis's ironies probed an established discourse for places to graft conservative materialism, places from where to begin fostering a different way of conveying charity, Munck sought merely to unite with and entertain an audience already familiar with such tropes. Humor was in no sense absent from Danish charity literature in general, and so it seems unlikely that Munck's witticisms were intended (or able) to challenge any conventions. Unlike Riis, Munck rather maintained an established discourse and never aspired to challenge it.

Bricolage Style

Riis supplemented his sense of humor with a second probing device. Astoundingly frequent and violent shifts in style and tone gave to Riis's writings (in particular his early works) a dynamic, if not a feverish rhythm. Authoritative quotations, firsthand observations, personal recollections, statistics, slander, sensitive euphemisms, enthymemic deductions, hefty declarations, insisting demands, aposiopetic cliffhangers, innuendos, rumors, parables and minutely detailing descriptions replace one another throughout and at a furious pace. At times, the rhetorical rollercoaster appears to have been constructed exclusively for the break-neck experience. In its own way, it broke radically enough with conventions to destabilize the very identity of

15. Ibid., 70.

the genre. It is the complex nature of this idiomatic rupture, and the powers it released to think otherwise, that will be analyzed henceforth.

Although Riis's peculiar style stands out among contemporary peers, his reviewers never commented upon it. In terms of rhetoric and style, Riis was considered factual, clear, and straightforward, fortuitously devoid of the "pathetic" language that otherwise plagued the charity genre. As one, reviewers welcomed his lack of superlatives, painterly adjectives, and emotional metaphors. Soon enough, his mode of address had earned him a reputation for "the simplest diction"[16]; "a simple and direct style"[17]; in short, for work that was "admirably narrated, in a simple, straightforward manner, without any mock sentiment or any mere striving after effect."[18]

Given that the genre extended rhetorically from sentimental fiction to academic objectivity, contemporary reviewers unanimously put *How the Other Half Lives* at the latter end of the scale. The *London Morning Post* said the book was "written calmly and dispassionately, and in the presence of a distracting wealth of highly-promising material [its author] has steadily resisted the temptation towards sensationalism."[19] For the majority of critics who similarly emphasized Riis's simplicity and clarity of diction, these were qualities that rather stood in opposition to ornamental pathos than to a discombobulating composition. Only a minority of readers found in his stylistic disarray a noticeable curiousity—and some did not even consider it a shortcoming. An anonymous reviewer of *The Critic* concluded rather disparagingly: "His book is literally a photograph and as such has its value and lesson, but also its serious limitations. There is a lack of broad and penetrative vision, a singularly warped sense of justice at times, and a roughness amounting almost to brutality."[20] But what the Christmas issue of *The Christian Intelligencer* in similar spirits

16. *New York Herald*, Nov. 23, 1890. LC, Riis Papers, box 10, Riis's scrapbook.
17. *The Spirit*, Feb. 1890. LC, Riis Papers, box 10, Riis's scrapbook.
18. *The Boston Gazette*, Nov. 22, 1890. LC, Riis Papers, box 10, Riis's scrapbook.
19. *London Morning Post*, June 3, 1891. LC, Riis Papers, box 10, Riis's scrapbook.
20. *The Critic: A Weekly review of Literature and the Arts*, Dec. 27, 1890. LC, Riis Papers, box 10, Riis's scrapbook.

euphemized as the book's "vivid word delineations"[21] was not a liability to everyone: a few even considered it a strength. *New York Independent Journal* wrote that "His desire for fact dominates entirely his desire for fine writing and this circumstance will commend his work to many. His facts are startling enough."[22] *The Churchman* even said that "he writes what he knows very much in the unsystematic way in which he seems to have learned it, and not by any means as methodically as he might. But to the ordinary reader this is no disadvantage—rather, perhaps, the reverse."[23] *The Brooklyn Eagle* simply stated the apparent: "He treats the subject like a statistician, an ethical philosopher, an orator and an artist in one."[24]

A comparison with one of Riis's closest peers may help to illuminate the particulars and the operative agency of his style. General Booth's *In Darkest England and the Way Out* was published in America only weeks prior to *How the Other Half Lives*. This circumstance provided critics and philanthropists alike with a welcome opportunity to juxtapose the tenement crises of London and New York and also to compare a Christian socialist and a conservative materialist. Rev. William Booth (founder of the Salvation Army in 1878) wrote in a temperate, patient, and charming style, sincerely engaged in his subject and mindful of the reader following him. Here is a representative passage:

> As I rode through Canada and the United States some three years ago, I was greatly impressed with the superabundance of food which I saw at every turn. Oh, how I longed that the poor starving people, and the hungry children of the East of London and of other centres of our destitute populations, should come into the midst of this abundance, but as it appeared impossible for me to take them into it, I secretly resolved that I would

21. *The Christian Intelligencer*, Dec. 24, 1890. LC, Riis Papers, box 10, Riis's scrapbook.
22. *New York Independent Journal*, Dec. 1890. LC, Riis Papers, box 10, Riis's scrapbook.
23. *The Churchman*, Dec. 13, 1890. LC, Riis Papers, box 10, Riis's scrapbook.
24. *The Brooklyn Eagle*, Nov. 21, 1890. LC, Riis Papers, box 10, Riis's scrapbook.

> endeavour to bring some of it to them. I am thankful to say that I have already been able to do so on a small scale, and hope to accomplish it ere long on a much vaster one. With this view, the first Cheap Food Depot was opened in the East of London two and a half years ago. This has been followed by others, and we have now three establishments: others are being arranged for. Since the commencement in 1888, we have supplied over three and a half million meals. Some idea can be formed of the extent to which these Food and Shelter Depots have already struck their roots into the strata of Society which it is proposed to benefit, by the following figures, which give the quantities of food sold during the year at our Food Depots.[25]

Then follows a list of 17 different foodstuffs, from soup and bread to meat and milk, complete with weight, measure, and additional remarks. One may compare the narration above to Riis's "simple diction," which, in as many lines, tells four different stories:

> The Street Arab puts his whole little soul into what interests him for the moment, whether it be pulverizing a rival who has done a mean trick to a smaller boy, or attending at the "gospel shop" on Sundays. This characteristic made necessary some extra supervision when recently the lads in the Duane Street Lodging-house 'chipped in' and bought a set of boxing gloves. The trapeze suffered a temporary eclipse until this new toy had been tested to the extent of several miniature black eyes upon which soap had no effect, and sundry little scores had been settled that evened things up, as it were, for a fresh start. I tried one night, not with the best of success I confess, to

25. General Booth, *In Darkest England*, 94-95.

> photograph the boys in their washing-room, while they were cleaning up for supper. They were quite turbulent, to the disgust of one of their number who assumed, unasked, the office of general manager of the show, and expressed his mortification to me in very polite language: "If they would only behave, sir!" he complained, "you could make a good picture." "Yes," I said, "but it isn't in them, I suppose." "No, b'gosh!" said he, lapsing suddenly from grace under the provocation, "them kids ain't got no sense, no-how!" The Society maintains five of these boys' lodging houses, and one for girls, in the city. The Duane Street Lodging-house alone has sheltered since its foundation in 1855 nearly a quarter of a million different boys, at a total expense of a good deal less than half million dollars.[26]

Between these two quotations may be glimpsed what *The Critic, The New York Independent*, and *The Churchman* viewed as a lack of methodology in Riis, possibly for the benefit of the ordinary reader. The vivid diction conveys the unruly boys and the opportunistic character of their self-appointed manager; it also samples their coarse language, testifies to Riis's familiarity with them and takes us personally into the washing-room. Whereas Booth writes about the poor from the temporal and spatial distance of his study, and compliant with the rules of description that this distance allows, Riis is a first person narrator who is physically present in the lodging house and who personally interacts with the boys, turning swiftly and conversationally from general characteristics to individual events, from micro- to macro-perspective, and does not shy away from follies like "black eyes upon which soap had no effect," if it conveys spirit and squalor in one phrase. Later in his career, he boasted of his improvisational style and derided his opponents: "The critics of my books complain that I am unsystematic, that I 'put things in' as I think of them. Perhaps so.

26. Riis, *How the Other Half Lives*, 158.

I find it somehow easier to put them in when I think of them than when I don't think of them."[27] What is here referred to as Riis's *bricolage writing* was a rhetorical device with a particular function in the mutation process that produced a new charity object.

While Riis's irony probed for the attractors of discourse, his style probed for its limits. *How the Other Half Lives* explored the exterior boundaries of charity discourse without, of course, strictly determining new borders for its knowledge production. As a piece of genre literature, written and marketed to a target audience, its diction must first of all be noticed for its weakening of genre identity. Reviewers' occasional remarks about Riis's unsystematic treatment of subject signal with sufficient clarity the presence of strong disjointing forces, which, at the same time, opened possibilities for generative impact from exterior genres and formats. This two-fold facilitation of the mutation event will be delineated in next chapter. The pressing question now is this: How did Riis's particular style emerge?

Although a number of sources might be considered, one must be regarded as primary: American newspaper journalism.[28] As Daniel Czitrom has argued, there can be little doubt that Riis' journalistic training turned him towards a motley mode of writing, but it is far less

27. Riis, *The Peril and Preservation of the Home,* 68.

28. Riis's newspaper career began in 1873, when he got hired from the street as a general reporter at the *New York News Association*, an agency that sold supplementary coverage to New York newspapers. The following year, he landed a job as reporter at the *South Brooklyn News*, a small four-page Democrat party paper that, within six months, found Riis as its editor. Six months again, in January 1875, Riis had bought the paper from its Democrat owners. Riis then sold it back in the fall with a net profit of $2,525, having successfully increased sales revenues and turned the editorial column in favor of the Republican Party. Riis stayed on as a reporter for another year before he went on to try his luck in the magic lantern advertising business. In the fall of 1877 Riis returned to reporting and began his career with the *New York Tribune*. Having become a police reporter in early 1878, Riis stayed with the *Tribune* until 1888 when he began writing for *The Evening Sun*. Riis would stay with *The Sun* for eleven years after which he turned to live off his lectures and books.

certain, in my opinion, that the work of one particular journalist, Charles F. Wingate, "anticipated much of the stylistic approach, tone, and organizational framework deployed by Riis."[29] It is true that Wingate, much like Riis, organized his writings around "'race' and place", that is, around ethnic character and downtown tours; it is also true that both shared a focus on particular social issues, but the bricolage style cannot be found in any of the articles by Wingate that Czitrom refers to (predominantly a series published in the *Tribune* during 1884-85). It is not at all certain that Riis's style should be traced to any one particular peer writer. More likely, it probably emerged out of three combining elements: a) a generally volatile time for news journalism, which, during the mid '80s , had developed new generic formats, target audiences, and styles; b) Riis's developing lecture oration, which he had chances to practice with increasing regularity and public support at the time; c) the sheer challenge of composing an extensive literary work in very short time. It is possible to see in Riis's bricolage style a mutated form of the challenged penny press journalism.

The 1880s have often been described as a turning point in the history of the American press, both in terms of style and readership identity. The instability of the period eventually settled into two more permanent journalistic genres in the mid-1890s.[30] 'Yellow journalism' on the one hand: an inexpensive, sensationalist, heavily illustrated, working-class newspaper format represented primarily by Pulitzer's *The World* and Hearst's *The Journal*. On the other hand, the traditional New York papers, such as *The Times, The Sun*, *The Tribune* and *The Herald*, which developed the old penny press format. Media historian Michael Schudson has attributed the turbulence of the '80s to the fierce competition that followed from a rapidly growing and

29. Daniel Czitrom, "Jacob Riis's New York", in *Rediscovering Jacob Riis: Exposure Journalism and Photography in Turn-of-the-Century New York*, (The New Press, New York: 2007), 70.
30. Daniel Czitrom, *Media and the American Mind* (University of North Carolina Press: Chapel Hill, 1982); Ted Curtis Smythe, *The Gilded Press 1865-1900* (Praeger, West Port, Connecticut: 2003); Michael Schudson, *Discovering the News: A Social History of American Newspapers* (Basic Books: New York: 1978).

unpredictably changing information market: "Newspapers tried to satisfy public standards of truth, public ideals of decency, and public tastes in entertainment. That meant, on the one hand, that newspapers had to be lively, colorful, and entertaining. It meant, on the other hand, that they had to be factual."[31] But it also meant that newspaper editors had to be acutely aware of veering readership values and mobile social positions. Riis's editor at the *Tribune*, Whitelaw Reid, relayed in an interview that, "Newspapers gather about them different constituencies with different wants. [...] The relation between a newspaper and its constituency, from the moment the paper becomes firmly established, is a reciprocal one. Each acts on the other. I don't think newspapers very largely lead public sentiment or create it."[32] Consequently, Reid maintained strict editorial control over published values and opinions, allowing such content only in the editor's column. Ordinary reporters were forcibly discouraged from making private conjectures and were severely reprimanded when overstepping the lines. Reid repeatedly castigated Riis for being both "editorial and presuming,"[33] and although Riis downplays the antagonism ("in the end the complaints died out. I suppose I was given up as hopeless"), he most likely remained a difficult and problematic contributor to the penny press paper.

The constituencies that Reid mentions were not as precisely monitored then as they are today; the task of identifying readers' demands, wishes, and expectations was a matter of intuition and experience rather than analyzing polls, surveys, and statistics. For commercial newspapers it was of course crucial to get it right. Editorial views, priorities of coverage, style of writing, line of advertisement, graphic design, illustrations, distribution, and, of course, the price were instrumental factors. Maneuvering a newspaper was not an easy thing to do with increasingly vacillating, heterogeneous, and disloyal readerships. The same churchgoing, middle-class readers, who

31. Schudson, *Discovering the News,* 71.
32. "Interview with Whitelaw Reid, Editor of 'New York Tribune'," in *Views and Interviews on Journalism* ed. Wingate (F.B. Patterson, New York: 1875), 28.
33. Riis, *The Making of an American*, 223.

with pietistic fervor publically rejected Sunday editions, reputedly both enjoyed and demanded them.[34] The information business was already quite volatile in 1883, when Joseph Pulitzer from St Louis, Missouri, took over *The Morning World* from the railroad magnate Jay Gould at a mere $346,000. Pulitzer lowered the retail price, illustrated heavily, and turned the *World* into a workingman's paper that topped the circulation figures within a few years.[35] During the period that followed until the Yellow Press informally consolidated in 1895 into as a distinct genre, the traditional regime of news veridiction was decidedly out of joint. This is the period when Riis's style evolved.

Riis explored the possibilities and the limits of news reporting from within the journalistic and editorial confines of his particular employer. Reid favored "politics, news, earnest controversial discussion" above "elegant writing for gentlemen, and agreeable general reading."[36] He knew that "each newspaper caters to its own constituency, and its success depends on reading with the utmost promptness every indication of what that constituency wants."[37] But while he exclusively targeted the economically promising segment of the rising middle class, he also understood the financial potentials of a market and a consumer group whose tastes and opinions he thought newspapers ought not to satisfy. In an address to the Editorial Association of New York and Ohio in 1879, Reid anticipated with contempt Pulitzer's later success at targeting the working class. "There is not an editor in New York who does not know that fortune that awaits the man there who is willing to make a daily paper as disreputable and vile as a hundred and fifty thousand readers would be willing to buy."[38]

34. James Melvin Lee, *History of American Journalism* (Houghton Mifflin, Boston: 1917), 379-80.
35. Smythe, *The Gilded Age Press*, 105-121.
36. *Views and Interviews on Journalism*, 28.
37. Ibid., 27.
38. Reid, quoted in Richard Kluger, *The Paper: the Life and Death of the New York Tribune* (Knopf, New York: 1986), 139.

Reid's attitude towards the working class grew increasingly derisive and incredulous.[39] In 1877 the *Tribune's* unionized printers had begun a massive strike that lasted until 1892. According to Richard Kluger, the newspaper's chronicler, the *Tribune* refused to meet the workers' demands and it sustained severe attacks from the union weekly *The Boycotter* in January 1884. Reid responded in the editorial column with categorical charges against the labor class and their liberal champions, targeted particularly against Felix Adler. In February, Riis found his editor issuing portrayals of the poor that represented the opposite views of his own:

> Felix Adler, for example, refuses to admit that any change is needed in the ways of life and the habits of certain classes that occupy tenement-houses. He insists that the fault lies in the debased nature of their environment. He says: "It is not the squalid people that make the squalid houses but the squalid houses that make the squalid people." Now this is by no means an accurate generalization, and it is one, insistence on which may have bad and discouraging results. [...] It would be most unjust to visit the squalor of these poor people as a fault. They cannot help it. It is their normal condition. They inherit acquiescence in it. They do not inherit any yearning after a better state of things. And when philanthropists build model lodging houses in the cities, or model cottages in the country for this kind of people, they do not at once welcome the change. They cannot in fact appreciate it. They really prefer the old ways.[40]

As a *Tribune* police reporter, Riis not only challenged the exclusivity of the editorial column, he also voiced opinions that were directly opposite of his superior editor. General conditions for covering police

39. *The Tribune* may have maintained a skeptical editorial attitude to "the tenement problem", but it was not an entirely dismissive one. *The Tribune* took over the Fresh-Air Fund in 1881 from the *Evening Post* and sent children from the tenements to private families in the country or to special summer camps. Cf. Lee, *History of American Journalism*, 358.

40. "The Tenement-House Question," in *The Tribune*, Feb 6, 1884, 4. This is a first editorial item in a series of three, all with the same title. The other ones appeared on Feb 19 and March 7.

matters, which often coincided with tenement coverage, were further complicated in 1884 with the successful rebranding of the competitor, *The World*, whose editorial profile was now more or less in line with Riis's views. Kluger puts it succinctly: "Pulitzer chose his side, and it was with the poor immigrant, the sorely used workingman, the brutally crowded tenement dweller. The plight of the poor was news, and the *World* alone told what life among them was like. It may not have made for pretty reading, but it was gripping when written up in simple, even slangy, highly graphic language so that the marginally literate had no problem absorbing it."[41]

Riis's style was not, however, directly adopted from *The World*. Its class-specific tone and mode of address would have seemed inappropriate to Riis's audience. Much rather, his way of writing developed out of two general and conditioning circumstances. The first was the turmoil among news institutions and the resulting discontinuation of the penny press tradition. The sudden absence of a strong regulating heritage opened possibilities for writing differently, and in this respect, Riis was already at the limit of what his editor could accept. For a second conditioning circumstance, one must remember that Riis had been challenged to publish his first book on a very tight deadline, while at the same time pressuring himself to master ad-lib lecturing before a paying audience. As a result he wrote fast and, in his own words, as things came to mind. The style that emerged was probably then neither consciously adopted from others nor minutely orchestrated for effect; it most likely sprung from the same source as his lecturing style: from frequent heuristic contact with live audiences.

The day after his first illustrated lecture at *The Society of Amateur Photographers of New York* on January 25, 1888, reviews said that he talked "in a conversational way" and that "Mr. Riis was so ingenious in describing the scenes and brought to his task such a vein of humor that after two hours every one wished that there was more of the exhibition, sad as much of it was."[42] In general, the early lecture re-

41. Kluger, *The Paper*, 147. Further, according to Kluger, the *World* readers "wanted both terseness and strong descriptive powers, humor where appropriate and originality that was not obscure, and the most assiduously pursued level of accuracy in the gathering of facts."

42. *New York News*, Jan 26, 1888 and *The Tribune*, Jan 26, 1888. LC, Riis papers, box 4.

views are more preoccupied with Riis's images than with his oral presentation, but a few brief comments suggest that Riis spoke freely and leisurely yet in a remarkably entertaining and engaging manner. If he already at this early stage had developed the oratory style that is handed down to us in the stenographed transcription from November 1891 (where Riis truly puts things in when he thinks of them), is impossible to know. No detailed descriptions have survived of Riis's early lectures, only vague allusions to a rhetorical vividness that nevertheless seems to offer the most likely candidate for what could have transmuted into a unique form of writing. Having developed a successful and apparently unique mode of oral address just prior to being confronted with the task of writing the manuscript, and having precious little time to complete it, it seems reasonable to suggest that the new style of writing emerged from a successful mode of lecturing combined with an unsatisfying journalistic practice mired deep in discursive disequilibrium.

This chapter has suggested that some significant new technologies were applied to the charity discourse with *How The Other Half Lives*. Irony was used to drape the social menace in a smart, tasteful garment that only revealed the horrors more succinctly. Humor was developed as a powerful new weapon against the ubiquitous tenement system, and it was employed proselytizingly by the author as he at first allies with his readers in poking fun at the tenement population, only then to immediately corner his affiliates with evidence of their active part in the system of oppression. Secondly, a much faster pace of argument was introduced into charity parlance, with rhetorical jump shifts between distinct modes of address and literary tropes. Both of these techniques disrupted the prevailing discourse and facilitated a grafting of new problems of greater urgency. Riis probed for unspoken public concerns and went well beyond the boundaries of the established charity genre. In the next chapter I will try to show how the migrating elements from Copenhagen adapted to and mutated the American charity discourse.

CHAPTER 5

The Mutation Event

One may easily identify areas of stagnation in the reformist tenement discourse in New York. Certain long ingrained antinomies, unquestioned notions, and naturalized causes granted to its topology these relatively dead domains. We have already noted one such undisputed opposition, between the worthy poor and the unworthy poor, which was conceptually maintained through a number of empirically recognizable signs and character features that indicated complaisance with the pauperizing processes. The distinction was accepted as unproblematic and incited little cause for debate or investigation. Similarly, the clear and undisputed contraposition between the *Sunshine and Shadow* genre and earnest philanthropic literature allowed many a gentleman to consume gory descriptions of spectacular downtown misery on one day and sentimental charity grievances with fervent calls for reform on the next, and without much consternation or sense of paradox. Meanwhile, there were other binaries that were decidedly uncertain and vagarious, for example the opposition that separated reformers into 'environmentalists,' i.e. those who held the environment responsible for individual privation, and 'essentialists,' who rather pointed to personal character as the most decisive

1. This distinction has often, and unfortunately, been described as categorical and simple. Riis is conventionally portrayed as a pioneer of the environmentalist perspective, which is far from the truth. Nor was his environmentalism as univocal as many commentators have argued, e.g. Peter Hales, *Silver Cities: The Photography of American Urbanization 1839-1915* (Temple University Press, Philadelphia: 1985), 167-68; James B. Lane, *Jacob Riis and the American City* (Kennikat Press, Port Washington: 1974); Rune Hassner, *Jacob A Riis: Socialreporter med kamera* (Lucida Pocket, Laholm: 1987); David Leviatin, "Framing the Poor: the Irresistibility of How the Other Half Lives," editor's introduction to *How the Other Half Lives* (Bedford Books, New York: 1996).

cause for social development.[1] Individual reformers sided very rarely with one camp exclusively, but would instead combine the two into a unique blend of endorsements and argue fiercely for their individual position. One may thus distinguish between charity concerns of low intensity (such as the former) and those of high intensity (such as the latter).

This chapter will look at how Riis took advantage of the particular topology of intensities which shaped the New York tenement discourse in the 1880s and defined its propensity to mutate. I will suggest that a number of discursive migrations, which arguably took place with his work (not only from Denmark to America, but also from journalism into charity writing, etc.) intensified certain public concerns and that this, in turn, provided fertile conditions for new discursive formations. It will be argued that the mutation event that followed transformed urban poverty as a conceivable and perceivable phenomenon. Of course, Riis did not invent mutating strands of discourse out of thin air. As we have seen, much of the transformative process relied on distinct differences between conventions, trends, and currents, which his writings exploited to chaperone new features into the idiom of reform. What is exceptional about Riis is that he let these lingual migrations run their course as affective agents, that he was not too quick to adapt his views and ways to established conventions, and that he worked as exceptionally hard as he did: his reputed stubbornness, integrity, and choleric assiduity should not be underestimated. The following analysis rests on a topological theorem which suggests that the integration of entities in a steady state system may cause invariants to destabilize, patterns of variation may deform or disintegrate, and new areas of disequilibrium may emerge, while formerly unstable areas may solidify.[2] Our analytical task is

2. For an introduction to cultural topology and morphogenesis, see Rene Thom, *Structural Stability and Morphogenesis: an Outline of a General Theory of Models* (W.A. Benjamin, Reading, Mass: 1975); Gilbert Simondon, *L'individuation psychique et collective* (Aubier, Paris: 1989); Peter Borum, *Structure et genèse: les questions d'individuation et morphogenèse entre Gilles Deleuze et Jean Petitot* (unpublished Ph.D.-dissertation, University of Copenhagen, 2005); Manuel DeLanda, *Intensive Science and Virtual Philosophy* (Continuum, London: 2002), 71-72.

to describe the most important transformations invoked by the migrations that we have identified.

It has already been argued that irony, humor, and a new bricolage style of writing helped to probe for uncharted resources both within and outside of the conventional charity vernacular. It has also been suggested that through Riis's sustained efforts at publically addressing the tenement problem, certain very strong charity concerns from Denmark confronted much weaker American ones. A viable hypothesis can now be formulated: the migrations that took place with Riis's writings capped the power and loosened the strict distribution of the doctrinal invariants that until then had buttressed the tenement reform cause in New York. A new set of relational invariants could then emerge to redistribute the entire field of charity. With one singular work, the tenements became a new object of knowledge, known by a new kind of popular scientist, articulated in a novel language, and held to be susceptible to an array of unfamiliar affects.

In the following, it will be examined how this new formation came about and how it could gain sufficient strength. Riis need not have been conscious of the processes involved: he did his best to achieve his goals, but was not in control of what he was able to do or the extent of his impact. In this sense, language develops autonomously and somewhat independently of the ones who intentionally articulate it.

The Making of the Will to Honesty

Riis's notion of a will to honesty had no comparable equivalent in contemporary American charity writings. Although a mundane notion of will was common and established—referring to an individual's desire to improve his or her social and material standing—the conceptual position which made the concept of will extraordinary in Riis's argument had no precedent. An infinite, God-given primary within every individual that measures his or her ethical and socio-economical capacity; this will to honesty was conceived uniquely by Riis. It was power of human existence, a power that may increase or diminish but never completely perish. By naming it, Riis invented a universal singularity, and by inventing that he called for a notion of justice to match:

> The poorest immigrant comes here with the ambition to better himself and, given half a chance, might be reasonably expected to make the best of it. To the false plea that he prefers the squalid homes in which his kind is housed there could be no better answer. The truth is, his half chance has too long been wanting, and for the bad result he has been unjustly blamed.[3]

To examine the conception of will in Riis's work, one should first map related notions already in use in the American charity literature. Will was conventionally regarded as a natural element of the human psyche, as something that belongs to the mind. To Charles Loring Brace, leader of the Children's Aid Society, will was a psychological resource for battling lower, biologically inherited drives. Of a nine-year-old girl he wrote:

> The 'gemmules' or latent tendencies, or forces, or cells of her immediate ancestors were in her system, and working in her blood, producing irresistible effects on her brain, nerves, and mental emotions, and finally, not being met early enough by other moral, mental, and physical influences, they have modified her organization, until *her will* is scarcely able to control them and she gives herself up to them.[4]

Like Riis's concept, Brace's will may also gain and lose power: another, luckier poor girl that he encountered in the tenements, enters school and "feels the profound forces of American life; the desire of equality, ambition to rise, the sense of self-respect and the passion

3. Riis, *How the Other Half Lives*, 20.

4. Brace, *The Dangerous Classes of New York*, 43.

for education. These new desires overcome the low appetites in her blood, and she continually rises and improves."[5] Dr. Stephen Smith, another vocal reformer, suggested a slightly different concept. Of the deprived he wrote: "we must remember that they have become so habituated to their methods of herding together in small, dark, unventilated rooms, that they have either no desire, or but the slightest disposition to improve their domiciles or mode of life."[6] Smith's concept of will is unrelated to blood inheritance, but much like Brace's concept it rises and falls with exterior influences, so much so that it presents a psychological mirror image of the environment. Josephine Shaw Lowell employed a similar concept when arguing for improved reformatories for fallen women: "The unhappy beings we are speaking of need, first of all, to be taught to be women; they must be induced to love that which is good and pure, and to *wish to resemble it*."[7] She too employs a concept of will that is directly malleable by exterior affections. All in all, will appears as a low-intense or 'weak' concept in the sense that its meaning shows little variation and stirs little controversy. Archives reveal no disputes about will and no attempts at developing the concept.

It is interesting therefore to observe a greater intensity pertaining to the question of how to stimulate will. Variations on this issue are surprisingly rich. But as it turns out, this wealth follows from the multitude of positions between essentialism and environmentalism. This diversity, in turn, derives directly from the problem of poverty's causes, where will plays but a minor role in the total makeup of an individual character. The manifold ways to stimulate will follow in fact directly from the multitude of positions on the causes of poverty, ranging from personal moral ineptitude to structural material deficiency. Reformers took issue with the strengthening of will some-

5. Ibid., 46.
6. Stephen Smith, *Methods of Improving the Homes of the Laboring and Tenement House Classes of New York*, (n.p. New York, 1875), 11.
7. Josephine Shaw Lowell, *One Means of Preventing Pauperism* (n.p., New York: 1879).

where along this scale of causes, and no one failed to declare which half they prioritized.[8]

Taking sides seems obligatory, notwithstanding the intensity of the issue. Which comes first: moral or material causes? Is the preacher mightier than the plumber when it comes to raising the will to self-help?[9] Riis's construction of will offered him a third position, and an axis perpendicular to the bipolar scale. The will to honesty is not a psychological element pertaining to character, but rather a life-force present in all humans from birth. It is an expression of God's perfection in human life, and although it can be weakened or strengthened from exterior influences, it cannot perish altogether. (This is why the most unworthy poor presented such a thorny problem to Riis.) Furthermore, will is not directly affected by exterior circumstances, only indirectly does its power raise or fall with events that impact on the individual. However, with every actual affirmation or negation of the family home, of labor division, or of neighborliness, will is either strengthened or weakened. It was stated earlier while introducing the

8. Brace, being one of the most explicitly pious reformers, argued that, "Christianity is the highest education of character. Give the poor that, and only seldom will either alms or punishment be necessary." (*The Dangerous Classes of New York*, 23). Similar, if more nuanced views are found in Washington Gladden, Edward Everett Hale, Rev. Charles H. Parkhurst and Elisha Harris. Marbled with more or less explicit acknowledgement of the need for material improvements, these authors prioritize religious moral support and guidance. Conversely, John Talbot Smith declared in "The Homes of the Poor," in *The Catholic World* July 1887, 509, that creed was unable to lend much of a hand in the battle against the tenement problem. He pointed out that "a sinner cannot be rightfully cheated or poisoned any more than a saint can —a doctrine which occasioned the landlords much surprise and grief," regardless that these "landlords were of all forms of belief, Jew, Christian, and atheist". Other reformers, such as Henry George, Lucy M. Hall, Felix Adler, Octavia Hill, Josephine Shaw Lowell, Roger S. Tracy, and Dr. Stephen Smith, contributed to the secular mode of argument, which, however, only rarely failed to grant at least some minor role to religious notions.

9. Rev. Charles H. Parkhurst is an interesting contributor in this respect, as his writings reveal an unsuccessful struggle against the necessity of prioritizing. See for example *The Question of the Hour* (Anson D.F. Randolph & Co, New York: 1886).

conservative triangle, that when any one of its nominal values is positively or negatively impacted upon by external forces, that impact affects indirectly also the other two values. It therefore makes little sense for Riis to take sides. If he privileges the plumber over the preacher, he merely suggests the preferred starting impulse, which immediately must be followed by neighborly spiritual nourishment. Riis's concept of will was able to mutate the meek American opposition into a dynamic tripartite structure, especially as it thereby introduced a revolutionary interdependency between materialism and Christian invariants.

What may have enabled such a construction? Why had previous charity writers not discovered this alternative approach before? On the one hand, the conventional American concept of will was both reliable and functional, and, importantly, it proved resilient to conceptual motility in its discursive vicinity. On the other hand, a concept like Riis's would have seemed vague or meaningless in isolation from his overall conceptual structure. It needed above all the nominal values of the conservative triangle to work.

The original public concern that pertains to this will had intensified gradually in Copenhagen during the 1860's.[10] To judge a poor man's will to improve was in Denmark considered necessary for correctly diagnosing his social conditions of life, and for prescribing the proper kind of assistance. But it seemed impossible to justly and objectively observe such a thing, let alone relying on it for measuring a man's worth. With Riis's appropriation of the problem, something extraordinary occurs to this concept, something which would be impos-

10. Riis's concept of will to honesty developed from an indeterminable psychological notion of will, which in Denmark was foregrounded not least by the sheer intensity of debate, but also thematically in Vilhelm Munck's writings. Especially influential were the widespread hesitations about how to diagnose will in another human being. Riis continued the broodings about how to awaken a seemingly dormant will through forced labor or solitary confinement. The divine nature of Riis's concept suggests by contrast an adaptation to the pious current of American reform discourse, which emphasized the Christian family as the ideal psychological environment. Merged with the radical indeterminability from Copenhagen, will detaches from the mind and assumes the nature of a life force.

sible to explain without the American context: it was employed for measurement of human worth with its indeterminable nature intact. Let this be illustrated with some quotations. Riis says, "the effort to be clean is the first and the best evidence of a desire to be honest,"[11] but the ethnic Italian, who is "content to live in a pig-sty"[12] is nevertheless "as honest as he is hot-headed."[13] The Chinese, on the other hand, are "clean as a cat" but his opium is the only means to effectively kill the desire to be honest: "From any other form of dissipation than that for which Chinatown stands there is recovery; for the victims of any other vice, hope. For these there is neither hope nor recovery."[14]

The necessary *and* impossible diagnosis of the poor man's will to improve presented an insurmountable problem to reformers in Copenhagen, but it was a productive problem too, prompting the development of an impressive palette of assessment practices, charity theories, protocols, and institutional recommendations. In New York, Riis turned the practical problem into a theoretical asset with an adjustment of the concept's relational position. The empirically indeterminable character of will made it suitable for a concept of *changing ethical capacities*—in other words, a concept pertaining to a body's fluctuating abilities to justly interact with other bodies. As a concept of changing ethical capacities, will unified the cleft between doctrinal and materialist categories of assessment, exactly as Riis's proposition of hope would demand. Riis accepted the impossibility of empirically deciding on someone's will to honesty, but in return he insisted on speaking of changes in the capacity to justly interact with others, regardless of whether or not any such actual interactions had been observed, or indeed could be.[15] He was obviously unable to define which interactions a given body was capable of engaging in, but that is insignificant. What was important was change: increase or decrease. The effects of such change altered the state of what he

11. Riis, *How the Other Half Lives*, 41.
12. Ibid., 43.
13. Ibid., 47.
14. Ibid., 83.
15. This hinge appears most explicitly in the attitude of hope, but traverses in fact the entire theoretical system.

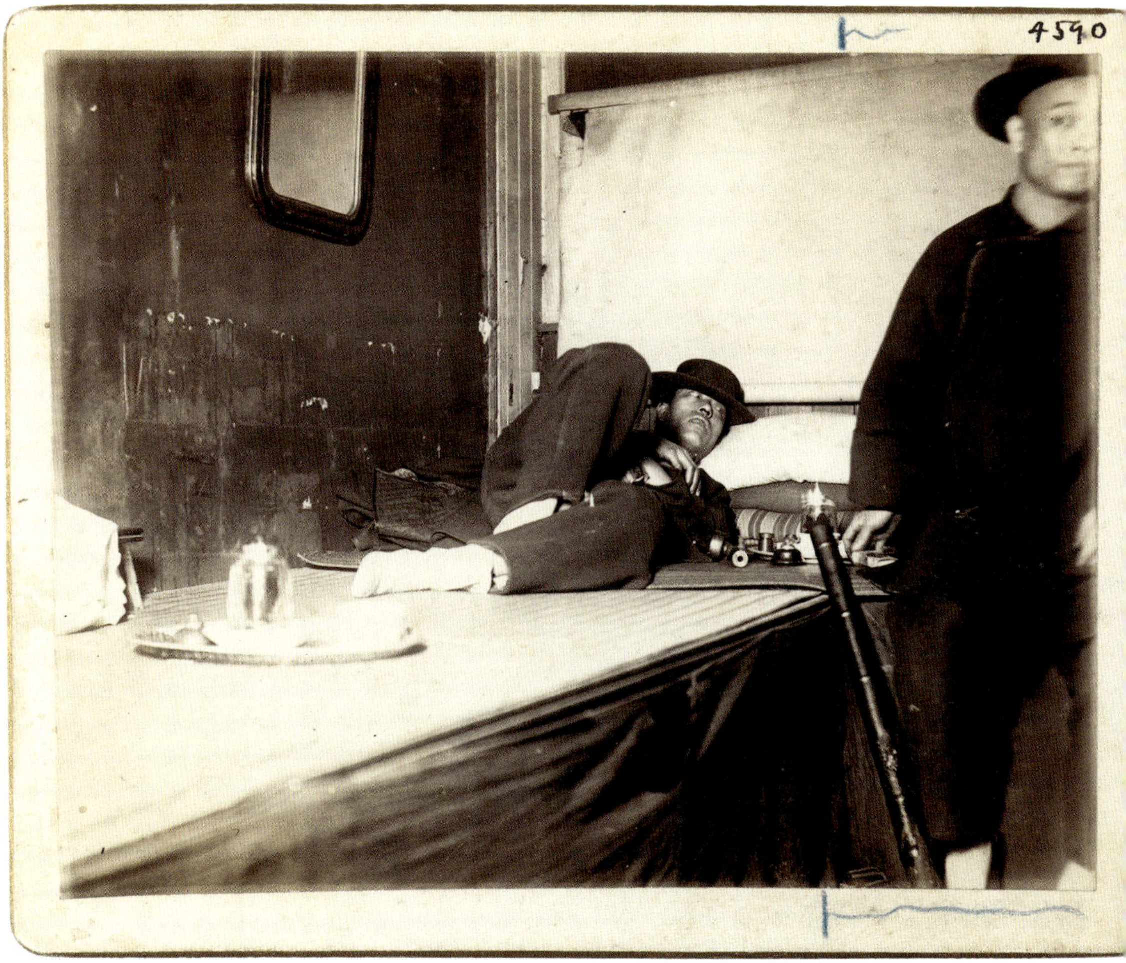

Figure 20. Richard Hoe Lawrence and Jacob A. Riis, "Chinese Opium Joint," [90.13.3.184] ca. 1890. MCNY.

called 'the inner man', and although this state could not be determined from outside, certain signs of its modification would be indicative. Hence, and most importantly: the existence of such a will required faith—not psychological knowledge—and faith in man. To acknowledge the will to honesty was a matter of faith; figuring out how to stimulate it would then rather be a matter of attentive individual observation, experimentation, and learning from experience. Each tenement dweller, each deprived family, each sordid tenement house, and each dysfunctional neighborhood must be observed, exposed to change, documented thoroughly, and be believed in. Will has no phenomenal form but may be diagnosed indirectly through documentation of repeated exposure to various kinds of impact and close monitoring of developing response symptoms. It is meaningless to debate if religious or material means of assistance are preferable. Will must be stimulated by both.

Riis's introduction of a foreign, Danish concern mutated a weak American concept of will and transformed it from a humdrum psychological notion into a new relational invariant. At the same time, the foreign concern mutated the strong bipolar scale of causes, turning its 'either/or' into an incontrovertible 'both/and'. If Riis's conceptual maneuvers seem petty under the magnifying glass, they were in discursive practice certainly not. They midwifed a new universal singularity and with it, everything changes. Affective relationships between the nominal values of the conservative triangle are possible and meaningful only with this singularity.

In order to clarify how an indeterminable will to honesty fits with the triangle's determinable nominal values, one may study a passage from *How the Other Half Lives*. This illustrative anecdote appears immediately after Riis's conceptual introduction of the will to honesty.

> There were nine in the family: husband, wife, an aged grandmother, and six children; honest, hard-working Germans, scrupulously neat, but poor. All nine lived in two rooms, one about ten feet square that served as parlor,

> bedroom, and eating-room, the other a small hall-room made into a kitchen. The rent was seven dollars and a half a month, more than a week's wages for the husband and father, who was the only bread-winner in the family. That day the mother had thrown herself out of the window, and was carried up from the street dead. She was 'discouraged' said some of the other women from the tenement, who had come in to look after the children while a messenger carried the news to the father at the shop. They went stolidly about their task, although they were evidently not without feeling for the dead woman. No doubt she was wrong in not taking life philosophically, as did the four families a city missionary found housekeeping in the four corners in one room. They got along well enough together until one of the families took a boarder and made trouble. Philosophy, according to my optimistic friend, naturally inhabits the tenements. The people who live here come to look upon death in a different way from the rest of us—do not take it as hard. He has never found time to explain how the fact fits into his general theory that life is not unbearable in the tenements. Unhappily for the philosophy of the slums, it is too apt to be of the kind that readily recognizes the saloon, and shapes its practice according to the discovery.[16]

In this passage, the indeterminable will to honesty contrasts glaringly with the observable values of the conservative triangle. Honest and hard-working Germans, short of space at home but neat, with a favorable division of labor in the family and good neighborly relations: all signs suggest a sound will to honesty. But suicide strikes, as unforeseeably to the bereaved family as to the reader, with evidence of the woman's lacking capacity to endure life in the tenements. Riis gives no reason why she killed herself, which is consistent with the indeterminability of will and crucial for the diagnostic function of the triangle. Her will to honesty is not determined by phenomenal causes,

16. Riis, *How the Other Half Lives,* 41.

nor is it redeemed with her death. Riis abstains from making a heroine of her, or a martyr. The meaning of the story is instead concentrated on the cleft between visible signs of relative accomplishment and the belated evidence of a defeated will. It is then not a question of friends and family failing to see the woman's plight. The unpredictability of her suicide is clearly underscored. Will is not a psychological element that mirrors the environment. It is rather a matter of the woman's exhausted capacity to be affected by the world, that is, a question of a life that could not any further erode her self-esteem. It is crucial to recognize that the limit of her capacities have neither been known to her nor to anybody else—indeed none of us can know what we are capable of—but while it became impossible for her to descend any further, as she has lost all faith in life, duty still made her endure some time. Riis's narrative is constructed to establish this gap between faith and duty. And what he wants to say is that you can only deduce from known impacts upon a body the *changes* that correspondingly affect the will to honesty, but one cannot thereby determine the actual state of another's will. From continuous detrimental impacts upon the nominal values of family home, of labor shared, and of neighborly relations, one may conclude that this woman's will weakened—evidently to the point of utmost inertia. As an individual, she remains exterior to her family, and the affective relationship between these two bodies must as well have negated her values. What to others may appear as respectable and steady advancements in the life of a family may be excruciating stagnation to someone who is unable to negate any values any further. For reasons that must be kept within the family, this mother was not capable of benefiting from the neatness of her home, or from the rewards of shared labor, or from the moral reciprocity of daily interactions with her neighbors. It is not a question of showcasing injured pride or failed expectations on her part. The only hint that Riis provides is the ultimate negating power of common ressentiment, of "taking life philosophically." The story testifies in the final analysis to the monstrous lack of neighborliness in the philosophy of the slums.

In the eyes of the city missionary and the neighboring women, the tragic event was not difficult to understand: the poor wife succumbed to her desire for better things to come. She was too ambitious, and her aspirations turned into deepest discouragement. Is that any different from Riis's interpretation? The distinction appears when their psychological view is taken to its perilous moral conclusion. Riis finds that if will is understood to be a psychological force that varies with the environment, it becomes a virtue to take life philosophically. Adapting to circumstances is to maintain a balanced rapport between perceived reality and one's expectations. One may even be prepared to admire the four stoic families who resided each in a corner of a single room. But at the logical conclusion of such a philosophy, it becomes non-contradictory to propose that death means less to the poor and, at the same time, that tenements do not provide unbearable life conditions. But this is clearly an ethical absurdity. To avoid it, will must not be understood as a psychological element reflective of the environment. Upon considering the Danish indeterminability of will as it migrated into a pious reform discourse that strongly emphasized the Christian family, it is not at all strange to find it developing into a spiritual life-force founded on a relational invariant that makes man aspire beyond the conditions that be. Will is too powerful to depend on the frail human psyche. It is figured the other way around. Considered as the expression of God's perfection in an imperfect being, will becomes synonymous with a ceaseless, but variably powerful strife for perfection. Successive affirmations and negations of values determine the ability of mind and body to find truth in sensuous impressions and to adequately intervene in a value-driven world. Against the conventional, psychological understanding of will, Riis posits an immanent expression of transcendence in every man.[17] Mere ambition may be curbed, but the poor woman suffered from the crippling of a will that must not be disciplined. Now, the passage above does

17. This does not mean that Riis condones suicide. To those who fight too hard or too impatiently for the reward there are disheartening moments to come. Suicide can never be justified because will, and in extension also hope, are inextinguishable. Cf. Riis, *The Making of an American*, 70-71.

not provide the whole picture. It is an extreme case that merely clarifies the indeterminable nature of will vis-à-vis the measurable values of the conservative triangle. For a more careful account of their relationship we first need a closer analysis of how the concepts came about.

Will and the Conservative Triangle

As we have seen, the conservative triangle consists of three nominal yet real values: the family home, the division of labor, and the Christian neighbor. Riis's concept of an indeterminable will forged them into a unique, dynamic entity.

For his idea of labor, Riis appropriated an American concept often used by social reformists to measure the worthy against the unworthy poor.[18] This notion of labor distinguished neither between kinds of employment nor between greater or lesser remuneration; in very general (and often in very Christian) terms, the concept signified any human processing of resources for collective sustenance. An example can be found in Charles Parkhurst as he writes, "Work is a man's normal condition [...] In the sweat of thy brow shalt thou eat bread."[19] Similarly, albeit in the far more secular writings of Henry George and Felix Adler, there is a concept of labor that signifies human activities in general insofar as they sustain communal life.[20] The unworthy poor are those who disregard such activities: beggars, loafers, prostitutes, thieves, and gang-members do not contribute to

18. Labor was obviously not the only factor involved in making this distinction: rational expenditure, wholesome leisure activities, sobriety, cleanliness and fidelity are equally often used for measure.

19. Charles Parkhurst, *The Question of the Hour* (Anson D.F. Randolph & Co, New York: 1886), 14.

20. Cf. Henry George, *The Crime of Poverty* (Land Values Publication dept., London: 1885), 26-27 "Nature gives to labour, and to labour alone; there must be human work before any article of wealth can be produced, and, in a natural state of things, the man who toiled honestly and well would be the rich man, and he who did not work would be poor"; see also Washington Gladden, "Christianity and Popular Amusements," in *Century Illustrated Magazine*, Jan. 1885, 384 and Felix Adler, "A New Experiment in Education," in *Princeton Review*, Jan-June 1883, 145.

communal life, and are therefore deemed unworthy. This concept of labor was generally undisputed, but it transformed radically when taken up into Riis's system; primarily, labor transformed due to its close connection to his concept of will, but also because of his preservation of the Danish uncertainties regarding a possible awakening of a dormant will through forced labor.[21]

From that contested notion and its structural position within the Danish tenement dispute, the meaning of labor assumed for Riis an active sense. Work was no longer merely something one either did or did not do as a condition of being a part of society; it was also, and more importantly, an activity that might intrinsically change a person for the better and make someone lost re-enter the ranks of civil fellowship. Related to the concept of will that Riis regarded an expression of divine perfection, the notion of labor assumed the meaning of activities capable of elevating one to a higher state of perfection. Labor was regarded as the practice of the will to honesty, hence an absolute nominal value.

Will and labor were thought to reversibly affect each other. A will to honesty was immediately weakened without the practice that sustains it and conversely, a weakened will meant reduced capacities to practice it. But this simple equation did not end in an ideal of maximized labor quantity. When Riis found a family of all wage earners, he said it was rather a corruption of will, that "all is lost". He meant by this that labor affects not only a person's individual will, it affects the will of the family too, as an autonomous body. A properly gendered division of labor strengthens another nominal value, the value of the family home, and it does so both directly and indirectly: indirectly by empowering the will to honesty of the family body, which, when increased, affirms the instinct of beauty and the dissemination of civic virtues throughout the republic. Directly, the proper division of labor affirms the family home by securing a sufficient income as

21. Forced labor for tramps and other unworthy poor was already an institutionalized practice in New York, most notably on Blackwell's Island, but it was first and foremost recognized as a form of judicial punishment and not a means to restore the subject's will to partake in social life.

well as mindful consumption habits, plus the time and the attentiveness needed for raising children. Riis observed that in the absence of a proper labor division between parents, families tend to pursue other sources of income as well, such as taking on lodgers or preferring child labor to schooling, which inadvertently corrupts the self-respect that their homes were meant to produce. This decay was considered coextensive with material depletions of the home, which, following Riis's materialist proposition, impact directly on the will to honesty of each family member.

Whereas Riis's concept of labor was appropriated from the American reform movement, his concept of family home seems to have been a modification of ideals touted in newspapers and Sunday magazines. Here, the distinction between good and bad tenement homes was clear and uncontroversial. A good tenement home was a safe haven, a shelter that provided care and comfort, whereas bad houses produced misery and crime.[22] Bad homes produce; good ones preserve. Furthermore, the established social correlation between bad homes and social depravation corresponded perfectly with the physiological correlation between poor housing and disease: what bred physical ailments also begot social illnesses, as poignantly expressed in a single sentence by women's reform champion, Lucy M. Hall: "Disease and its offspring, drunkenness, degradation, vice, and crime, are engendered and propagated in these environments."[23]

Riis's mutated conception of home ascribes to bad ones and good ones alike a producing capacity. Good homes nurture civic virtues and affirm the instinct of beauty, both of which are needed to further a democratic republic. Bad homes breed vice and disease, essentially by negating the good that decent homes produce. The instinct of beauty is for Riis as much a token of God's perfection in man as is the will to honesty, but, impervious to rational or even moral curbing, it affirms without restraint the desires of life and the joys to be had. No

22. Cf. John Talbot Smith, "The Homes of the Poor," in *The Catholic World*, July 1887, 45: 268, 509.

23. Lucy M. Hall, "Tenement-Houses and their Population," in *Journal of Social Science*, June 1885, 93.

to keep comfortably filled up to the advantage of their host. But to look thoroughly miserable they must keep awake. A tramp placidly dozing at the fire would not be an object of sympathy. To make sure that they do keep awake, the wily bartender makes them sit constantly swinging one foot like the pendulum of a clock. When it stops the slothful "sitter" is roused with a kick and "fired out." It is said by those who profess to know that habit has come to the rescue of oversleepy tramps and that the old rounders can swing hand or foot in their sleep without betraying themselves. In some saloons "sitters" are let in at these seasons in fresh batches every hour.

On one of my visits to "the Bend" I came across a particularly ragged and disreputable tramp, who sat smoking his pipe on the rung of a ladder with such evident philosophic contentment in the busy labor of a score of rag-pickers all about him, that I bade him sit for a picture, offering him ten cents for the job. He accepted the offer with hardly a nod, and sat patiently watching me from his perch until I got ready for work. Then he took the pipe out of his mouth and put it in his pocket, calmly declaring that it was not included in the contract, and that it was worth a quarter to have it go in the picture. The pipe, by the way, was of clay, and of the two-for-a-cent kind. But I had to give in. The man, scarce ten seconds employed at honest labor, even at sitting down, at which he was an undoubted expert, had gone on strike. He knew his rights and the value of "work," and was not to be cheated out of either.

Whence these tramps, and why the tramping? are questions oftener asked than answered. Ill-applied charity and idleness answer the first query. They are the whence, and to a large extent the why also. Once start-

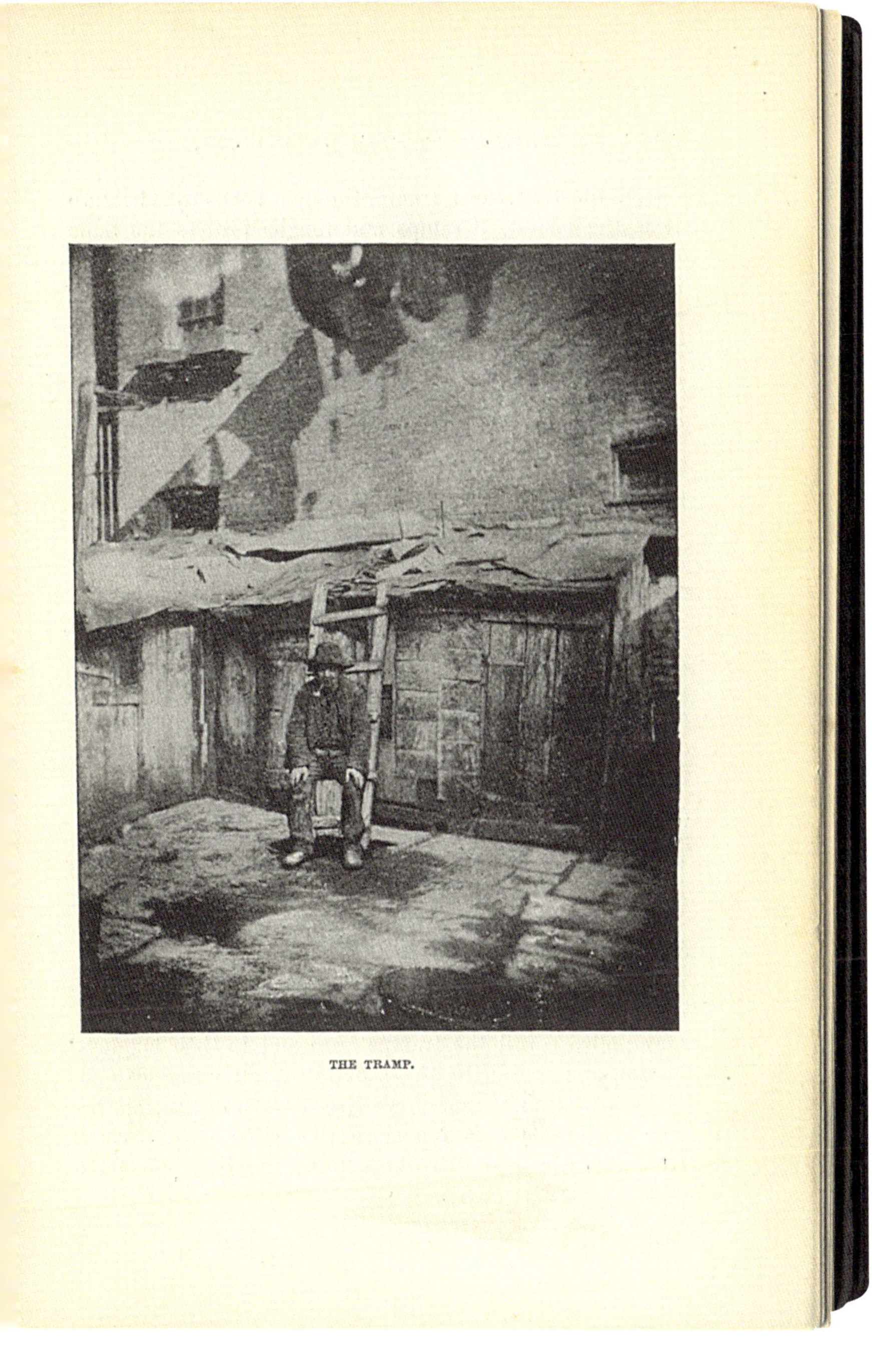

Figure 21. Jacob A. Riis, "The Tramp," from *How the Other Half Lives*, 1890 edition.

republic, no city, and no tenement home can foreclose the beauty, the freedom, and the fun of life, and still put value and trust in the self-esteem of its dwellers. To restrain one's selfish desires out of respect for a fellow neighbor is a task only for the 'inner man'. This tenet is at the core of the proposition of conscience. By contrast, to politically move forward toward a strengthened republic means, in the name of solidarity, to bestow on all children the civic virtues that the republic rests upon, a gift that is first given at home, with beauty and opportunities to play, then with schooling and education, and eventually with adult dialogue and democratic participation. Bad family homes negate thus both the sense of beauty and the production of citizen virtues: and thereby they also weaken the will to honesty in any body, large or small, who comes into contact with them.

Proponents of the popular model tenements in Copenhagen emphasized the productive capacity of good homes. Better than associated pawnshops, workers' savings banks, insurance associations and small-scale business support, model homes offered a nurturing seedbed for the most vulnerable subjects and a veritable greenhouse for the more robust workers and other worthy poor. Model tenements were in Copenhagen considered capable of cultivating social, moral, and economic (if not yet democratic) responsibilities. Suggestions that family life should be temporarily restricted for the worst of the unworthy poor, in an attempt to squeeze out the last remnants of their will to self-help, show just how intimately the will to improve was associated with the agency of a family home. Other Danish disputes —for example whether observable domestic conditions bear witness to the dwellers' moral state or rather to their need to be taught how to lead an urban life—also rest upon a presumed productivity within the walls of a family home. Both alternatives presume productive domestic capacities yet fundamentally differently so, which itself offers a hint of the intensity of this Danish concern. It certainly harbored sufficient powers to challenge an uncontested notion of merely preserving good homes. Only when good homes produce civic virtues may the concept become an absolute nominal value.

Relationships of reversible impact have now been identified between the family home, the division of labor, and the will to honesty. It has also now been established that Riis's conceptual architecture includes several elements that were indigenous to the American reform discourse, but, as novel concepts, appear to have been conceived with the help of transformative concerns from Copenhagen. The same process does not, however, adequately describe the conception of Riis's neighborliness.

The conceptual design of Riis's will to honesty requires an element that secures the emphasis on honesty. This is needed in order to restrict a more general 'will to improve,' which may include ways to personal furtherance that are motivated by selfishness or greed. This protective element is neighborliness, or brotherhood, a concept whose conventional meaning among American tenement reformers may be gleaned from Charles Parkhurst's appeal to "the brotherhood of mankind founded in the revealed fatherhood of Almighty God."[24] Its universal scope holds true also for Riis, whose appropriation of the concept nevertheless reveals a different discursive function. For while the majority of Christian reformers envisioned a necessary Christianization of the poor, Riis conceived of neighborliness as an unconditional, absolute, yet nominal value. The difference is this: the brotherhood of man must for Parkhurst and others first be exported to the tenements—not just as an idea, but as an actual Christian social foundation. These reformists must first capture the hearts of the poor in the name of Jesus Christ, and can only then administer the needed material means to self-help. By contrast, Riis's neighborliness needs no primary theological framework; he does not promote missioning in the tenements; he has no need for one church or another; in fact, neighborliness transcends formal religion. What kind of reform concept is this? How did it come about? Unlike the mutations already analyzed, this one did not germinate from Danish intensities that confronted and transformed an American discourse. It seems

24. Parkhurst, *The Question of the Hour*, 8.

rather that a minor American trajectory reacted to the transformations already described and offered a stabilizing concept of neighborliness.

It is tempting to consider Riis's neighborliness as a concept derived directly from Felix Adler's concept of *conscience*. They share being conceived of as nominal yet real values in every individual.[25] But Riis would too firmly disown Adler's contention that "the idea of Jehovah, as described in the Bible, was the result of a moral process."[26] To Riis, God is not entirely man-made. Riis might have admitted that the *immanent existence* of God—in other words, the God that creeds and congregations address in prayers, oaths, and confessions—has emerged as a result of the moral development of man, but he does reserve a place for the *transcendental existence* of God, which alone may warrant the brotherhood of man. Just as the will to honesty has a transcendental side and an immanent side (God's perfection is transcendent to man, but its expression in man as his will to honesty is immanent and variable in strength), neighborliness too has two sides. Its transcendental side, which warrants its universality, would extend from God through his image in every man (the expression of which is hope for all) whereas the immanent side of neighborliness is expressed in all acts of love that humans do unto each other and wish reciprocally were done to themselves. The image of God warrants the universal, loving kinship of man. Now, unlike the immanent will to honesty, which is *immediately* connected to its transcendental side, and directly measured against God's infinite perfection, the immanent acts of neighborliness are only mediately related to the image of God, and the mediator between the two is conscience. This mediated nature is why neighborliness, unlike will, is an absolute nominal

25. "The morality of the world rests upon its own evidence. If to-morrow every dogma which the masses of mankind hold sacred, could be blotted from their memories, the voice of Conscience would still sound as before, from the depths of human nature; wrong would still be wrong, and good good." Felix Adler, *Conscience: A lecture delivered before the Society of Ethical Culture* (Lehmaier & Brothers, New York: 1886), 10.

26. Ibid., 9.

value and not a relational invariant. Any increase or decrease of an individual's neighborly values is due to external interactions (which include longstanding relations). Affirmation of neighborliness is only possible through interaction with other individuals—strangers as well as friends and family members. Affirmation takes place not 'inside' a person but rather in the inter-subjective sphere. A person will perceive it, however, with his or her conscience. Conscience senses inter-subjective events, and it measures (and thereby mediates) the moral meaning of a situation against the universal warrant of the human brotherhood. It senses whether a particular event is in agreement or in disagreement with that which makes us all kin. Permanent negation may numb our conscience and bring us to atrocities or to suicide. Riis always sought to shepherd his audiences and his readership toward an affirming, conscientious experience of the tenement situation; first and foremost it was the public neighborliness that had to be affected and affirmed through his publishing and lecturing efforts. More than that, he sought literally to affirm the neighborliness of his audience with every piece communicated. This was effectively his battle with the slum. It was also what brought about the mutation of discursive forms.

Neighborliness protects will from selfishness and greed, and it protects every individual from seeking advantages merely for one's own benefit. It was first and foremost this value that Riis set out in public to fortify for the benefit of the tenement dwellers. Neighborliness became for Riis the third absolute nominal value in every individual, of course with reversible affective relations to the will to honesty, to the family home, and to the division of labor.

Occasionally, one finds in nineteenth-century reform pamphlets a concept of hope that is reminiscent of Riis's . It is a Christian term, but much more fragile and conjectural than divine providence or trust in God, and the texts that invoke it usually infer stronger principles, such as the Golden rule, to promote a proper Christian way of life. The following example is from an article by Rev. J. Francis Morgan from 1883:

> There is in man a spiritual nature, which is constantly onging [sic] for a better existence. We believe there is no man, no matter how degraded and darkened by sin, who does not sometimes hope, yes long for a better existence. But the infidel says, 'Live for this world, and hope not for one you have never seen,' but it is an undeniable fact that no man proves so great a blessing in this world as the one who is constantly fitting himself for the society of the blessed in the home of God. Knowing the spiritual nature of man, the kind Father has given him a revelation and a religion which exactly meets the wants of his soul. So we see God has not left us in the dark, but given us the light of life, and laws by which to be governed.[27]

The man who is constantly fitting himself for the society of the blessed in the home of God: is he not also a man of the ideal society that Riis pursued: a man who will always be attentive to the neighborly values of his actions and intents? If he is not yet that, if he wallows in sin and depravity, at least he need not be Christianized first and materially rescued later. There is hope for all, for hope exists in every soul. Such an edict would have appealed to Riis, who would have recognized in it a concept worthy of his battle with the slum, particularly as it demands that absolute hope be joined with expectations of concrete action. Not God, but his needing subjects must provide. Hence, questions of social responsibility are insistently raised on the basis of a hope for all, a hope which He alone warrants. The actions prescribed in these minor pamphlets are not directly commanded by a transcendental God, but are rather suggested from an ethical principle of responsible and conscientious human judgment, which in turn is conditioned on a mediated relationship to divine redemption. When Riis invented the value of neighborliness, it had a precursor in these minor pamphlets. They in a sense intensified Riis's concepts of the family home and labor division (understood as the practice of the will to honesty), grounding these notions in established universalist territory.

27. J Francis Morgan, "What is Man," in *Herald of Gospel Liberty*, 75:51, 810.

Perhaps the process of conceptual intensification might explain why the articulation of neighborliness was late in the making. In *How the Other Half Lives*, it is not yet discovered. What will be named neighborliness in later writings and lectures is only glimpsed here as a negation of selfishness and greed; occasionally, it is expressed as 'public conscience':

> The remedy that shall be an effective answer to the coming appeal for justice must proceed from the public conscience. Neither legislation nor charity can cover the ground. The greed of capital that wrought the evil must itself undo it, as far as it can now be undone.[28]

Although the concept of neighborliness is not yet articulated here, there is a place reserved for it. The repeated question: "How shall the love of God be understood by those who have been nurtured in sight only of the greed of man" is posed as if in anticipation of its formulation. Likewise, Riis's defense of settlement projects and model tenement investments were from the beginning meant to affirm neighborliness and the family home. Business and industry too were praised and supported for their opportunities to affirm neighborly urban livelihoods through fair wages, safe labor environments, and viable consumption opportunities. Even municipal offices might contribute by securing available educational institutions, proper law enforcement, clean parks, streets and playgrounds, and most of all, a crackdown on corruption—all in view of affirming the value of neighborliness.

Some brief conclusions may now be suggested. All of the three nominal values are affected by social interactions, but they also affect each other reciprocally. These affections increase or decrease the power of the will to honesty. The will to honesty is the expression in every man of God's perfection, which thus extends to mankind as such. To this divine element in man belongs the indeterminable nature of its expression. The infinite hope in others that thereby is

28. Riis, *How the Other Half Lives*, 2.

conceptually secured does not restrict itself to Christian subjects, but reaches out coextensively with the will to honesty. Theoretically it is possible to raise any individual from pauperism—not in spite of, but rather because we are unable to know the strength of his or her individual will to honesty.

One may also conclude that Riis's invention of neighborliness was not—unlike the will to honesty, the family home, and the division of labor—the result of an American charity concept being transformed and intensified by foreign influence. It was rather the outcome of a minor strand of established American charity vernacular reacting almost invasively to Riis's perplexing construction. This response must be viewed in light of the slow, but thorough, discursive mutation that Riis's conceptual apparatus effected on American reform language. We know that Riis impacted fundamentally on what could be said and shown in terms of tenement reform activism. But we do not yet know how that mutation occurred.

To work out a viable hypothesis, it is important first to establish that the conservative triangle operated above and beyond its mere diagnostic functions of describing and analyzing social structure and individual relations. Its main purpose was rather to index an individual's ascending or descending will to honesty. This movement corresponds analytically with the affects exerted upon and between the three nominal values. One should, however, observe that the conservative triangle is rarely presented as a proper 'object' in Riis's writings. Its most common articulation is with the composition of narrative. As we are about to find out, Riis often composed by means of series of data and anecdotes, and it was through such serial variations and junctions that his narrative conveyed an impetus upon the nominal values presumably present in each of his audience members. In other words, he composed serial variations and junctions not only to describe life in the tenements, but also to affect his audience. Through this affect mainly, the mutation occurred. One must acknowledge the performative caliber of Riis's conceptual apparatus and relate it to his public appearances; only then will it be possible to understand how the American tenement discourse mutated: how new values emerged, how problems changed, and how novel means of expression were generally assumed for the cause.

Serial Junctions and Literary Affect

Let us first look at two quotations where the conservative triangle appears in uncharacteristically brief and objective form. Both show how the three nominal values impact upon each other. The most succinct quotation is extremely short: "The remedy [...] must proceed from public conscience. [...] Homes must be built for the working masses by those who employ their labor."[29]

The affirmation of values above commences with neighborliness. Public conscience is affirmed by the construction of good workers' homes; good homes increase the residents' will to honesty—it is the 'remedy'—and strengthen their commitment to honest labor, which in turn is a long-term asset for those who invest in their homes. It is furthermore implied by context that good homes also facilitate a proper division of labor in the family, which helps to remedy the social structure, increases self-esteem, and inspires new acts of neighborliness. Riis argues that any act of public conscience will continue to have an impact, also on other social bodies than the ones directly affected, but that such mediated effects may easily be countered or cancelled out by interests exerting force in the opposite direction. This would come from actions that negate the triangle's nominal values. Thus, the triangle can be imagined to rotate around its central axis, turning from impacting forces that tug in the affirmative or in the negating direction, a little like a threaded nut would ascend or descend with its rotation (Diagram 2). These movements of the triangle always represent value changes pertaining to an individual, which is not necessarily a person. It might as well apply to a family or a neighborhood, an ethnic group or the entire 'system'.

29. Ibid.

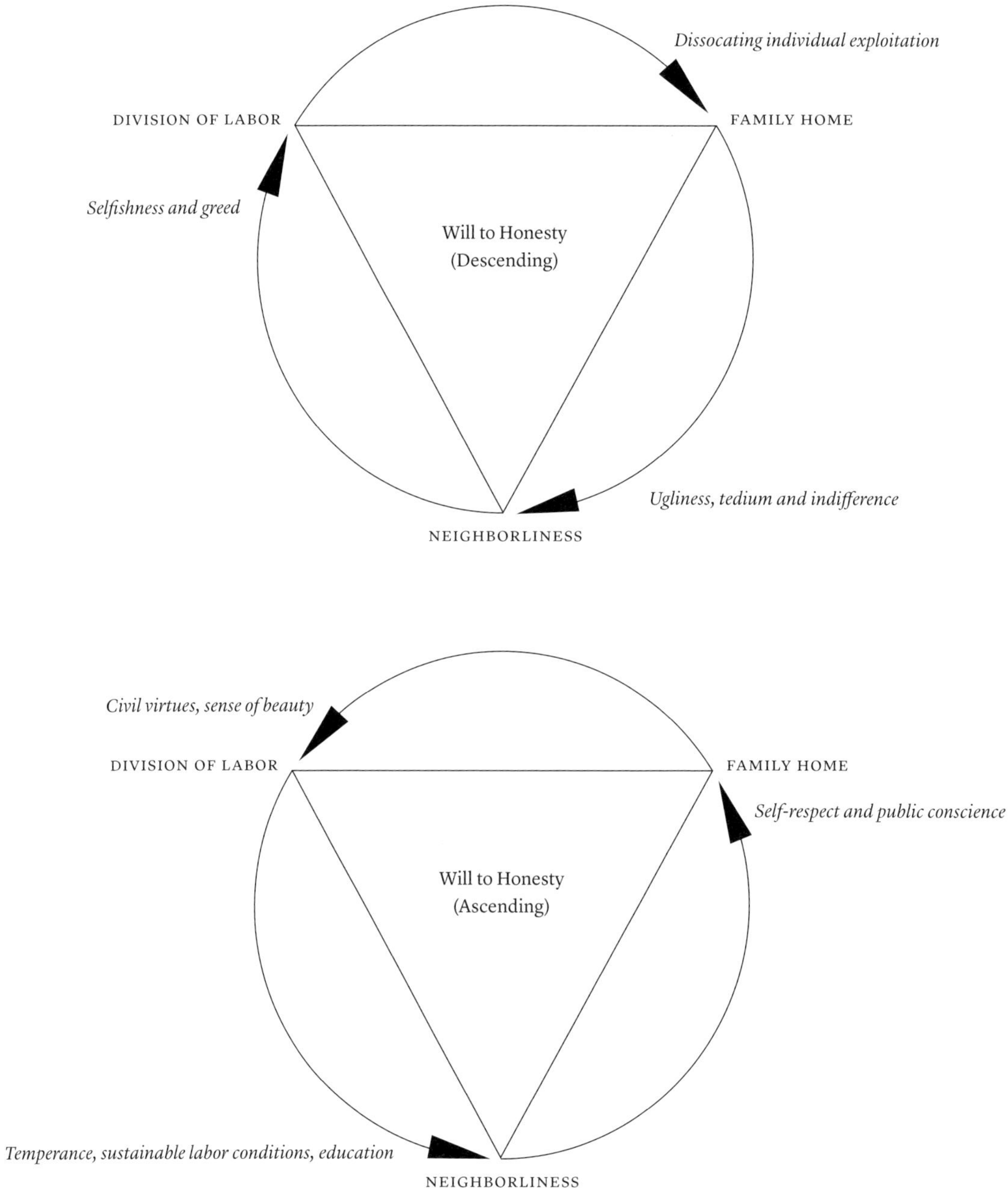

Diagram 2. Negating and affirming impacts on the conservative triangle

The meaning of the arrows in Diagram 2 might require some clarification. In a remarkable passage, Riis brings to view the affective relationship between nominal values, and here he also distinguishes clearly between the ascending and the descending effects on will. The first half of this lengthy quotation describes the 'miracle' of ascent, whereas the second communicates the more common descent.

> It is true that they tell only one side of the story; that there is another to tell. A story of thousands of devoted lives, laboring earnestly to make the most of their scant opportunities for good; of heroic men and women striving patiently against fearful odds and by their very courage coming off victors in the battle with the tenement; of womanhood pure and undefiled. That it should blossom in such an atmosphere is one of the unfathomable mysteries of life. And yet it is not an uncommon thing to find sweet and innocent girls, singularly untouched by the evil around them, true wives and faithful mothers, literally 'like jewels in a swine's snout,' in the worst of the infamous barracks. It is the experience of all who have intelligently observed this side of life in a great city, not to be explained —unless on the theory of my friend, the priest in the Mulberry Street Bend, that inherent purity revolts instinctively from the naked brutality of vice as seen in the slums—but to be thankfully accepted as the one gleam of hope in an otherwise hopeless desert.
>
> But the relief is not great. In the dull content of life bred on the tenement-house dead level there is little to redeem it, or to claim apprehension for a society that has nothing better to offer its toilers; while the patient efforts of the lives finally attuned to it to render the situation tolerable, and the very success of these efforts, serve only to bring out in stronger contrast the general gloom of the picture by showing how much farther they might have gone with half a chance. Go into any of the 'respectable' tenement neighborhoods—the fact

> that there are not more than two saloons on the corner, nor over three or four in the block will serve as a fair guide—where live the great body of the hard-working Irish and German immigrants and their descendants, who accept naturally the conditions of tenement life, because for them there is nothing else in New York; be with and among its people until you understand their ways, their aims, and the quality of their ambitions, and unless you can content yourself with the scriptural promise that the poor we shall have always with us, or with the menagerie view that, if fed, they have no cause of complaint, you shall come away agreeing with me that, humanly speaking, life there does not seem worth the living.[30]

To be as clear about this as possible, the "inherent purity" represents the divine will to honesty; "laboring earnestly to make the most of their scant opportunities" is its practice, what raises the families ("the innocent girls" and "faithful mothers") to a courageous fight against the exploiting influences of the barracks. The strengthened neighborliness that is conveyed here as "heroic men and women" is a "miracle" that is "not to be explained" by anyone but a man of faith. By contrast, the second part describes the negating affections that cause descent: "a society that has nothing better to offer its toilers" conveys a systematic exploitation of laborers whose "aims and quality of ambitions" become separated from their laboring practice; the many saloons and the lack of opportunities depress family life, rendering families "attuned to" the lowest levels of subsistence, forcing them to "accept the conditions of tenement-life", in short, to take life philosophically. The easily quenched will to honesty, their lost "half a chance" negates Christian neighborliness and perpetuates poverty. Accepting the conditions that be, the neighborhood descends to a level where life "does not seem worth the living."

The triangle is only rarely encountered in this type of condensed formats. Far more common is it to find expressions of ascent and

30. Ibid., 122.

descent articulated through extensive compositions of text. An example suitable for analysis may be found in Riis's description of the Bohemians. One should keep in mind that Riis here treats the population as an individual that relates externally to its constituent members.

The chapter called "Bohemians—Tenement-House Cigarmaking" is divided into two narrative parts. The first part presents the generic conditions that shape the specifically Bohemian abilities to cope with tenement life; it paints a complex picture of an ethnically individuated body, which is affected by numerous impetuses that thrust in both directions. The second part describes the same complex of affections once again, but this time through a series of visits with Bohemian families on the East Tenth and Seventy-Third streets. This ensuing serial composition brings about the perhaps most important function of Riis's narrative: its performative effect upon the neighborliness of the reader. It may be gleaned from press reviews of Riis's books and lectures, that such a serially induced message was perceived as a much lighter and more attractive kind of reformism than the boisterous, semantic pathos of his peers.

The first part of the Bohemian chapter argues that the singularly most detrimental influence upon this ethnic group is the circumstance that cigar industry managers (who employ more than half of the Bohemian population) also own the apartments where their workforce live and labor. Wages and rents are thus paid from and returned back to the same local employer, which conspires to render the Bohemian labor force the cheapest one on the market. Uncoordinated strikes are common and result either in a minimal raise of wages or in mass evictions and unemployment. Bohemians have accepted wages far below the union rates and this, combined with a common neglect at learning English, makes the adult population one of the most isolated ethnic groups in New York. Riis is very explicit about this assemblage of impacting forces: the labor exploitation is "a slavery as real as any that ever disgraced the South."[31]

31. Ibid., 109.

But there are also beneficial forces. These emanate primarily from an historically forged sense of neighborliness within the population. Riis notices a surprisingly resilient will to honesty and makes several casual remarks about it throughout the text. He touches for example upon the scarcity of Bohemian criminals, notices their racial pride, their cleanliness, and appreciation of aesthetic pleasures. A native clergyman remarks toward the chapter's end upon the Bohemians' troublesome religious past, from which the nation's proud endemic neighborly spirit blossoms as a blessing and a curse. Bohemian roots, he explains, grow deep into a history of "fierce contention [...] between Catholics and Protestants on Bohemia's soil, of bad faith and savage persecutions in the name of the Christian's God."[32]

In the second part, Riis redraws the portrait by, so to speak, putting the reader into the picture. The section is composed of six visits to various Bohemian families. These bring the reading down to a domestic scale, where each family is slightly differently affected by the factors that shape their communal way of life. While describing these Bohemian visits, Riis diagnoses each of the triangle's values in turn. Labor conditions and labor division is the focus of the first three visits. Domestic family life is the primary object of the following two, whereas neighborliness is treated with special care in the final visit. Value-negating affects are predominant in the first visitations while affirming ones become increasingly dominant in the latter. Not only, then, does the serial narrative enable Riis to examine small-scale impacts upon all sides of the triangle, it also gives to the succession an optimistic final tone.

Furthermore, these iterations do more than merely describe the social conditions of an ethnic group. Being constructed to also affect the reader's nominal values, which are exposed to the author's affirmations, the content of his analyses appeal to the reader's conscience and solidarity whereas the iterations serve to strengthen the will to

32. Ibid., 113.

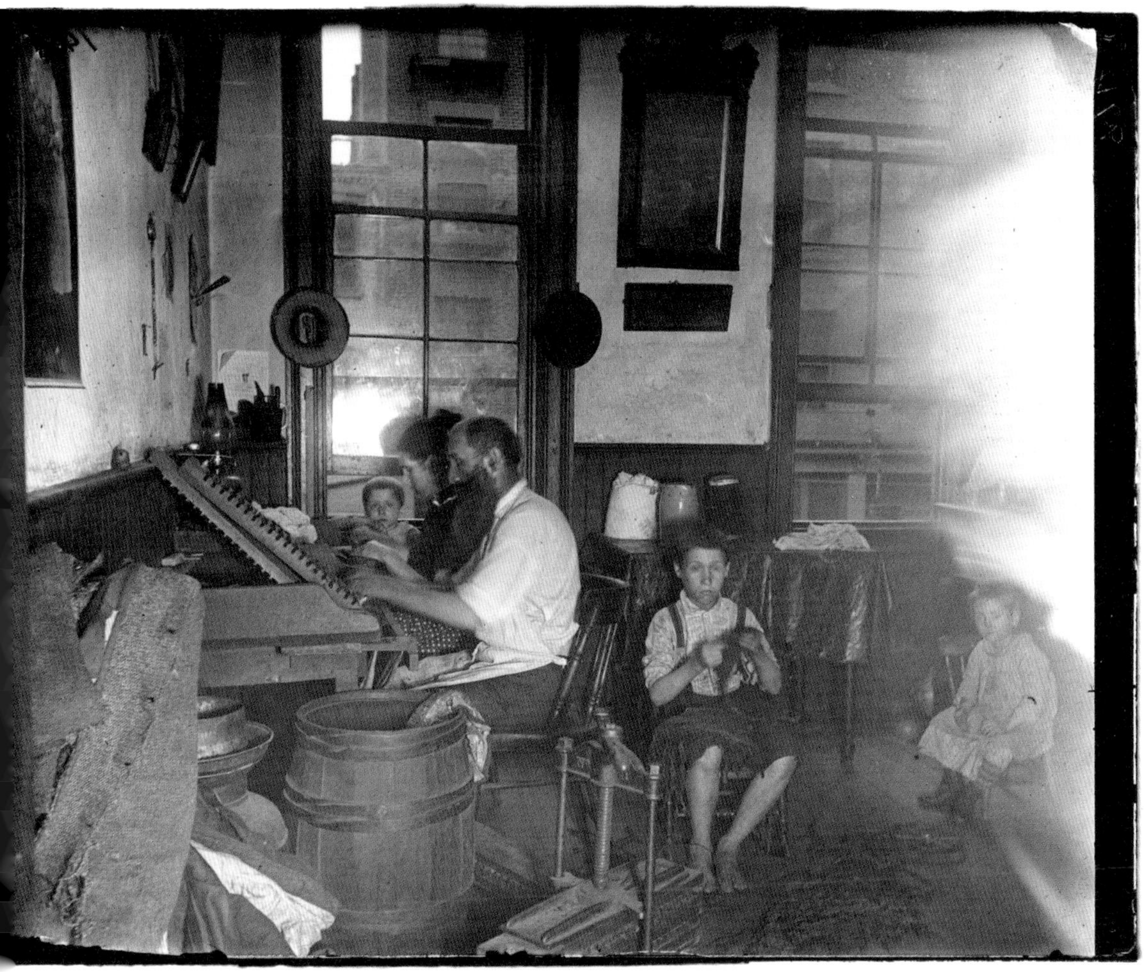

Figure 22. Jacob A. Riis, "Bohemian Cigarmakers at work in their Tenement" [90.13.4.150], ca. 1890. MCNY.

honesty.[33] Like any other form of social interaction, reading affects the nominal values of those who engage in it, and in this case, on this level of readership, it installs a differently identified object of knowledge and differently established knowers, who make sense otherwise of the conditions in the slums. Riis's technique of repeating case variations exerted a new kind of discursive force on his readers and painted a more convincing picture than what conventional pilings of adjectives and superlatives could muster. Iterated variations of absurd wage and rent ratios, for example, or account after account of variously absent English skills or tobacco-related diseases at different stages of development worked inchmeal upon the reader's neighborly values. But as rhetoric goes, this iterative technique served not only alarmist purposes. Importantly, toward the end of the Bohemian chapter, a number of agreeable descriptions interrupt the depressive perusal and strengthen the reader's sense of moral hope and political solidarity. Riis's descriptive text becomes then, through its iterative composition, a performative vehicle for communicating will to honesty, or rather, for raising it in the reader through affirming his or her neighborly values. It is a remarkable feat. More than any other feature, this will-strengthening capacity of Riis's factual analyses exerted mutating force on the existing discourse. The act of reading induces an ethical movement in the reader, which is sympathetically analogous with the impetus exerted on the narrated subject in each case variation. Appealing to an ever-widening readership, this technique redirected the curve of urban charity and established other possible truths about tenement life.

A most important aspect of Riis's writing technique is thus its ability to affectively connect individuals through descriptive cadences of

33. On the effects of this kind of iteration, see Gilles Deleuze, *Repetition and Difference* (Columbia University Press, New York: 1994), 70: "Repetition changes nothing in the object repeated but does change something in the mind which contemplates it." Roland Barthes elucidates the performative function while analyzing the proairetic code in *S/Z* (Hill and Wang, New York: 1974). For a revue of other relevant serial techniques, see also Gilles Deleuze, *Logic of Sense*, 39-41.

value negations and affirmations. It aspires to an ethical strengthening of will and an increased power to act among readers. As a general method of diagnosis, this triangular value analysis can be applied to any urban group. The Italians, the Chinese, the Jews, and the African Americans are then all analyzed in much the same way as the Bohemians, and as each group shows distinct grievances and strengths, Riis prescribes to each a reform program specific to its conditions and capacities. (Correspondingly, each one also affects the readership in its own particular way.) For Bohemians, whose will to honesty is far from extinct, there are particular remedies. Their endemic sense of neighborliness and limited English skills, combined with a strong specialization in a highly exploitative and dangerous trade, one that is associated both with terminal diseases and unfair wage labor at home; together, these conditions may explain why the Bohemians have become reputed to foster political hostilities against society at large. For a remedy, Riis first appeals to his reader's conscience, asking him to consider the social and historical reasons behind this reputation; second, he suggests that the churches be more actively engaged in battling the isolating tendencies of this community, and that means focusing on improving English skills and helping its members to access a wider labor market. If the churches were to succeed in recruiting a significant Bohemian congregation in spite of their tradition, Riis believes that their strong sense of brotherhood might impact positively on other immigrant communities as well. The status quo of a much battered will to honesty might then begin to ascend to become a powerful ally in the battle against the slum.

Similar performative analyses with ensuing concrete reform suggestions are methodically being worked out for every tenement community: the Italians, the Chinese, the Germans, the Irish, the "color line"—each are shown to possess particular conditions for prosperity and beneficial social interaction, depending, of course, on the formative impacts regularly exerted upon their labor division, neighborliness, and domestic family life. Then again, ethnicity was not the only differentiator of social bodies: children, drunkards, gangs, working girls, paupers and beggars are similarly attended to before Riis sums up *How the Other Half Lives* with the chapter "How the Case Stands," in which he outlines a prescriptive program for the heterogeneous system as such.

For a concluding remark, one must note the discursively formative, or settling capacity of Riis's performative technique. Particularly, one should focus on two of its most important component features, which derived from two firmly distinct genres of writing. The first one, the serial mode of composition, without which the iterative technique would not function, was a feature characteristic of the popular, but ill-reputed *Sunshine and Shadow* literature. As we have already noted, this genre thrived on delivering to the middle class the excitements of gambling, gang-life, intemperance and illicit entertainments which ostensibly flourished in the tenements. Its characteristically serial form of narrative was essentially a trope evoking nightly excursions to a string of tenement bars, dance halls, opium dens and cheap theaters. One might notice a similar promenade in *How the Other Half Lives*, which is also loosely narrated as a walk downtown.

But Riis rejected the slum guides' monotonous horror stories and was careful to include accounts of hope and progress whenever he found reason for it. The second element of Riis's performative technique, his balancing between good and bad influences, was typical of the opposite end of the tenement literature; particularly, it was a hallmark of the official tenement reports. These scholarly analyses gained credibility and public attention by accounting for signs of both peril and progress in the tenements.[34] Similar attention to balanced facts safeguarded the conservative penny press newspapers against

34. Cf. *Report of the Council of Hygiene and Public Health of the Citizens' Association of New York Upon the Sanitary Condition of the City* (D. Appleton, New York: 1865); The New York State Tenement House Commission, *Report* (New York, 1884); For examples in charity monographs see Octavia Hill, *Homes of the London Poor*, (London, Macmillan and Co: 1883), 23; Josephine Shaw Lowell, *One Means of Preventing Pauperism*, (n.p. 1879), 11; Felix Adler, "A New Experiment in Education" in *Princeton Review*, Jan-June, 1883, 148.

the popular sensationalist rivals of the Yellow Press. When Riis took into account the progressive as well as the corrupting tendencies, he took a stand against sensationalism, thereby enabling the observed labor conditions, family homes, and signs of neighborliness to be understood as markers of values to be realized rather than objective conditions of tenement life. As interlinked values, real yet also absolute and nominal, the three exposed corners of every individual diagram might both be affirmed and negated, and the forces that impact on them may thus both strengthen and weaken the associated will to honesty. This immediately communicated dynamism was essential for engaging the ethical sensitivity of the reader or the lecture audience. It was therefore also the decisive element of the formative, 'congealing,' and preserving moments of the mutation process. As a diagnostic and rhetorical device, the conservative triangle had been invented to exert direct emotional and normative influence; being structurally embedded in a narrative order, its affective sequentiality would operate immediately upon the audience. As these normative movements were then becoming real and palpably present, its powers to confirm and publically settle The Other Half (while at the same time disseminating associated concepts, methods, and propositions) grew stronger with every iterated analysis. With irony and humor, Riis effectively shot through sequestering borders between established idioms, which he then probed into for other ways of addressing the tenement problem. And with the resulting novel assemblage of tropes and concepts, which belonged exclusively to his diagnostic and engaging value analyses, he circulated a new tenement picture that radically and permanently recast the identities of beholder, observed, and representational media alike.

Having reached thus far in the analysis of the making of The Other Half, I hope to have sufficiently described its mutation of a discursive regime of veridiction. In the following two chapters I will attend to the visual elements that worked upon Riis's novel concepts from a non-discursive register. This world of percepts and images has its own forms and regularities, its own processes and capacities, and its own thresholds and relational invariants. In part, this realm of gazes and light, of looks and illumination, worked semantically upon the codes and signifiers of the text; in part, however, and not to be forgotten, it impacted directly upon the sensuous order of his audience.

CHAPTER 6

Iconic Syntax and Reproduction Media

In this chapter, we will turn toward Riis's photographs and let them slightly modify the analysis proposed so far. What has been suggested until now in terms of migrating concerns, fluctuating intensities, conceptual transformations, and emerging relational invariants has been salvaged exclusively from Riis's words; only a minimum of attention has been paid to the illustrations that, to an equal extent, contributed to the making of The Other Half. It is time now to take into account the visual part of his message, to allocate its proper heritages, its ways of making sense, and its non-discursive functions.

When in the two final chapters a separate analysis is reserved for images, it is to emphasize—too literally, perhaps—an epistemological distinction between irreducible modes of knowledge: on the one hand visibilities, that is, orders of light that make knowable the world as it appears, and on the other, statements, which have been analyzed in previous chapters.[1] The word 'visibility' is used here to designate forms of appearing: ordered variations of display and presentation which, much like the discursive curves, are concerted

1. In this, I follow Deleuze's Spinozean interpretation of Foucault, an interpretation primarily substantiated by Deleuze's rendering of power in Foucault. However, Spinoza's parallelism between mind and body is not continued in Foucault's genealogy, which reserves for language a determinable primacy over visuality. But parallelism maintains the crucial battle between the sensuous and the articulable, what Deleuze calls the "complementary space" (9). I believe that this Spinozean perspective distinguishes the present theoretical approach from the phenomenological slant that the genealogy has often assumed in many recent Foucauldian works of art history and visual culture. Gilles Deleuze, *Foucault*, 47-69;

around individual singularities. A singularity serves to relate variations to each other and to preserve their relative regularity and openness. A singularity is a virtual element that gathers possible ways (including ones never actualized) in which things, people, and events are able to appear to each other as phenomena. In New York of the 1880s, there were several visibilities that ordered sequestered ways of looking at tenement life. Riis's images helped generate a new modality of looking by manipulating those that subsisted already. This does not mean that Riis had full control over the generative process: it depended also, of course, on developments far beyond his scope of influence. The aim of the following two chapters is therefore to identify both the tactical manipulations and the public concerns that eventually led to the emergence of a new visibility (one that would subsequently inform the genre of social documentary photography). Before the analysis may commence, however, some theoretical comments may be helpful.

In the following, I call visibility the order that in each instance situates a beholder relative to the beheld, or rather, the regularity and regulation of their relationship. Hence, it is less a structure in the sociological sense than the structured conditions of appearance in a phenomenological sense. Visibilities have complex life spans. They emerge, thrive, wilt, and die from changes in actual practices of appearing, displaying, and staging—changes that are typically driven by technical, social, aesthetic, scientific or economic developments. Hence, while they condition the possibilities of appearing, they are at the same time exposed to change from that which they condition. Unlike statements, visibilities are not active but reactive. Without being inert, however, or readily shaped or defined by the statements, visibilities have an agency of their own: one which determines what they may be responsive to. This agency is neither determined by discourse nor by changing appearances: it is rather what makes the phenomenal world irreducible to the realm of discursive knowledge.

The visibilities that Riis manipulated were predominantly those that regulated appearances of human otherness. These visibilities were obviously a part of everyday civil culture, distributing certain variations of appearance into continuities and clusters, and others into distinct categories. Among the established visibilities that Riis's photographs unsettled, a couple of them may deserve particular mention. One furnished a gaze and a mode of display which properly situated the appearance of low-life characters in cheap theater melodramas or during guided slum-safaris to the lower Manhattan. The ordered presentation of curiosities in dime museums and sideshows belonged also to this visibility. Indeed, tenement dwellers occasionally appeared in such venues before a paying audience, sometimes as wax dolls and sometimes in live tableaux, and then often recognizable as characters known from the stage and from live slum-tour encounters. This typecast, yet variegated mode of appearing reproduced itself also in daily newspaper illustrations, in Sunday magazine cartoons, and in the *Sunshine and Shadow* literature. It was sustained by ingrained practices—social, economic, and technical—which, consistently and systematically coordinated the postures, the light, the movements, the perceptions, and the rules of interaction. Now, a completely different set of practices and perceptive regulations sustained the ordered appearance of tenement residents before social reformers, doctors, philanthropic organizations, commissioners, and journalists. This mode of appearance, or visibility, also involved a theatrical aspect, a play of representation, and was none the closer to 'reality' or 'the truth' than the first one. But its clinical regard was able to detect other phenomena, identify other deviations and norms, and make different connections between them. A third visibility that Riis engaged with had emerged with the growing public interest in scholarly anthropology. This visibility allowed the ostensibly uncivilized, as well as the merely slightly less civilized, to appear and be academically scrutinized as specimens of evolutionary development. The practices and regulations that sustained this encounter oriented appearance after determining hierarchies of race, measures of commercial advancement, assessments of social structure, knowledge forms, technical proficiency, and artistic skill.

These three visibilities do not form a complete list, but they suggest some of the most important modes of appearance that Riis's photographs would challenge. What, then, does it mean to challenge an established visibility? First of all, conditions of appearance are dynamic, both in the sense that they allow a more or less motley array of possible variations and in the sense that this scope of variation is exposed to change. Visibilities exhibit fluctuating degrees of freedom to expand or restrict those variations. But all of them have limits beyond which their practices infringe on rival visualities that prevent expansion. To challenge established visibilities is to enlist practices in such a way that a new visibility can organize appearances differently.

This is usually very difficult. Appearances on the fringes of a visibility are often confronted with adverse forces and are unlikely to maintain their marginal position for very long. For example, the architect Edward T. Potter's 1887 proposal for a functionalist tenement house offered solar orientation and cross ventilation that secured a maximum of sunlight and fresh air.[2] As a particularly progressive feature, all apartments had an oblique view to the street. But a tenement building that optimized visual access to public life was an expensive reform initiative that took space away from potential revenue. Potter's beautiful house was weak against the dominant financial interests and could not be actualized until after the market crash in the 1930s, when other political forces were dominant. Another type of fringe phenomenon occurs when incompatible visibilities intersect. It begs to be noticed that visibilities are usually normatively invested, and that the associated values determine their social differentiation. In Riis's time, it was expected of a sagacious city-dweller to be able to engage with mutually incompatible visibilities

2. Cf. Richard Pluntz, *A History of Housing in New York City*, 29-31.

and to traverse social spheres; urban life demanded skills at navigating mutually conflicting phenomenological regimes. Handling such contradictions could be a more or less pressing part of everyday life. For example, a socially respected citizen of the lower bourgeoisie, whom friends and acquaintances expected to see at charity lectures, should also, assuming different standards, be able to enjoy an occasional dime museum, where the same intemperate paupers, previously pitied, were now perceived as ghastly, fascinating examples of undeveloped nature. But this demand for flexibility also meant that a serious *faux pas* lurked somewhere among the thresholds. Certain charity societies exploited this risk and occasionally raided brothels, dance halls, and pleasure clubs, evoking through their mere physical presence a gulf of visibilities too shameful to endure for many respectable patrons.[3] Such raids were reportedly often enough to disturb the economy of the illicit businesses and to force them to move elsewhere. A third kind of fringe phenomenon occurs when discourse and visibility bifurcate. Venereal diseases, for example, were among the bourgeoisie often not treated by the family house doctor although, discursively speaking, these alliments belonged to the same clinical regime of knowledge as any other infectious condition. Signs of syphilis and gonorrhea were rather taken to be examined by quacks practicing at anatomic museums.[4] These establishments operated on the lowest rungs of the entertainment hierarchy, frequently offering displays for adult males only. Medical examinations here would be kin to practices that sustained visibilities of sexual desire, and they would take place, so to speak, on the outskirts of clinical modern medicine.

Visibilities do not follow discursive delineations; visibilities are not bound to individual subjects or to specific social groups or organizations; they do not follow categories of empirical objects. Further-

3. Timothy J. Gilfoyle, *City of Eros* (W.W. Norton, New York: 1992), 188-190; 298-302.

4. Michael Sappol, *A Traffic of Dead Bodies: Anatomy and Embodied Social Identity in 19th-Century America* (Princeton University Press, Princeton: 2002).

more, they have no intrinsic meaning although their practices and normative signatures provide a foundation for interpretation. They are few in number, but always a multiplicity. Disturbances in their iterative reproduction, caused for example by impulses from changing technologies and economies, make visibilities mutate, differentiate and sometimes redistribute their cultural dominance. Visibilities may be disturbed if a single series of appearances is being forced to respond differently to discursive determinations, for example, or if its social norms are made to spread to other, differently valued appearances which then establish a new sustainable series.

The mutation of visibilities that occurred with Riis's photographs rests on two formal conditions. The first is found in the normative conflicts that arose on the fringes of three incompatible visibilities. In particular, Riis's illustrated lectures ventured out into these outskirts, where images and diction allowed appearances that would reconcile irrecusably divergent norms. The reordering of variations that settled with these excursions will be examined in the next and final chapter. The second condition for the mutation of visibilities is found elsewhere: in the serial nature of Riis's visual displays. The significance of Riis's photographs—their emotional power as well as their individual meaning—was in fact largely dependent on their serial composition. Until 1947, when the Museum of the City of New York curated the first exhibition of Riis's photographs, these had never been displayed individually, devoid of extensive verbal narrative or commentary, as singular works of art. Prior to this remarkable event they had been objects of use, and their essentially syntactic seriality, whether they were reproduced in books, articles or shown during lectures, was fundamental to their meaning and impact. A sample of thematically related magazines and books from the time is enough to corroborate Maren Stange's observation that the generic tenement image might easily have included any of Riis's photographs[5]—but the generic tenement visibility could hardly have accommodated the

5. Maren Stange, *Symbols of Ideal Life: Social Documentary Photography in America, 1890-1950* (Cambridge University Press, Cambridge: 1989).

structure of composition that ordered his presentations. It is befitting to speak of 'series' when the task is to highlight the extraordinary variations in sequencing that Riis applied to image and word composition: far beyond mere illustrations he operated with an impressive blend of various corroborating, ambivalent, and conflicting juxtapositions. Such an intense variety of visual rhetoric was in itself able to affect and transform the reproductive iterations that maintained the conventional visibility of tenement charity.

The first thing to notice about this condition for a mutation of visibility is that possibilities to explore serial composition and iconic variation varied with different public media. In the following, the photographs will therefore be examined relative to the particular syntactic possibilities afforded by books, magazine articles, and illustrated lectures. A second issue to be noticed is how far Riis's images exploited the ostensibly unique ability of photographs to *represent* reality as such. Regardless of whether or not the printed reproductions preserved any of the visual characteristics of the photographic image, and irrespective also of the disputes toward the end of the nineteenth century concerning the value of photographic veracity, Riis presupposed the avowed testimonial quality of the technical image and provided raw, unpolished witness accounts that showed the underworld as it really was. His photographs fully embodied the ideal of technical and objective veridiction. This is important to notice for other reasons than the obvious one: that no previous photographs had been made in the slums under similar circumstances, and that his ones apparently unveiled the objective truth for the first time. Beyond this pioneering quality, what begs to be noted is Riis's iterative rhetoric, whose neighborly impressions from real life made the use of iconic syntax even more decisive. Exploiting each medium's distinct abilities to string together objective reality fragments over a complex verbal narrative proved a decisive technology for changing visibilities—being the first one in the slums with a camera did not. One may, however, benefit from a little historical background to appreciate this.

Photography's 'naturally induced' images implied from its earliest days a set of values, which soon claimed a certain distance to those pertaining to the established fine arts. The painter's sense of coloration and texture, the sculptor's rendition of form and body, the draftsman's creation of perspective and movement—these were categorically untranslatable into photographic virtues. Instead, truth to detail, instant momentariness, natural objectivity, strong alliances with the sciences and with other disciplinary institutions: all of these, plus an extraordinary reproductive capacity, were soon recognized as distinct photographic values. In the relative absence of an artist's unique touch, photographs developed a stronger, more differentiated bond between represented motif and adjacent discourse. Registers, protocols, anecdotes, legends, captions, instructions, greetings—photographs subjected almost promiscuously to the world of words, to stories, to chatter, to history, to archives, to law, and also, eventually, to news. This promiscuous will to couple with almost any story, any archive, would more than anything dissociate photography from the other visual arts. It speaks of a remarkable syntagmatic ability to nestle with discursive productions of meaning.

The semantic quality of a photograph is found in its capacity to function as a sign. A photograph can be considered a semantic entity insofar as it signifies. The vast majority of photographs contain visual elements that signify, but they also contain elements that do not. Such elements are, for example, the photochemical traces, the support of the image (paper, metal, glass), the reproduction technologies (halftone, wood engravings, photogravure, woodbury prints), the frame of the image, and its size. These non-semantic elements can be said to condition the semantic function of a photograph, but they are not reducible to that function. There are iconic qualities that do not operate as signs but function autonomously in relation to the elements that do.

Syntagmatic relationships between photographs (and words) tend to intensify their capacity to function as signs. Paradigmatic relationships, on the other hand, have no such intrinsic impact. Early police records, for example, invested photographs with several semantic functions, but although some of these relied heavily on the strong paradigmatic relationships evoked with the Rogues' Gallery, these relationships required discursive investment for the semantic functions to be operational. Paradigmatic image series merely form a trajectory of visual variations. Such variations may increase the semantic capacity of certain images, but again, this is not an intrinsic function of paradigmatic relations. Paradigmatic relations are relations of *non-semantic* image elements. For example, the relationship between a photographic print by Riis and a published wood engraving of the same image is paradigmatic. These variations of an image do not function as a sign, nor do they produce signs. Of course, it is possible that such non-semantic variations may act upon a sign or upon a syntagmatic series and influence their possible meanings. If, say, during a lecture a hand-colored slide would appear amongst a series of black and white images, it would certainly affect its signifying function. But a black-and-white slide lying next to a hand-colored slide on the light table does not form a syntagmatic relationship.

It has yet to be explained why certain paradigmatic variations impact on semantic functions while others do not. Such an investigation must, however, be postponed for another occasion. The sketched conceptual distinctions and definitions proposed above might hopefully still suffice for proceeding with the task at hand, namely to look at the serial composition of Riis's images in various media. The present chapter will continue with a study of how various media afforded different types of syntagmatic series, and how these impacted upon the rhetorical performance of Riis's photographs. The ensuing final chapter, which proceeds with a study of paradigmatic series, will look at relevant non-semantic relationships, focusing particularly on Riis's reconciliation of incompatible visibilities and the fringe phenomena that these offered him.

Syntagmatic Image Performance during Lectures

The public lecture was Riis's most visually intense medium.[6] Today we are able to appreciate Riis's performance technique thanks to a stenographed account of "The Other Half and How they Live; Story in Pictures." This lecture was delivered on November 9, 1891 at the "Christians at Work" convention in Washington DC, and was subsequently published complete with image references in the January 1895 issue of the monthly *The Temple Builder*. More than a century later, this publication enabled a Scandinavian team of curators to reconstruct the lecture event for an exhibition, allowing visitors and researchers alike to experience its persuasive style and syntagmatic structure.[7]

Like many previous Riis lectures, the Washington performance began with a short welcome address and a brief introduction. On other occasions a hymn or a prayer had followed to warm up the audience, but reviews mention no such entertainments at the November 9 lecture.[8] Riis immediately took the stage for some opening remarks, whereupon the lights were dimmed and the lantern projector lit up. After approximately one hour, Riis finished without taking questions from the audience. The stenographed Washington DC lecture identifies 61 lantern slides, shifting at irregular intervals, but often with a sense of timing and suspense that suggests an intimate collaboration between the orator on stage and the lantern operator.

6. Cf. Bonnie Yochelson, *Jacob Riis* (Phaidon, New York: 2001), 10.
7. The reconstruction of the lecture was made in 2008 for the exhibition *Jacob A Riis* at the National Museum of Photography in Copenhagen. An abridged lecture manuscript was published with a selection of images in the catalogue, cf. Dag Petersson, *Jacob A. Riis* (The Danish Royal Library, Copenhagen: 2008). Originally, the stenographed record was published in Riis, "The Other Half and How they Live: Story in Pictures," in *The Temple Builder; Christian Work and Method in all the World*, 2:5, Jan 1895, 405-429.
8. "Slums of a Great City," in *Washington DC Post*, Nov. 10, 1891; "A Reporter's Experience," in *Washington DC Star*, Nov. 10, 1891. Both in Riis's Scrapbook, LC, Riis papers, box 10.

Although Riis spoke without a manuscript, the lecture followed a prearranged narrative, as is evident from the ordering of slides. Two particulars about this narrative became apparent upon experiencing the lecture reconstructed: firstly, that the images enjoy narrative primacy over the words; secondly, that the narrative was organized into three distinct parts. Let us dwell on this second aspect. Not only did it become clear that there were three parts, but also that each of the three parts forms a complete composition with a clear beginning, middle, and end. What is more, each part deals with a particular side of the conservative triangle. The first part visualizes the decaying tendency of the family home. Here, Riis balances carefully between woeful domestic grievances and light jokes marbled with brief digressions; his diction is simple and conventional, and images and words correspond like synchronic couples. The second part then describes the decay of labor division, dedicating a major section to the orphans and street urchins that are destined for the gangs but in the meantime operate from overcrowded sleeping quarters downtown. Here, the tone is increasingly ironic, the jokes are more sinister and the brighter moments are fewer. Also, the temporal complexity increases with a greater portion of diachronic analyses and motley narrations of generic events. Finally, the third part portrays the decay of neighborliness, which only stops at the labor house and the anonymous mass graves at Potter's Field. Although the descending affections greatly outnumber the ascending ones, there are still expressions of hope in this part, with the Florence Mission as the brightest interruption. But even as such positive glimmers perform in this lecture as they do in the books, the seriality that grinds the lecture experience to a complete descent is vastly different.

Unlike *How the Other Half Lives*, which is organized as a sequence of population analyses, each being structured after the triangular model, the lecture employs the triangle from beginning to end, structuring its first, second and final part accordingly. Mounting indignation upon evidence with each individual represented on the screen lays bare the various ways in which they are challenged by the corresponding nominal value. Each part is furthermore governed by a narrative principle that ensures syntagmatic cohesion and continuity between subjects visited. In the first part, the principle is topographic; the value of family home is continuously being impacted upon by a lineup of places that, one after the other, string together into a narrative of domestic decay. The series of sites that make up the first part resemble a tour downtown. Each stop on the tour discovers a locality which, more often than not, belies the value of a family home: views into apartment interiors, cellar dives and outdoor alleys, streets and doorways serving as playgrounds, etc. But there are ambiguous sightings too, such as the streets adorned with clothes-lines that bear witness to a shortage of linen and insufficient washing facilities, but also of "some one trying to keep clean, and cleanliness, you know, is next to godliness."[9] Another view of hope is given with a peek into an improvised classroom with neat little girls posing for the camera, proving that runaway children, given up by the public school, are not beyond reach. Riis's sequence of slides clearly intensifies the semantic function of the images: the views are syntactically framed by a topographic grammar that orders iconic complexes into meaningful propositions, for instance by juxtaposing certain particular, real slices of life, *hic et nunc*, with generic, value-determined categories of the metropolitan cityscape: private and public spaces, commercial and social spaces, adult spaces and spaces for children, and so on. This topographic grammar structures the verbal-iconic order of sequencing, which in turn controls the communicative 'logic', or the common recognizability of what each image really refers to and how it impacts on other story elements. In this case, the narrative of places impacting on the tenement home reveals only a rather simple set of syntactic rules for how images may engage with words. To each photograph belongs a story or a comment that begins and ends with the picture displayed; the discursive order, evinced by this string of narrative units amounts quite simply the the cicerone's veridiction. It implies a tour guide's knowledge, the truth of the pointing index,

9. Riis, "The Other Half and How they Live," 410.

its descriptive explication, site after site, engendering a syntax of topographic events. Toward the end of this first part, a particular anecdote breaks with the established order and ties no less than three images together into an illustrated set. From a bird's view of the Bend in broad daylight, Riis's audience descends into the shady gloom of the nearby Bandit's Roost and proceeds down into the perpetual darkness of a neighborhood two-cent restaurant. Down here, Riis commences with the second part of the lecture, shifting the nominal value from the family home to the division of labor. The narrative principle is then no longer topographic, but physiognomic.

The second part presents the laboring bodies of pauperism, and it begins with the physiognomy of an idle tramp on strike before the photographer. This vagrant, Riis says, demanded another quarter for putting the emblematic clay pipe back into his mouth. The story moves on to street boys asleep after a day's work of peddling dirt from Castle Garden "as Holy Earth from Jerusalem at fifty cents a clod". Continuing the narrated decline from the first part, the images and anecdotes now combine into progressively more complex semantic structures. For example, Riis attributes the "problem with the children" to exploitative labor conditions, and underscores the claim with the physiognomic documentation of "Antonia Candida," a little girl photographed before and after she was taken in by the Society for the Prevention of Cruelty to Children. Presented to the audience over brief accounts of her background, this double image forms a syntagmatic unit that produces scores of signs, literally a catalogue of symptoms, and hence it also serves as the opening image to a portrait story of children salvaged from the corrupting paths of gang life or child labor. Here, the ironic jokes begin, the rhythm becomes increasingly jerky and irregular, as if the narrative was itself an expression of the hapless contingency of the narrated rescue operations. Eight views into the lineup of rescued children playing, praying, attending class or washing up for dinner comes a second sharp break and a return to "the poorest children, whom the public school rejects or cannot find room for." None of these palpable visual negations

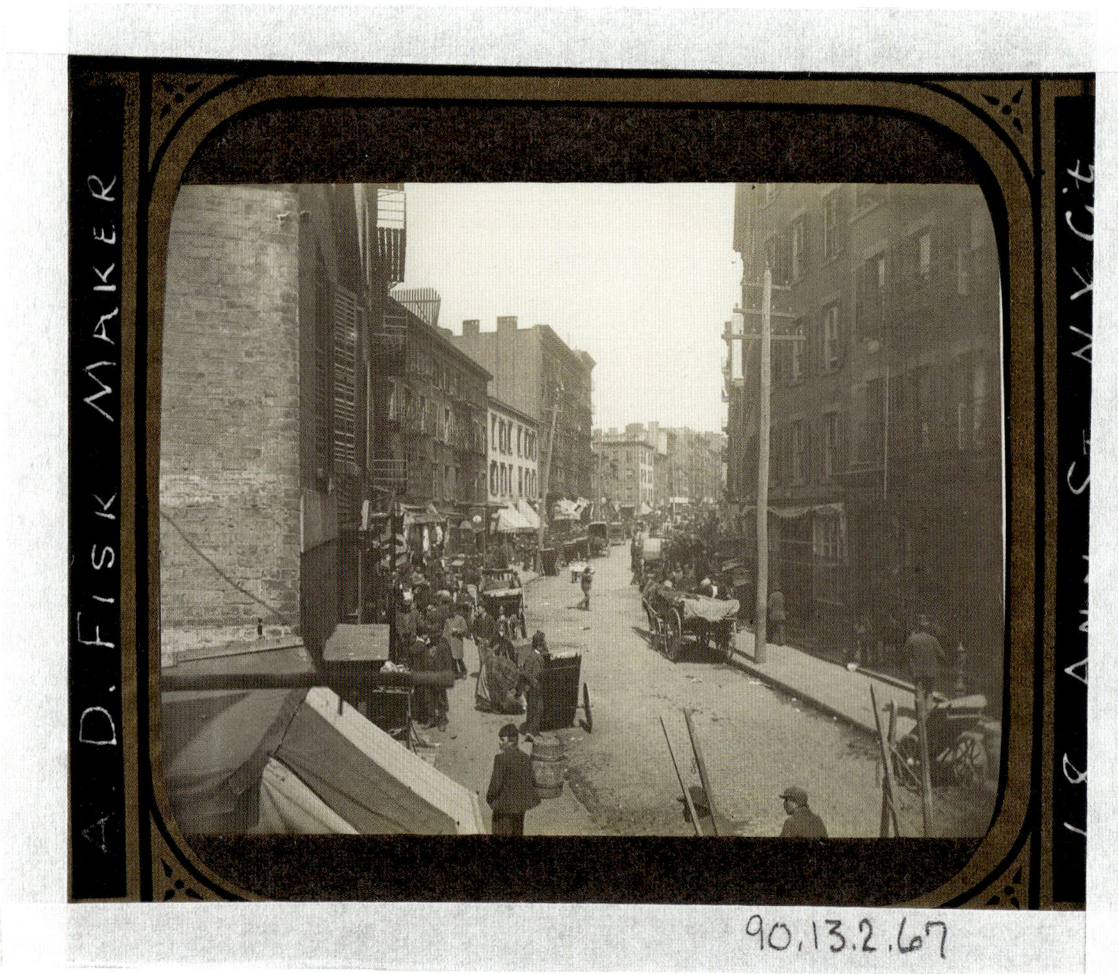

Figures 23. Jacob A. Riis, "The Mulberry Bend," [90.13.2.67] ca. 1887. MCNY.

"Here you are with the Italians. They live out of doors most of the time, and that is why they are healthy though dirty, and the death rate is not so large. Go there at sunset some evening and you will see an army of men and women slouching along with the unmistakable gait of the tramp. Where they all go will puzzle you. One by one they disappear, even while you look and before your very eyes. You will be troubled to find what becomes of them, till you look sharp and find doorways leading into side alleys."

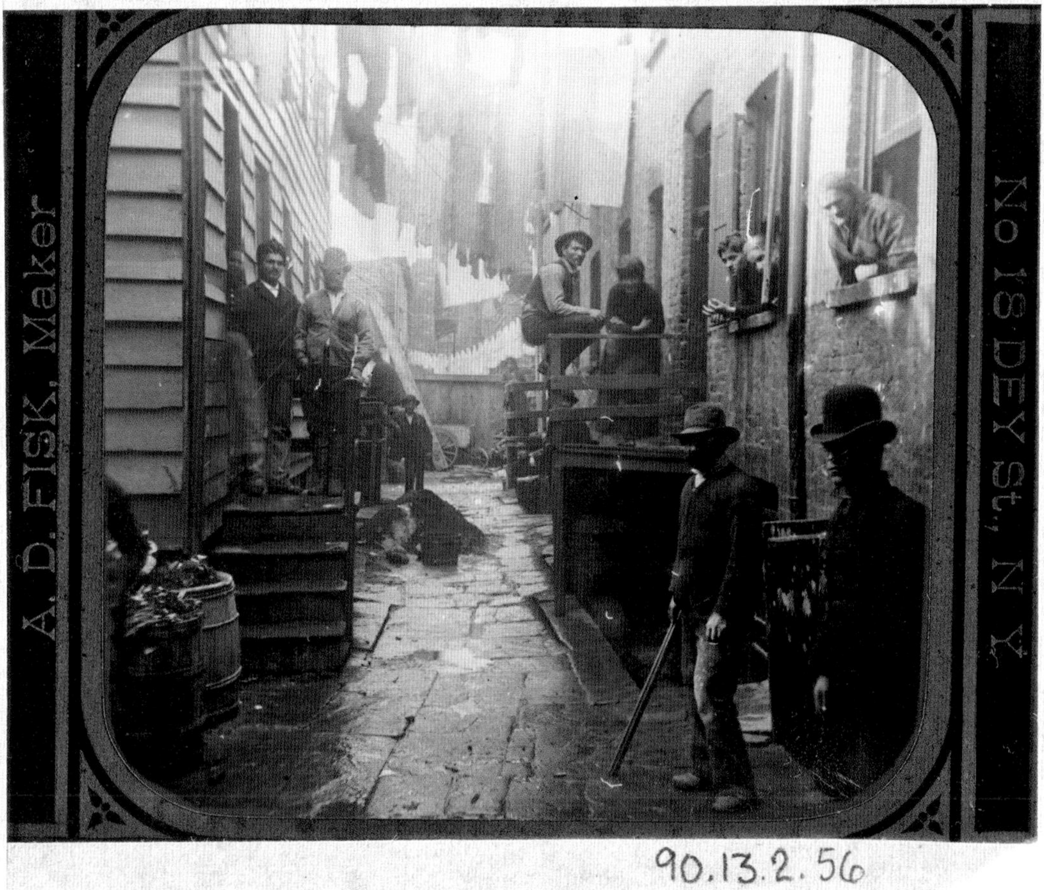

Figure 24. Richard Hoe Lawrence and Jacob A. Riis "Bandit's Roost, 59 ½ Mulberry Street," [90.13.2.56] ca 1887. MCNY.

"This one was called Bandit's Roost from an old Neapolitan bandit who lived there and died there. Since then the "Roost" has been filled up with rather inoffensive Italians, who do no harm except on Sunday, when they take to playing cards and generally in the end to the knifes, when murder comes in to finish the business. Let us go into one of the alleys and down into one of the under-ground rooms and see what goes on at three o'clock in the morning."

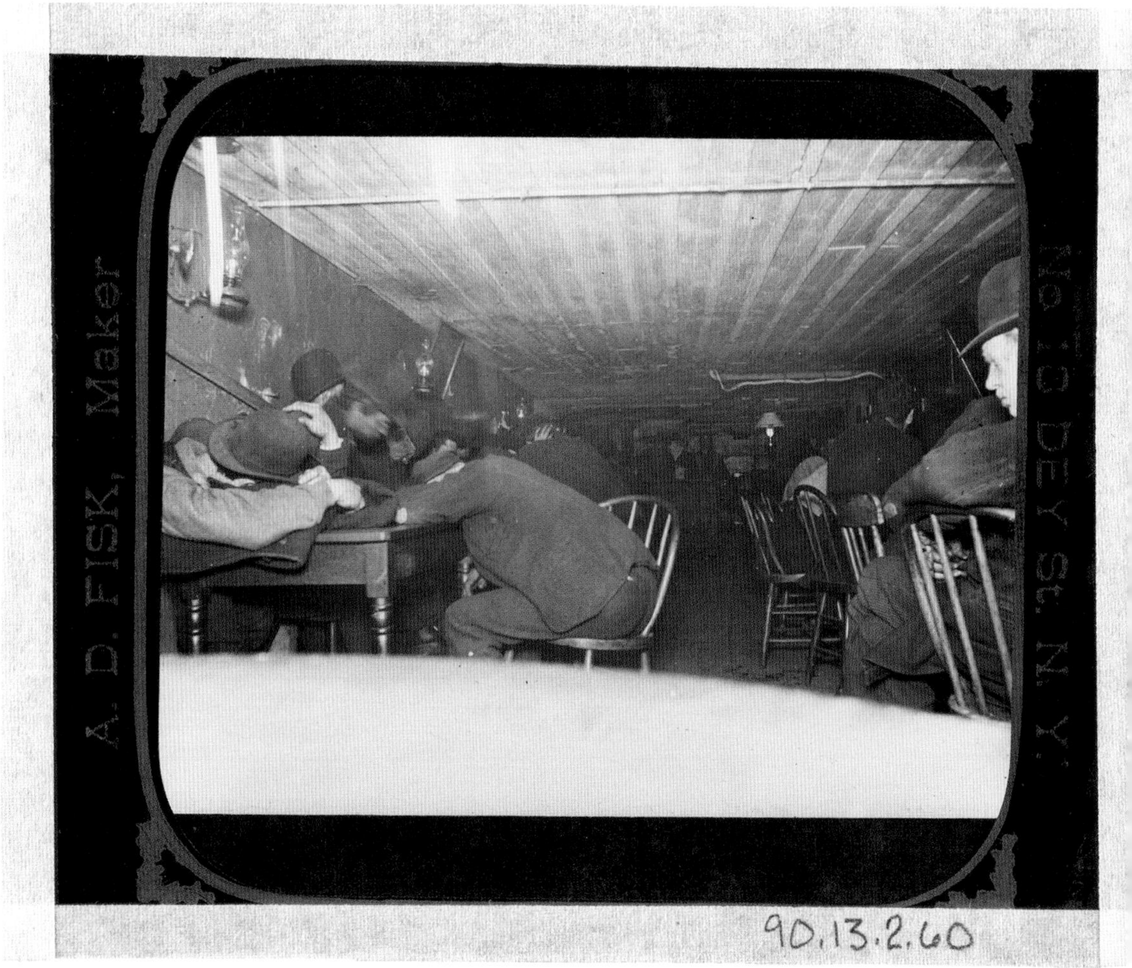

Figure 25. Jacob A. Riis, "An All-night two-cent restaurant" or "Bandit's Roost —In a stale Beer Dive in Cellar—Flashlight at 3 a.m.," [90.13.2.60] 1887. MCNY.

"There you have a stale beer dive. They call it with a nice name, a "Two-Cent Restaurant". For two cents you can get a round of drinks, such as it is, and have the privilege of sleeping all night at the table, or of lying under the table. Tramps, all of them! They are not thieves. They have not spunk enough for that. At most they might summon up courage to rob a clothes line, when no one is looking. Once I went down to raid such a place with the police, and we found there forty-two men and women in a room not more than twelve feet square, and in the corner on a heap of dirty straw lay a woman with a new-born baby."

of proper labor division are individualized by corresponding anecdote, as in the first part, but are rather woven into each other and into a parallel account of biting sarcasm and despair. An intense narrative assemblage has commenced that soon includes the adults, the parents, and the employers who have disowned their basic labor responsibilities. The cicerone's veridiction is now exchanged for an order of friendship, a truth that comes out of intimate personal knowledge and affection. The physiognomies displayed tell a story of betrayal, a story of how the life of drunkards, thieves, and prostitutes betrays the tenement children and reproduces behavior that negate the republic. Self-esteem and will to honesty are reduced to a level where society, quite naturally, hands over the tenement youth to the gangs. By thus approaching the cultivation of selfishness and greed, Riis opens the question of neighborliness.

Before commencing with the third part, Riis offers a remarkable interlude: a juxtaposition of Mrs. Stewart's extravagant marble mansion on Fifth Avenue and a squatter's shack on the upper Eleventh. The point is that happiness is independent of wealth, and that the jolly squatters live better as a family than the Stewarts do in their palace. These remarks move the lecture from the sociological register to the pious domain. Only with that in place will Riis descend into New York's inferno, to the rungs of the hopeless. The narrative principle here is conscientious; during this third part, what ensures syntagmatic continuity between visitations is the affective nature of human relations, which here for the most part negate the value of neighborliness. A normative grammar is at work here: a set of communicative regulations that steer and tailor semantic meaning by repeatedly juxtaposing the photographs' irrecusably real, objective, and singular human countenances with the live relationship in the lecture hall between Riis and his audience, to whom the narrator addresses himself in increasingly direct and personal ways. After three initial images that each show brave but insufficient attempts to counter the misery (foundlings registered at the police station; Sister Irene's Asylum for Orphans; the Florence Mission for Fallen Women), Riis plunges into

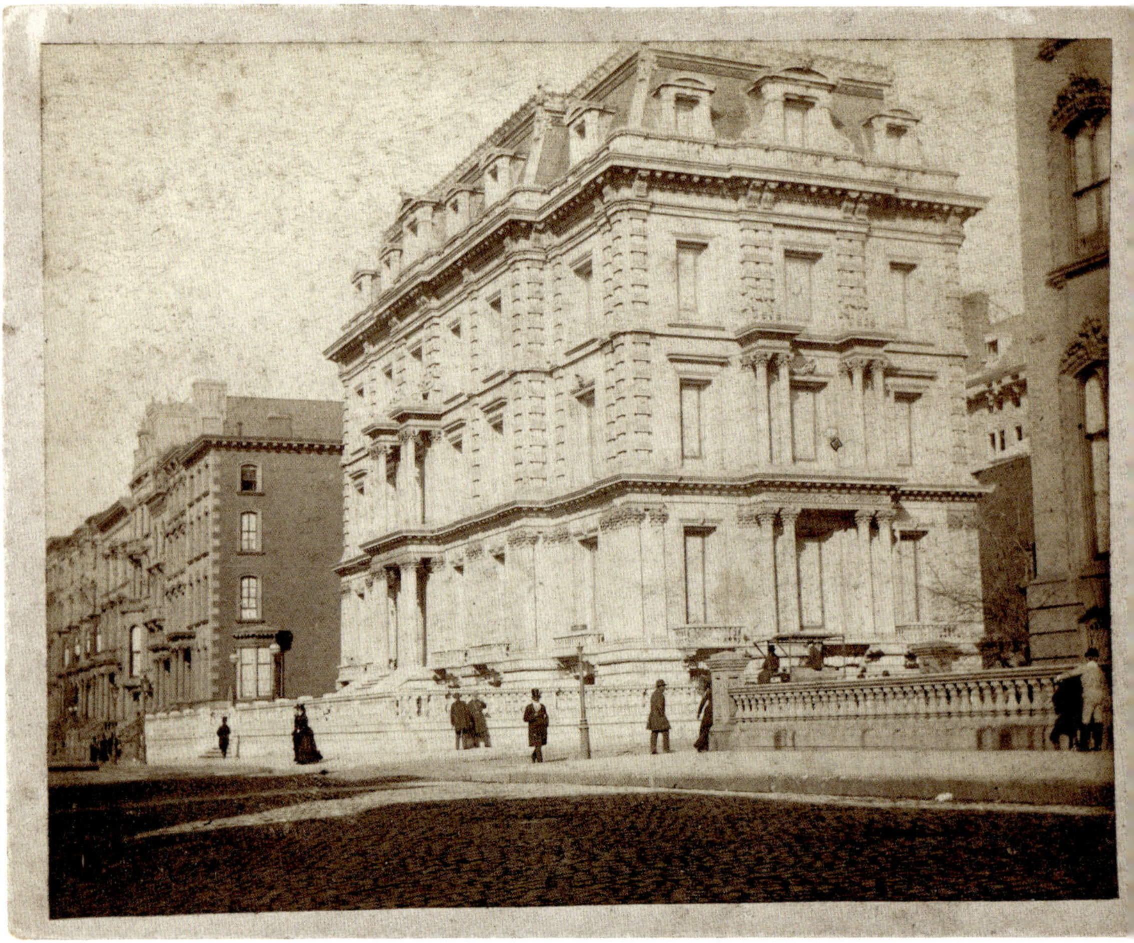

Figure 26. Anonymous photographer, "A.T. Stewart House," [90.13.3.133] 1895. MCNY.

"Since the last stone was put on that house and the last dollar of the two millions was expended, I do not think there was one happy hour in that big building. After all, wealth does not make the difference. That was Mrs. Stewart's on Fifth Avenue. Now let me introduce you to Mrs. Flanagan's over on Eleventh Avenue."

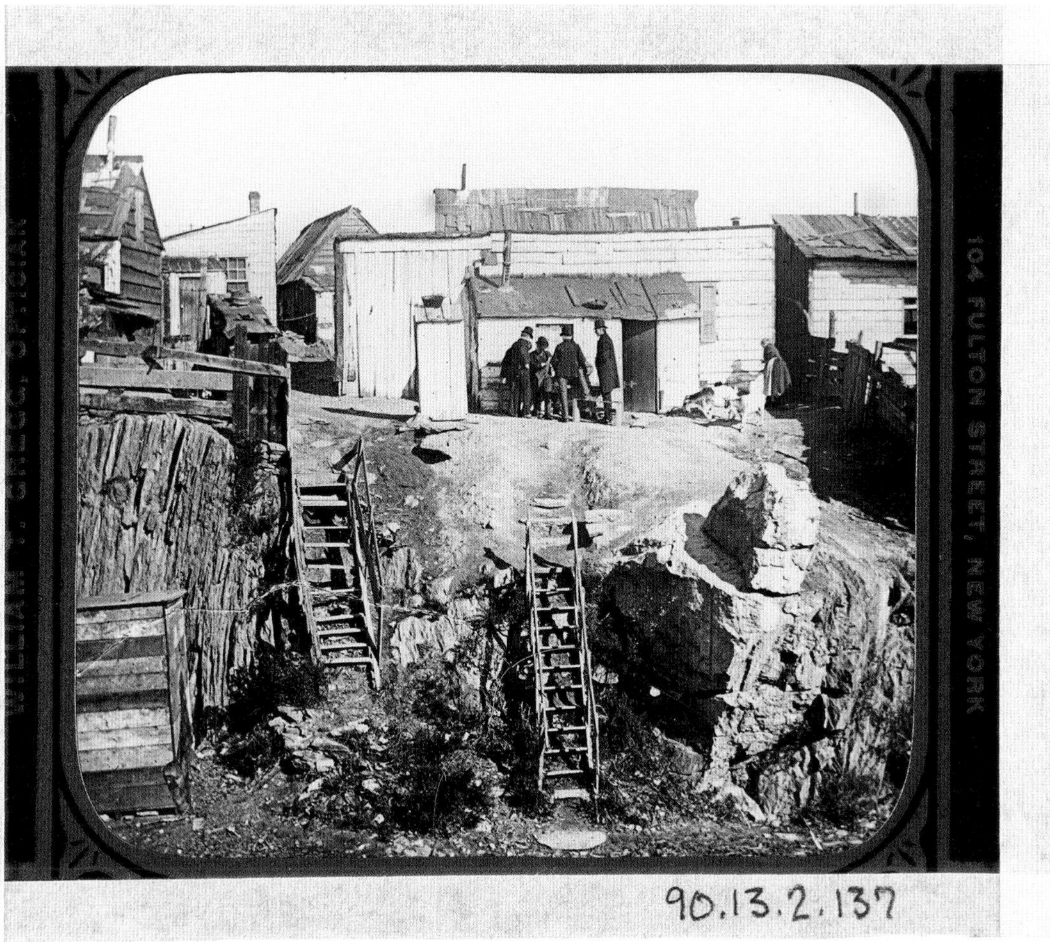

Figure 27. Jacob A. Riis, "Shanty Town," [90.13.2.137] 1896. MCNY.

"Happiness enough there, and why not? They are squatters and don't care whether school keeps or not. With the strong love for the soil that characterizes the Irish everywhere, they fight for their rock, even though it does not belong to them, until they are driven away and the rock is blasted from under them with dynamite. [Laughter] Then they will go to somebody's else rock and fight for that. The tax-gatherer has no show with them. They take the steps away, if he bothers them too much, and let him stand below and jaw as much as he likes."

chaos: "But, friends, here is one (shows picture of Chinatown) whose heaven is not the same as ours. He wont [sic] have it at all. This Chinaman, you can't do anything with him. I despair of him altogether. I give it up." Through five successive images Riis mocks the rituals in the Chinese temples, he ridicules their primitive communication skills, and gasps at the sights of the opium dens. Three exterior views and two interiors: the former show a sunny desolate street with a solitary figure walking down the sidewalk or picking among some garbage on the curb. The interiors picture an altar close up, bewildering in its display, and a man sprawled out numb on an opium bunk, his faced covered by his hat. It is a story of solitude and selfishness that negates the value of human relationships as such, and with it community feeling and neighborliness.[10] Next circuit contains the lodging houses and the black-and-tan dives, where "black and white of both sexes meet." There are no families in these windowless interiors or among the anonymous throngs and crowds: even Riis's staccato syntax helps to stamp them out of this environment. None of the subjects pose standing on their own but are either laying flat on the floor or stand leaning up against a wall. The flash finds them burrowing like cave dwellers. At this point, all ridicule has stopped and Riis holds back on the blood and thunder; resignation or relinquishment dims his metaphors and his overall diction, as if to give free rein to the audience's indignation. Toward the end of the lecture, Riis addresses New York's municipal institutions with a few cynical puns up his sleeve. Meanwhile, Blackwell's Workhouse looms behind him as an isolated compound towering on an anonymous terrain; the Female Almshouse and the Penitentiary rear ignominiously over their inmates and convicts. Potter's Field is the penultimate stop, grim in appearance with its sullied and hard-working men loading coffins into mass graves. But with these men, these honestly laboring men, the descent into hell on earth turns back to social life and further

10. Riis probably deliberated the barren feeling of these Chinatown images: long shadows suggest an early morning expedition with chances of empty streets; the view from an opium den originally included a Chinese man sitting next to the reclining smoker (see figure 20), but cropping marks and verso comments indicate that Riis wanted him excluded from the frame.

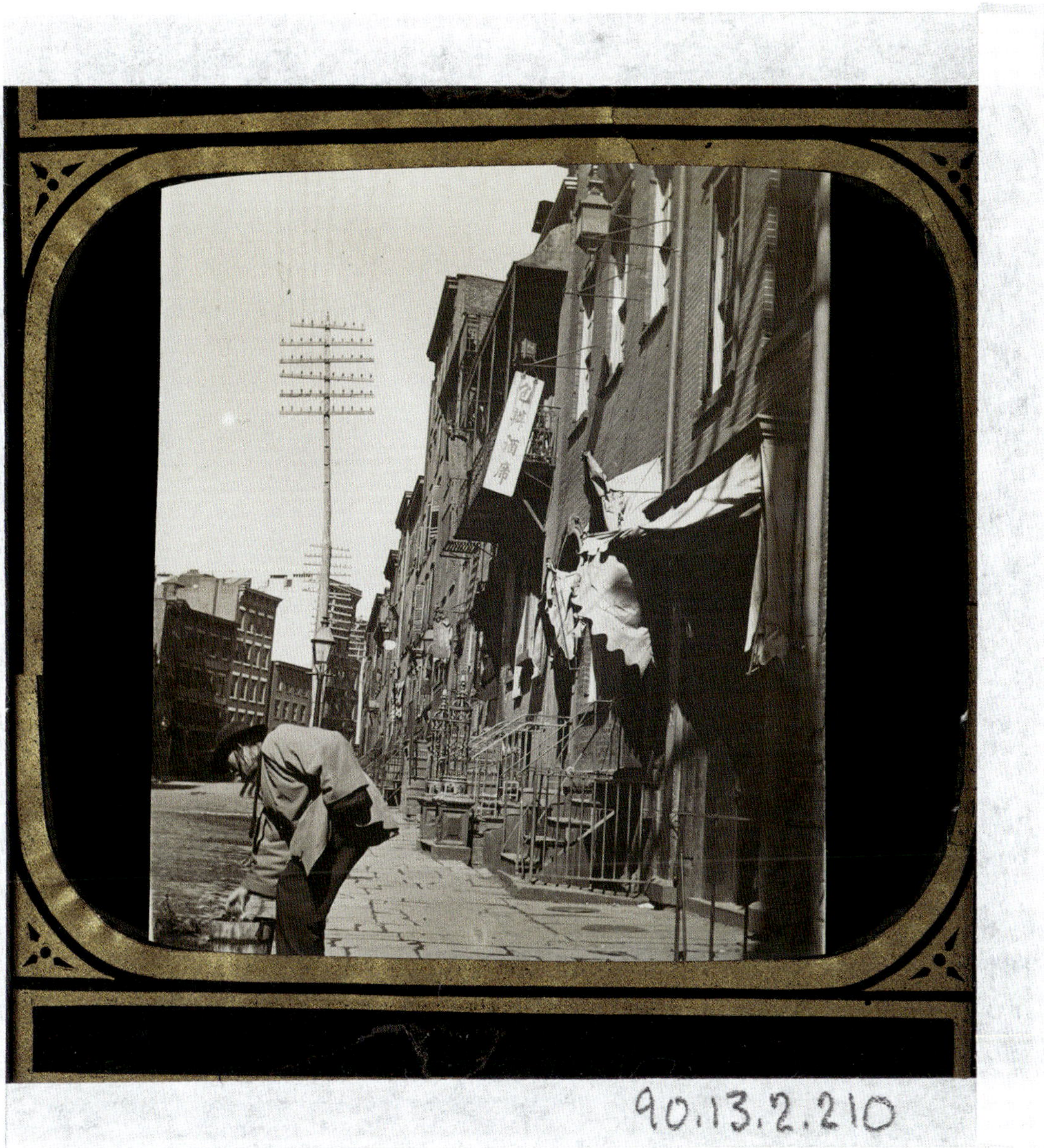

Figure 28. Jacob A. Riis, “Chinatown,” [90.13.2.210] 1895. MCNY.

toward the explicitly religious domain of the afterlife. For the great finale, Riis casts an image of Christ upon the screen and reminds us of the duties to any of God's children. "Thank God! There is something beyond even the Potter's Field, for out of its gloom, and misery, and desolation, there comes a voice of our Saviour, with the promise, 'Inasmuch as ye have done it unto one of the least of these my brethren, ye have done it unto me,' and also the command, 'Go out into the highways and hedges, and compel them to come in.' [Applause]"

If we are now ready to consider the thesis held forth above, that "the significance of Riis's photographs—their emotional power as well as their individual meaning—was largely dependent on their serial composition," and if one further concedes that their significance intensified with the developing complexity of narrative composition, then a proposition seems close at hand regarding how these lecture slides contributed to challenging the existent visibilities of the tenement poor. This singular lecture has revealed a great variety of narrative principles, syntagmatic regulations, image-word relationships, rhythmic intensities, and veridictional variations. It has also been observed that it was visually driven, with the series of photographs in the lead of the narrative progression. Indeed, never before had a charity lecturer invested such great rhetorical diversity in images. More than anything else, Riis's lecture suggests that it was its sheer rhetorical variety, wealth, and wonderful weave of verbal-visual tropes, many borrowed from unexpected corners of the cultural ecology, that discontinued the visibilities conventionally reproduced by the charity community. One singularly powerful device, which was not exclusively used in lectures, would prove particularly mutagenic.

Occasionally, Riis tells the story of the making of the photograph that he shows. When he does, it sometimes produces a very special effect, almost a sensation of time travel. What happens is that the diction splits the photograph into two diachronically different representations. One represents the motif in its singular past moment. It offers a view in time frozen still. This allows the audience to see things which in the past moment were too fleeting or insignificant to behold. Viewers are given the time to ponder the meaning of such things, to have them pointed out, explained, and talked over. The other representation appears instead contiguous to the discernible motif and is timely. It describes circumstances, thoughts and conversations that occurred before and after the photograph was taken, elements that may have impacted on the motif, but which are not visible in the picture. If two such representations successfully compose a joint narrative, it may present a time nucleus in the sense that Walter Benjamin intimated in several of his works.[11] The story of Riis accidentally setting fire to an attic room full of blind tenants with his flash powder is one example. The resulting photograph, "Upstairs in Blind Man's Alley" is certainly not one of his most accomplished works, but with the narrative of its making, it produces one of the lecture's most memorable passages. Other time-warp images are more complex and may even involve two photographs, such as the story of The Montgomery Guards. But when this kind of image device appears in books, or in journal articles, the verbal-iconic affordances of these media impact on the time-warp effect, reducing the historico-ontological drama to a level that only permits a mere anecdote.

Although Riis's photographs and their compositional variations "made a most profound impact upon those present,"[12] as one reviewer had it, the lecture events could hardly by themselves have produced enough significance to mutate a visibility in the sense suggested above. Riis's lectures, unique as they were, confronted an iconoclastic charity institution of vastly greater reproductive powers than they alone could overturn. Only a broad and above all else iterative media strategy, one that encouraged repeated dissemination of the images, might have created a sufficient impulse. The iterability of several media with distinctly different affordances might together have created enough visual significance to establish a new visibility.

11. The most concise description of the nucleus is perhaps found in The Arcades Project, where the concept seems modeled after a photographic representation: "The present determines where, in the object from the past, that object's fore-history and after-history diverge, so as to circumscribe its nucleus." Benjamin, *The Arcades Project*, 476 [N11,5]; see also 463 [N3,2].

12. "Filled with Misery," in *New Haven Palladium*, July 20, 1891. LC, Riis papers, box 10, Riis's scrapbook.

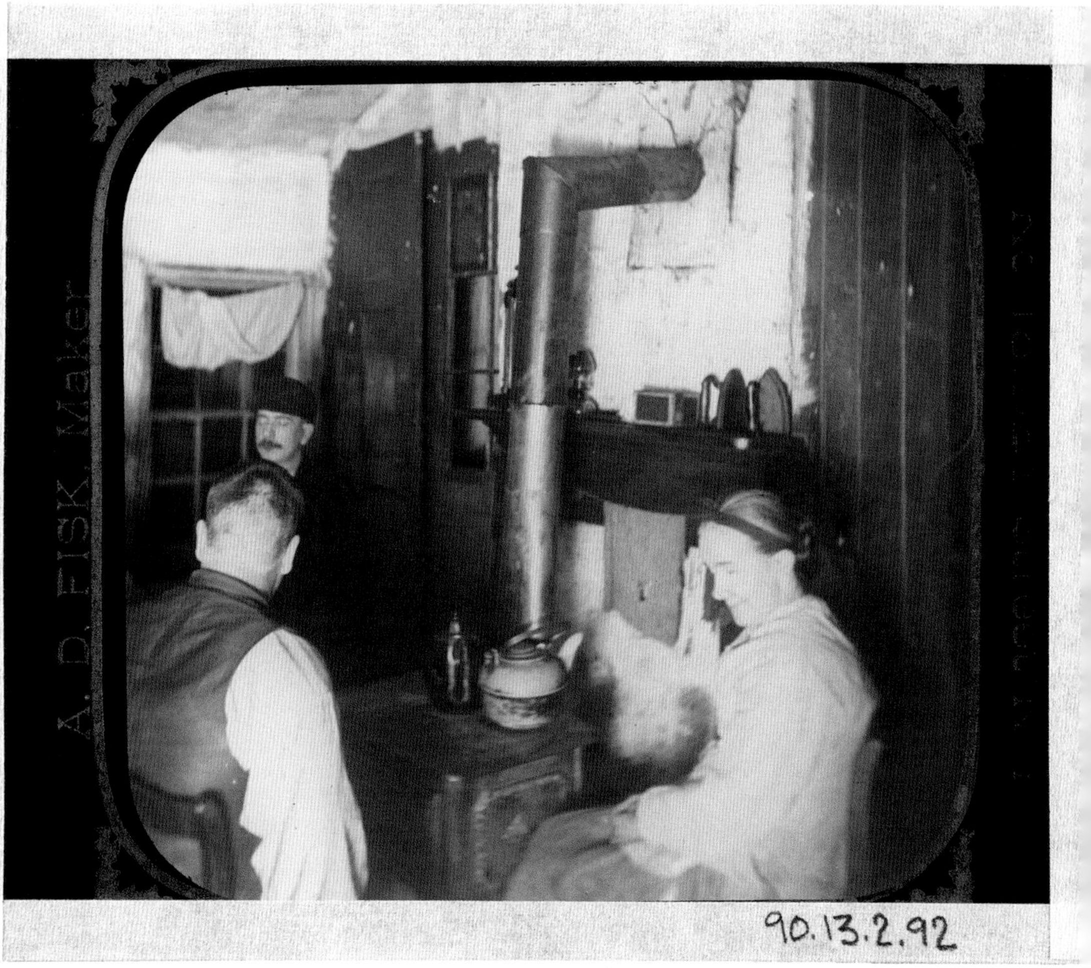

Figure 29. Jacob A. Riis, "Upstairs in Blind Mans' Alley" [90.13.2.92] 1888. MCNY.

"Let me take you upstairs and show you some of those tenants. There were five of them in all, but only three of them got into the picture. This is from a photograph by flash-light. With unpracticed hands, for I was new at such work then, I managed to set fire to the house. When the flash died away I saw the rags and boards in the wall burning pretty lively and I did not feel at all happy about it, for there were five blind people, who had not the least idea of their danger, and four or five flights of stairs between us and the street. I put it out though, and burned my hands and clothes in doing it. When I had it out at last, I went down into the street and tried to get a policeman to go up there, but instead of sympathizing with me he laughed till the lamp-post he leaned against shook. "What, that place burn!" he sad. "Why, certainly it did," I said, "I ought to know. I set fire to it myself." He said, "That place burn! Nothing of the kind! They call the house the 'Dirty Spoon.' It caught fire six times last winter but could not burn. The dirt was so think on the walls it smothered the fire." [Laughter]"

Syntagmatic Image Series in Books

From a strictly visual point of view, the 1890 edition of *How the Other Half Lives* offers a far less intense experience than the lectures. Its 41 images (and five floorplans) are fairly unevenly distributed over the 304 pages, where they also perform a rather different repertoire of communicative functions. For example, whereas the slides of a lecture were actively engaged in the diagnostics of the conservative triangle, the book assigns this key function entirely to the discursive register. However, there is one unique image function afforded only by the book medium, which plays a significant role with respect to the triangle's performativity: certain singular images provide the text with something like inflection points or centrifugal centers. As previously noted, Riis pursued a mode of analysis where observations, authoritative remarks and statistics communicated not just information about the various demographic groups, but also a palpable impression of the regular impacts that individuals and their nominal values were exposed to. Certain illustrations in *How the Other Half Lives,* as well as in *Children of the Poor* and *The Battle with the Slum* function as points of anchorage for these performative impressions. These images tie together the iteration of impacts that shape a given community and hold them in a single comprehensive view. Offering a sensuous, concrete particularity, they gather in a glimpse a piece of mundane tenement reality, photographically charged with deep symbolic significance.[13] The *intended* purpose may have been otherwise straightforward: perhaps to merely illustrate the analysis or to increase the conscientious effect upon the reader. Nonetheless, thirteen images, not all of them reproduced as halftone photographs,

13. In the 1890 edition of *How the Other Half Lives,* the following images perform this function: "Bandit's Roost," "A Downtown Morgue," "In a Chinese Joint," "At the Cradle of the Tenements," "In the House of an Italian Ragpicker," "Five Cents a Spot," "A Market Scene in the Jewish Quarter," "Knee-pants at forty-five Cents," "Bohemian Cigarmakers at Work in their Tenement," "A Black and Tan Dive in 'Africa'," "The Trench in Potters Field," "Street Arabs in Sleeping Quarters," and "A Flat in the Pauper Baracks."

have sufficient 'density' to gather a tenement individual's generic affections and to sensuously convey their ethical particularity to the reader. Some of these illustrations have supplementing satellite images that relate paradigmatically both to the text and to the mother image. In *How the Other Half Lives*, satellite images are for example "Coffee at one cent," "Hell's Kitchen and Sebastopol" and "Dispossessed." To the category of satellites belong also the emblematic pictures, which are never halftone photographs, and which often conclude or open a chapter. The ash barrel, for example, that concludes the first chapter, "Genesis of the Tenements," had functioned epigrammatical already Riis's 1889 article published in *Scribner's*, "How the Other Half Lives", and would eventually, after many iterations, become a logotype of sorts for the very concept of The Other Half. The opium pipe that ends the excursion to Chinatown similarly heralds the entire community, whose iterated affections are gathered together with the image "In A Chinese Joint." The portrayed washerwoman that ends the chapter "The Italians in New York" is a special emblem insofar as it heralds the fundamental concept of will to honesty.

Here is what that particular emblem does: the will to honesty, says Riis, is signalled in the tenements by the clothesline. As a concept, the will to honesty is introduced toward the end of the chapter, "The Down-Town Back-Alleys", where it is juxtaposed with a wood-engraving of clotheslines, reproduced from the photograph "An Old Rear Tenement in Roosevelt Street". Image and concept correlate unanimously. The next chapter, "The Italians in New York" ends with the image of the washerwoman, printed mid-page, underneath the following concluding remark: "These vile dens flourish and gather about them all the wrecks, the hopelessly lost, on the lowest slope of depraved humanity." At this point, image and text are counterpoised as mutually contradicting. However, the washerwoman has the last word, which makes of her a bulwark against hopelessness. She resists hopelessness emblematically, and her power to do so derives from the Madonna in the photograph "In the Home of an Italian Ragpick-

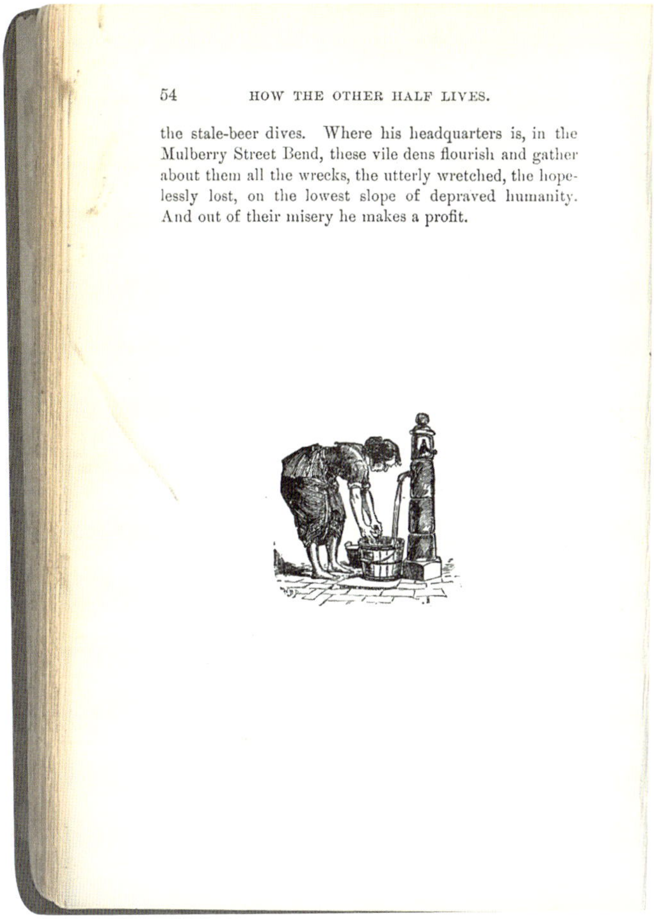

54 HOW THE OTHER HALF LIVES.

the stale-beer dives. Where his headquarters is, in the Mulberry Street Bend, these vile dens flourish and gather about them all the wrecks, the utterly wretched, the hopelessly lost, on the lowest slope of depraved humanity. And out of their misery he makes a profit.

Figure 30. Anonymous illustrator, "Washing Woman" from *How the Other Half Lives*, 1890 edition.

er in Jersey Street", the image that gathers the Italian affections. This image is dense enough to hold together the various impacting forces that shape that neighborhood. And how is that?

Two elements seem conditional for an image to perform the gathering function. Firstly, it must create an apparently immediate presentation, i.e. it must sacrifice its own iconic being and resolutely sluice the gaze past itself and on to the present past. Thus the first element: a conjuration of the reality of past beings. The other conditional element is the density of the image, and this must not be mistaken for profoundness or photographic quality. Density does not derive from the motif. Density, in this case, is a concentration of trajectories. An image may attract problematic notions and contradictory views from its immediate context and assemble these into a concentrated symbolic expression that betrays iconic density. In the case of "In the Home of an Italian Ragpicker," the trajectories convey in different ways the ambivalent Christian neighborliness among the shoddy, insouciant, festive, family-oriented, but occasionally violent Italians, symbolically gathered here in the perfect Madonna pose with infant, complete with the familiar Christian iconography of the ladder, the empty vessel on the floor, and the revered asceticism. Will to honesty, as the expression of God's perfection in man, is manifested in this image by its unification of on the one hand, Italian trajectories concentrated in symbolic form, and on the other the conjuration of a singular, past moment's reality. The implicit proposition of infinite hope then provides its satellite emblem with the power to resist hopeless depravation and despair.

Not all of the images in Riis's books perform this gathering function. Many images are neither anchor points nor satellites, but simple illustrations of adjacent text. A small number of these describe the making of the images and reproduce thereby the time-warp experience described earlier, albeit in anecdotal form. In *How the Other Half Lives* this occurs with images such as "The Tramp," "Getting Ready for Supper," "Upstairs in Blindman's Alley," "A Growler Gang in Session," and "Prayer Time in the Nursery." Whereas the time-

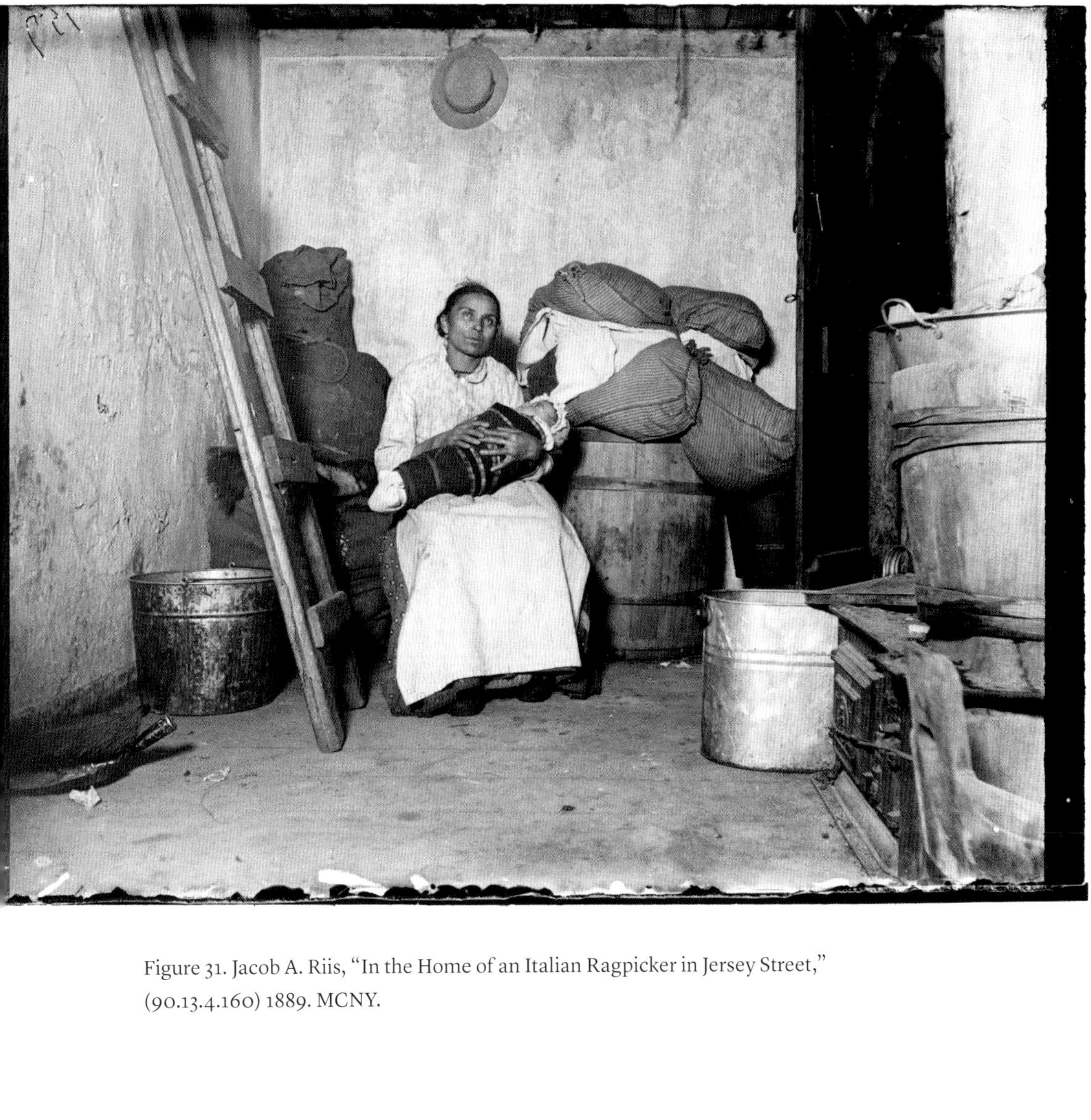

Figure 31. Jacob A. Riis, "In the Home of an Italian Ragpicker in Jersey Street," (90.13.4.160) 1889. MCNY.

warp experience may be very strong during lectures, where the images enjoy a narrative primacy, the books fail to reproduce the effect and supply at best a mere curious anecdote. Other images that serve as illustrations in *How the Other Half Lives* include: "The Bend," "Bottle Alley," "An All-night Two-cent Restaurant in 'the Bend'," "Seven Cents Lodging," "The Official Organ in Chinatown," and "A Tramp's Nest in Ludlow." Many of these form syntagmatic relationships not only with the text but also with other images, some of which are high-density anchor images. For instance, "The Bend" and "Bottle Alley" are both related to "Bandit's Roost;" "An All-night Two-cent Restaurant" is syntagmatically related to "A Downtown Morgue;" "The Official Organ of Chinatown" belongs to "In a Chinese Joint."

Not only are there fewer images in the books than in the lectures, different kinds of word and image combinations also make them perform other semantic functions. The previously highlighted function of gathering serial variations is particularly intriguing as a performative act. It may have been an unintended effect of images meant merely to illustrate a given situation, and indeed, this is how Riis's illustrations are traditionally interpreted. But they could also have been intended to play a part in the performative ploy that Riis's rotating triangles executed upon his audience's neighborliness. The literary construction is too consistent to be dismissed, as is the distribution of high-density images, one of which appears in each chapter. Consistency would suggest that the individuating series of affections (exemplified earlier with the Bohemians) were a deliberate performative device. For the casual reader, such a series of affections may seem nothing more than an account of the regular circumstances and events that shape life conditions of an ethnic group, but at the same time, through the act of reading, this reader will be exposed to repeated conscientious impulses on his or her own body. Believing perhaps to learn only about someone else's life conditions, the reader is affected morally through the experience of reading. These normative impulses are meant to affirm the reader's own neighborliness, which —unless the reader is "something worse than a cynic who can lay it down without serious reflection"—increases the individual's will to honesty and brings a collective readership closer to Riis's goal. This goal, obviously, was to make the middle class assume a more actively engaged involvement in the life conditions of the tenement population. A photograph dense enough to hold a series of affecting impulses on a particular body (e.g. the Bohemians), would, through the reversibility of communicated affect, also impact on the neighborly values of the reader. Conversely, if Riis's text had instead conveyed a series unfit for symbolic concentration, for example describing affecting bodies rather than bodies affected, the iconic effect upon the reader would be lost. Without a doubt, the anchoring images served an important topical function.

It is not, however, very likely that Riis premeditated the scheme suggested here, or even that he composed the images in his books for this effect. I describe formally what the images in his books and lectures are actually doing, what Riis discovered in terms of persuasive strategies; it is clear that Riis meant to affect his readers, and that he was recognized for using more sophisticated means than his peers. However, he may not have been in charge of the graphic design of his illustrated books; in fact, it is even uncertain if there were a conscious strategy behind their design or if it happened more or less routinely in the course of an industrialized printing process.

What the images are actually doing—that is the relevant object of this investigation. That, and nothing else, is what may help us understand their creation of urgency, argument, and meaning, i.e. their iconic significance as conceived through verbal and visual compositions. The variations of syntagmatic relations (even of syntactic orders) that the images helped to explore are a measure of their use value, i.e. of their applicability in creating semantic meaning. On the other hand, the consistency of performative functions measures their impact value, i.e. the intensity of rhetorical affection as afforded by different media. Having discovered and identified several methods of creating significance in the lectures and in the books, we shall now look at Jacob Riis's magazine articles.

Syntagmatic Image Series in Articles

Riis's lectures had no trajectory-gathering, high-density images. The photographs that served as anchor points in the book had no similar function in the lectures. In fact, the iconic syntax of the lectures was fundamentally different from the one afforded by the book medium, and the distinction continued with the illustrated magazine articles and newspaper items. These pieces were neither as consistent and complex as were Riis's books,[14] nor as novel and emotionally engaging as the lectures. Every journal and magazine had a graphic profile of its own and Riis's articles had to comply with the particular style sheet. His articles in *The Golden Rule* and in Gen. Booth's *The War Cry* from 1893 were, like other items, illustrated with crude drawings, outlining merely the main elements of the original photograph (reminiscent of the first 1888 budget prints of Riis's photographs, which had appeared in *The Sun* as "Flashes From the Slums"). By contrast, The *Century Magazine* made fine wood engravings and juxtaposed Riis's images with original drawings by Jay Hambidge and others.[15] *The Review of Reviews*, another pro-reform illustrated monthly, used both halftone and wood engraving technologies to render photographs, sometimes adding further graphic effects such as ripping

14. I am referring here exclusively to the uniformity of Riis's tenement monographs, i.e. to *How the Other Half Lives, The Battle With the Slum, A Ten Year's War, Children of the Poor,* etc. Other publications by Riis, such as *Theodor Roosevelt, the Citizen* and later works about Scandinavian history and mythology vary in visual expression. The volumes of collected short stories (e.g. *Out of Mulberry Street* and *Children of the Tenements*) are scarcely illustrated and contain no photographs.

15. The illustrating policy of a magazine was not always entirely consistent, as three articles by Riis published in *The Century Magazine* may reveal. "Merry Christmas in the Tenements" (Dec 1897) mixed original artwork by Jay Hambidge with a few halftone reproductions of photographs by Riis; "Light in Dark Places" (May 1899) brought several detailed and profoundly altered renderings of Riis's photographs, also made by Hambidge; "In the Gateway of Nations" (May 1903) was illustrated with original artwork by G.W. Peters, none of which has since been associated with Riis.

the edges of the reproduction and even lifting out a figure from its background (see for example "A Scrub" in the August issue, 1895).[16] *Scribner's* did not print halftone photographs by the early 1890's. Instead, they illustrated Riis's articles with wood engravings and halftone reproductions of drawings and watercolors produced from the photographs. In 1901, *The Churchman* printed halftone photographs with ominous black frames in the article version of "The Battle With The Slum", whereas *The Christian Herald*, four years later, saw fit to decorate their printed halftone photographs with *art nouveau* inspired frames. Such ornaments were increasingly common, but had already peaked with a newspaper publication in 1900.

Between March and April that year, the Sunday edition of *The Chicago Tribune* spent six consecutive front pages on "The Story of the Slum," featuring headlines that added *Jugend* frills to *art nouveau* adornments with every issue. The extraordinary visual expenditure granted to these pages have sadly not survived the archive politics of later years and may today only be guessed at from the visually insufficient scans at ProQuest's Historical Newspapers. With the exception of some crumbling fragments in the "Miscellaneous Files" in the Jacob A. Riis Papers at the Library of Congress, which are here digitally pieced together to give an idea of installment #3, we are left to imagine what the whole series looked like. Nonetheless, these few pages may reveal a few important aspects of the iconic grammar that pertained to reform magazines and periodicals at the time. For one thing, it appears that an exceptional paradigmatic capacity for iconic variation was affirmed and unleashed. It went far beyond established norms in lectures and books, where, although a certain degree of modification was allowed, one rarely challenged the identity of an image once it had been published. (Posthumous editions of Riis's books, however, learnt from the magazines and altered the images more or less at will.) *The Chicago Tribune* displays startling graphic variations of photographs previously published by Riis: these appear now as

16. Riis, "The Clearing of Mulberry Bend," in *Review of Reviews,* August, 1895.

The Story of

HOW WE ARE FIGHT

BY JACO

AUTHOR OF "HOW

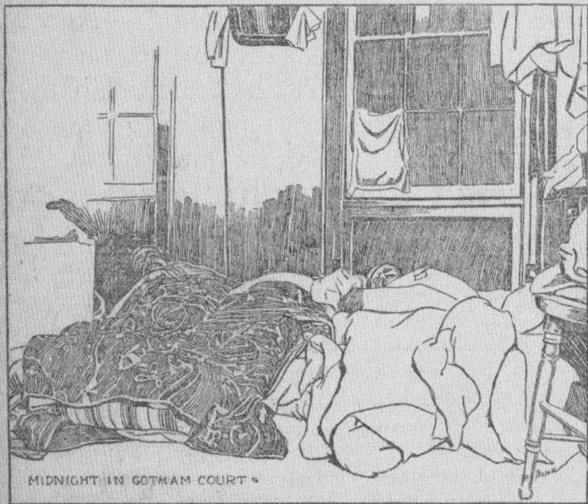

MIDNIGHT IN GOTHAM COURT

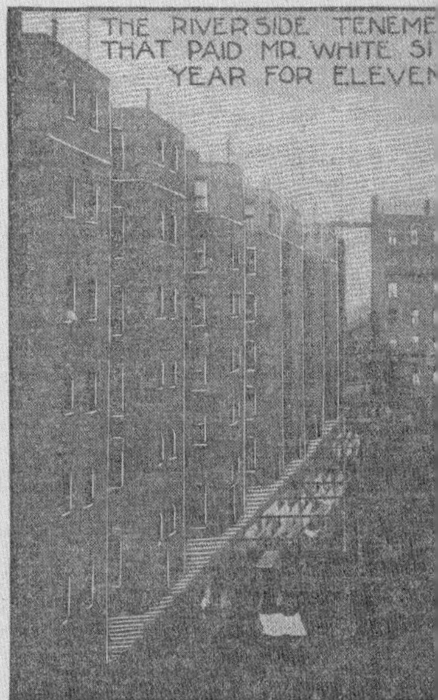

THE RIVERSIDE TENEME
THAT PAID MR. WHITE SI
YEAR FOR ELEVEN

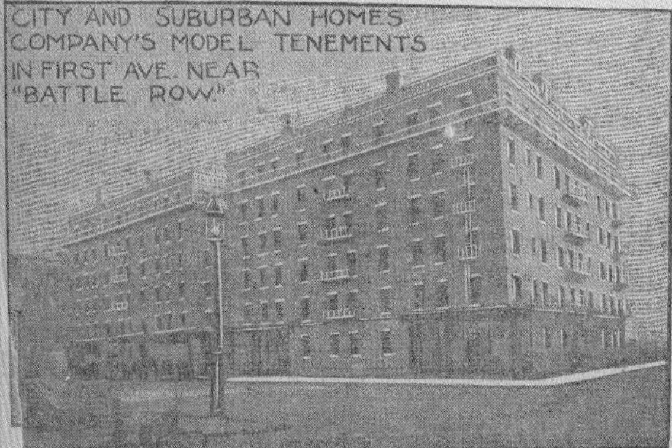

CITY AND SUBURBAN HOMES
COMPANY'S MODEL TENEMENTS
IN FIRST AVE. NEAR
"BATTLE ROW."

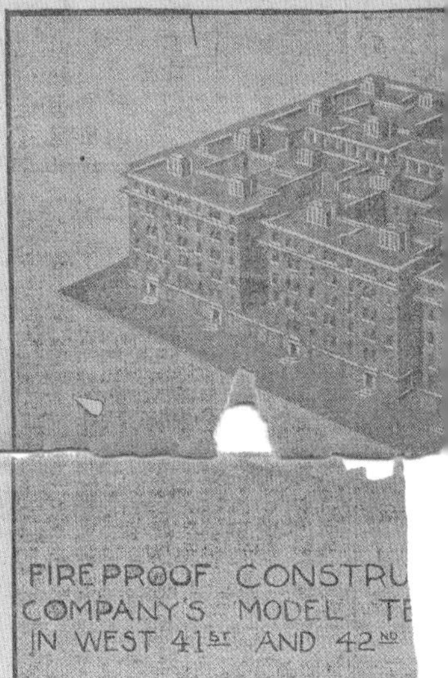

FIREPROOF CONSTRU
COMPANY'S MODEL TE
IN WEST 41ST AND 42ND

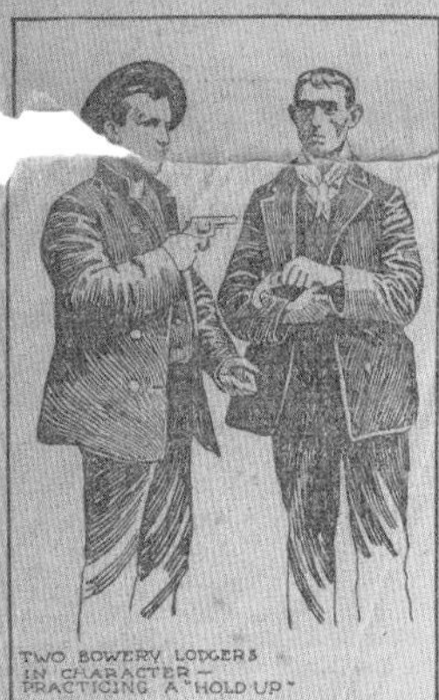

TWO BOWERY LODGERS
IN CHARACTER—
PRACTICING A "HOLD UP"

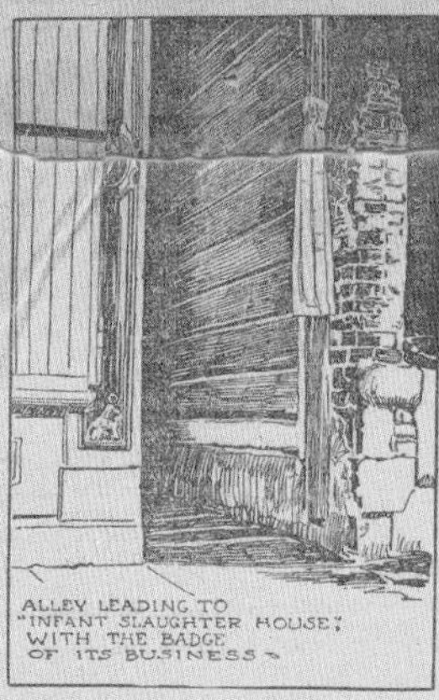

ALLEY LEADING TO
"INFANT SLAUGHTER HOUSE,"
WITH THE BADGE
OF ITS BUSINESS

[WRITTEN SPECIALLY FOR THE CHICAGO TRIBUNE.]

I HAVE told how the awakening in 1879 left behind it a company of philanthropic builders with some hundreds of thousands of dollars to spend in showing us how tenement-houses might be

I remember as though it were yesterday the convention of clergymen held in Chickering Hall some twelve or thirteen years ago to devise ways of laying hold of the mass of people that was sliding out of reach of the churches—I spoke of it before—and Mr. White jumping up and crying out:

the test. We enacted a law upon the basis of the arraignment of the slum by the Tenement-House commission of 1894, which gave the Board of Health the power to seize "unsanitary property" and destroy it. We trod in that simply in the footsteps of London and other English cities, but it was a step it took us years to make up our mind to, and even when we had taken it we were slow to act under the powers given us.

TOO MUCH "DISCRETION."

The old notion of "vested rights" is a big stumbling block for the Anglo-Saxon mind, hard to surmount. For years our Health department had possessed the power to order

and an
seized s
city an
its purp
lords r
woe. T
the tax
commun
their re
But fo
Tamma
for a co
the Hea
tled the
rights c
Tracy m

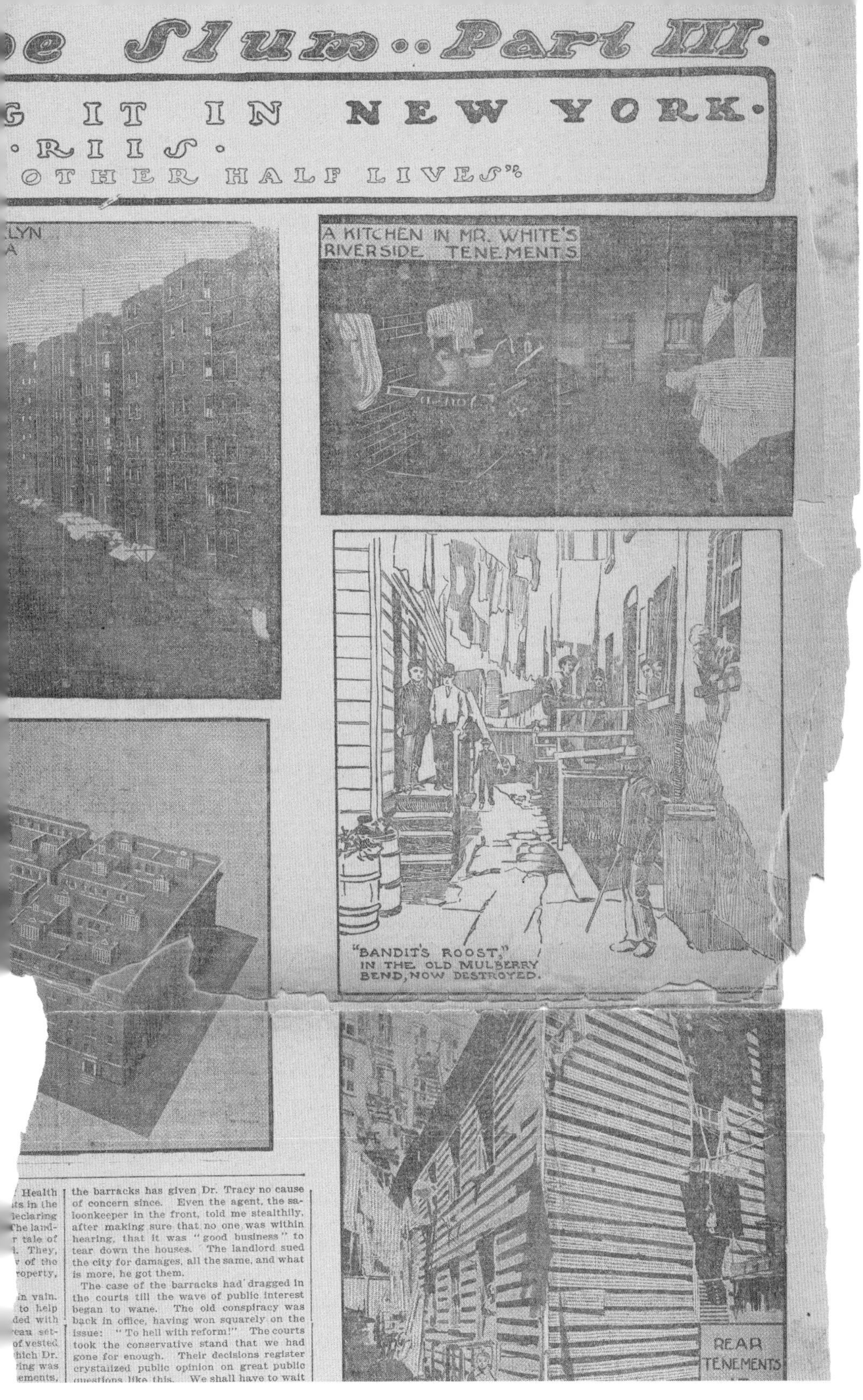

…e Slum.. Part III.

…G IT IN NEW YORK.

…RIIS.

…OTHER HALF LIVES".

A KITCHEN IN MR. WHITE'S RIVERSIDE TENEMENTS

"BANDIT'S ROOST," IN THE OLD MULBERRY BEND, NOW DESTROYED.

REAR TENEMENTS

the barracks has given Dr. Tracy no cause of concern since. Even the agent, the saloonkeeper in the front, told me stealthily, after making sure that no one was within hearing, that it was "good business" to tear down the houses. The landlord sued the city for damages, all the same, and what is more, he got them.

The case of the barracks had dragged in the courts till the wave of public interest began to wane. The old conspiracy was back in office, having won squarely on the issue: "To hell with reform!" The courts took the conservative stand that we had gone for enough. Their decisions register crystallized public opinion on great public questions like this. We shall have to wait

Figure 32. Jacob A. Riis, "The Story of the Slums," *Chicago Sunday Tribune*, March 25, 1900. Library of Congress.

simple drawings, now as careful wood engravings, now in halftone reproductions, at times being reproductions of ink renditions made from photographs, often heavily retouched or even with drawn or painted image elements added onto them and occasionally with framed captions inserted into the image. The visual identity of a photograph is indeed put to the test here as motif, technique, framing, and detail are open to unrestricted manipulation. It follows from such exceptional mutability that images, when thus able to engage in open-ended syntagmatic variations, become more versatile in terms of use. The promiscuous quality of photographs is accentuated, which means that each photographic signifier increases its number of possible signifieds. This in turn affects the image's normative identity, relaxing it, leaving it more open, which further invites editorial measures for establishing value and meaning, e.g. by applying captions, collage-techniques, thick sinister frames, etc. Favoring applicability, it is no surprise that the reform periodicals boosted the use value of Riis's images at the expense of their individual impact value.

A number of remarks should be made to clarify the above. First, to avoid misunderstandings, the emphasis on use value in magazines does not mean that these image reproductions were devoid of power to impact upon the established visibility. It is true, however, that Riis's article illustrations had little of the affecting capacity of images in books or in lectures. The impact of magazine illustrations was rather bound to circulation and distribution. Among the wealth of illustrations printed in a given issue, Riis's pictures could hardly stand out, but they affirmed broadly and unambiguously the shared reform values of a readership already sympathetic to the cause. Rather than impacting directly upon existing visibilities, Riis's magazine illustrations increased by iteration the affecting capacity of book and lecture illustrations.

Second, some of the 'crude' reproduction techniques favored by journals and newspapers should not be considered inferior to the elaborate ones but rather faster and more succinct. These images needed a mere glean to convey the message and would thus supplement more detailed renderings or support a written passage with a distinct function. Peter Hales once bemoaned the crude reproduction of "Bandit's Roost" in the 1888 item "Flashes From the Slums," which he found lacking compared with the rich original photograph.[17] Such quality judgments do not sit easily with the editorial values of a nineteenth-century reform magazine. A number of adequate reasons justified reproductions that were fast, casual, even a little dingy, small, and lacking in attention to detail.

Third, one should be careful not to conclude from these editorial liberties that illustrations were generally disregarded or considered of minor value. Riis's 1889 feature article in *Scribner's* Christmas issue, "How the Other Half Lives,"[18] appeared with minutely executed wood engravings by Otto H. Bacher and Kenyon Cox. These highly respected illustrators (who signed their reproductions in print) took extensive liberties with the original photographs. The photograph "Gotham Court," for example, had the boy pictured to the far right replaced with a family scene, and the gang of urchins that once eyeballed the photographer got exchanged for a group of children playing and comforting each other. Another engraving simply removed the two adults who feature as the main motif of the photograph "A Flat in the Pauper Barracks, West 38 Street, With All Its Furniture." Perhaps the decision was made due to their blurred faces, but removing them was far from a neutral intervention. It altered drastically the illustrating function. In Riis's *Scribner's* piece, where the figures are missing, the image of an empty deleterious interior supported a general critique of insufficient housing policies. In the lecture, where the photograph was shown unaltered, Riis had the following to say: "That is a flat in Hell's Kitchen out of which McGloin, one of those

17. Hales, *Silver Cities*, 172. Several of the other crude illustrations in "Flashes From the Slums" are rendered with even greater liberty than "Bandit's Roost", for example "A Black and Tan Dive," and "Women's Lodging Room," which are both mirror reversed and have, like the oddly titled "White Slaves," significant image elements added to the original photographs.

18. Riis, "How the Other Half Lives: Studies Among the Poor," in *Scribner's Magazine*, December 1889, 6:6, 643-662.

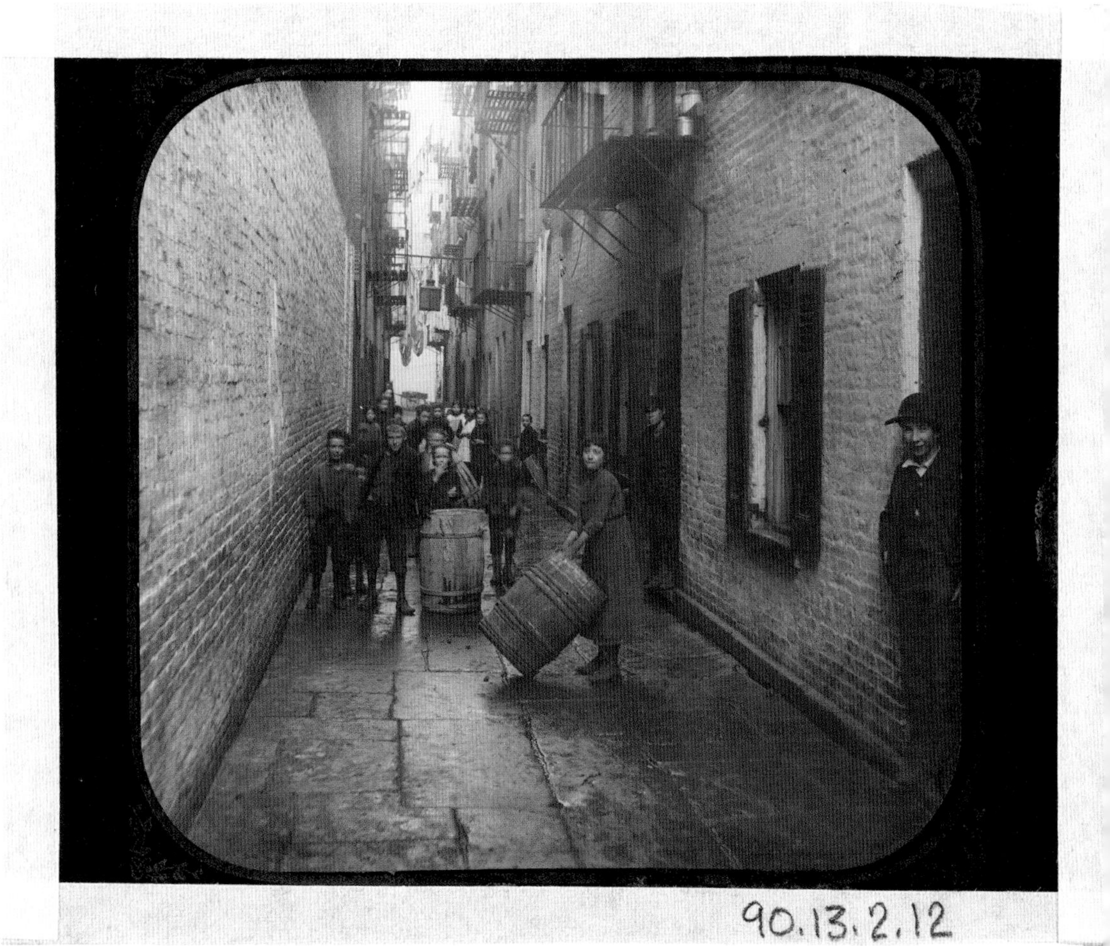

Figure 33. Richard Hoe Lawrence and Jacob A. Riis, "Gotham Court," [90.13.2.12] 1887. MCNY.

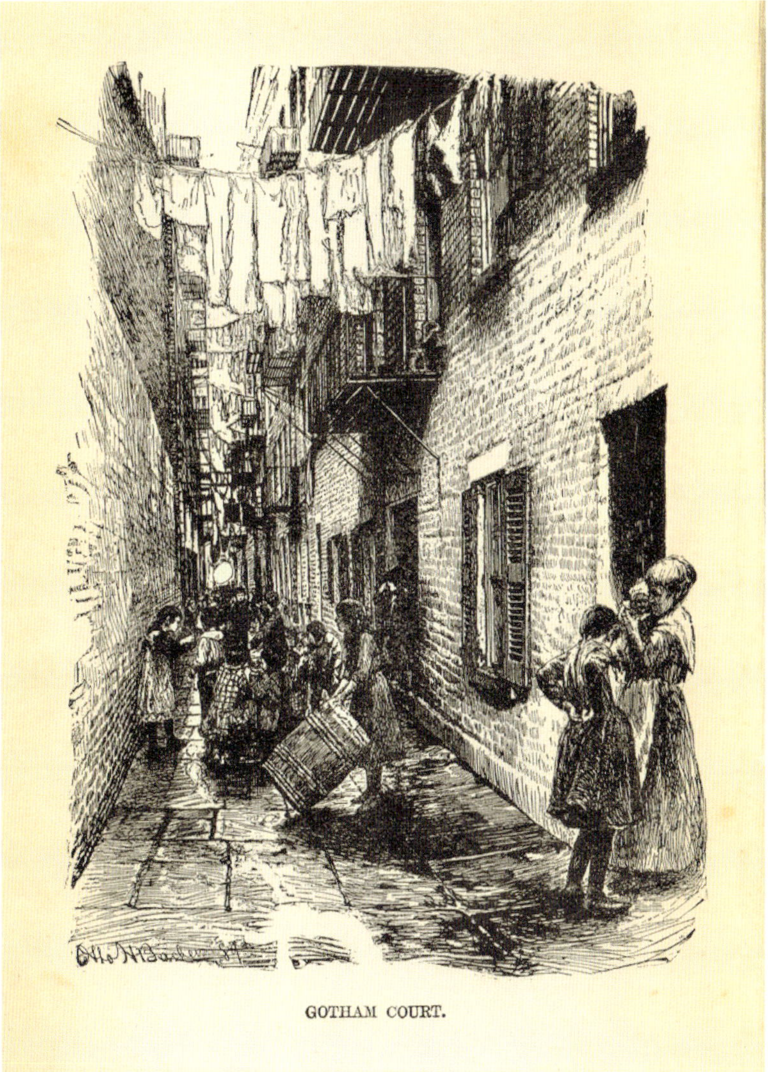

Figure 34. Otto H. Backer, "Gotham Court" published in *Scribner's* 6:6, Dec. 1889, 645, and frontispiece in *How the Other Half Lives*.

murderers who died on the gallows, came. You do not expect a rose to grow out of a swamp, and you could hardly expect anything but such a tough to grow in such a place."[19] In short: editorial liberties taken with original photographs were in all likelihood justified by the perceived demand to accommodate content to the desired narrative and to streamline the message according to prevailing tastes among the magazine's buyers. If anything, the many far-reaching manipulations underscore the political force commonly attributed to images in the public domain and the concern among editors to harness this power for the good of their paper.

Fourth, as already noted, visual manipulations involved not only alterations inside the frame, they also meant other possible syntagmatic relationships to the text. Magazines thus allowed an exceptionally wide array of syntagmatic structures. Occasionally, these were open to the extent that syntax became rather tenuous. For example, "A 'Black and Tan Dive' in Thompson Street" was once used to merely set an ignominious mood to an otherwise unrelated story of suicide in the article version of "How the Other Half Lives." In the book (where the same story is told in a different context), the image appears in the chapter "The Reign of Rum," where the motif effectively underscores Riis's argument of "all the evil the saloon does."[20] Similarly with the image "In a Chinese Joint," which, in the article version, bore little upon the adjacent descriptions of housing shortage, whereas, in the book, it gives credence to rumors of abducted girls, lethal opium dens, and white slaves of Chinatown. It is important to note, however, that not all of Riis's images were equally mutable as magazine illustrations. "Pietro Learning to Make an Englis' Letter" was first published in *Scribner's* article version of "The Children of the Poor." The essay tells of a crippled Italian boy named Pietro who had learned to write in spite of his maimed hand and hoped to teach his father. Riis had known the boy personally and the image was never

19. Ibid., 660; Riis, "The Other Half and How They Live," 423.

20. Riis, *How the Other Half Lives*, 215.

published without reference to that story. Likewise, the photograph "The Tramp," picturing a loafer posing with a clay pipe in his mouth, was never published or shown without the story about how, before the photograph was taken, he had removed his pipe and demanded extra money for putting it back. Riis's personal experiences defined the narrative limit of these pictures and their authorized interpretation would always follow them.

With regard to illustrations featured in newspapers, magazines and journals, syntagmatic regulation was generally lax and permissive, yet thoroughly dependent on the ideological regimentation of magazine editors. Their frequent and often far-reaching image manipulations occasionally transgressed the identity of some images, and so the practice generated extensive chains of paradigmatic image variations. Considering the dominant use-value of these images, the paradigmatic series have come to sit uncomfortably with presumptions of an original. Images like "Bandit's Roost," "A Black and Tan Dive" and many others have from their first appearance presented themselves as a paradigmatic multiplicity. It is for this reason historically awkward to comply with traditional art-historical practice, which for each image seeks to identify its original title or caption, cultural context, production technique, publication venue, author and date of completion.[21] Such details might tend to conceal in retrospect the commodity nature of these images and their fundamental use value, which in no sense were based on authorship or artwork attribution. Graphic power and rhetorical performance were definite priorities for Riis. The remarkable syntagmatic freedom of his images reveals instead something that was far more essential and conditional for their market value, what Elizabeth Edwards has referred to as the 'deep context' of photographs, that is, their capacity to be applied to very different, sometimes counter-directed narratives.[22]

21. Cf. Alexander Alland, *Jacob Riis: Photographer and Citizen* (Aperture, Millerton, New York: 1974); Yochelson, *Jacob Riis*, passim.

22. Elizabeth Edwards, *Raw Histories: Photographs, Anthropology and Museums* (Berg, Oxford: 2001), 107.

The pursuit of tracing diverse syntagmatic relations in this chapter has perhaps revealed an unexpected richness: myriads of different verbal-iconic templates whose application served to engage Riis's images in distinct modes of meaning production, modes that furthermore varied with the media that brought them to public attention. Some of these syntagmatic relations occasionally engaged his pictures in provocative contact with audience values, performing on occasion rather advanced rhetorical functions. Throughout, I have tried to focus on what the images appear to be doing. This is what the term iconic significance should suggest. All the iconic functions and filaments that have been outlined in this chapter should amount to a measure of their significance. To grasp the multiplicity and the distribution of various measures of significance is vital to the task of explaining how a new visibility could emerge. When the task is to unearth how a mode of looking could reorient its subjects vis-à-vis the objects, how the phenomenological appearance of tenement poverty could change, and to what extent one particular body of work could be pivotal to the mutation, one has to assess its gathering of variations and the forces that enable the gathering. It could be referred to as the power of an iconic mode of appearance.

I have proposed that new visibilities may emerge when a series of significant appearances gather enough power to reorganize a conventional set of variations, and when the links that a series owes to exterior powers enable it to stabilize its iterations into a sustainable identity. The first condition of emergence is certainly fulfilled with the syntagmatic variations that Riis explored. The second is what we are about to investigate next. It is time to look at the value conflicts on the fringes of neighboring visibilities.

CHAPTER 7

Paradigmatic Series and a New Visibility

Riis's images were only partially semantic, that is, only to a certain extent should they be considered as signs. Non-semantic image elements are, of course, present in all images, furnishing an iconic articulation which is not bound to the lingual function of signification (thus distinguishing the iconic articulation from the first and second articulations of signs[1]). Amounting to a purely visual differentiation of a sign, or a set of signs, these non-semantic elements form rather variations of appearance, variations that 'make sense' out of signs with iconic means. I will refer to this articulation as the 'visuality' of an image, a term not to be confused with visibilities. Visualities do not form syntagmatic series of elements and do not organize signs into complex utterances. Still, they articulate a meaningful order, or coherence, one which is structured paradigmatically. The visuality of an image is able to affect other images, and it may have an impact on its semantic elements, its signs, as well as on its non-semantic elements. This affective capacity should not be attributed to an image as its property, but must rather be considered a situated

1. The first articulation of a sign consists of its morphemes, the smallest signifying entities. The second articulation of a sign consists of partial elements that do not signify but that differentiate the meaning of the sign. The third articulation that I propose is perceptibly a part of the signifying entity and, like the second articulation, it differentiates the meaning of a sign while it does not signify in itself—however, unlike the first and second articulation, the third is not bound to the signifying function. It may affect the act of signification but is not determinable on such grounds, as it may also amount only to a mere sensuous differentiation of the signifier, a differentiation that alters its sense but not its semantic meaning.

and singular affordance, a capacity that is exercised only relative to another entity's ability to be affected. In the following analysis, I will deal with Riis's photographs being impacted upon and impacting upon paradigmatic as well as syntagmatic elements. At first, it will be explored how certain technical and material advances made during the late nineteenth century facilitated some of Riis's most unique visualities. Once these have been described and their genealogical sources are identified, subsequent interest will be directed toward the non-semantic impact that these visualities had upon syntagmatic series. It will be necessary, in a final moment, to decide upon the role that—with an anachronistic phrase—Riis's "recasting of the distribution of the sensible"[2] actually played for the creation of a new visibility of tenement poverty.

Three distinct domains were crucial to the emerging visuality of Riis's images: a) new photo-technical developments; b) the cheap entertainment industry, and c) the lantern lecture business. Although the latter two require somewhat more complex analyses to explain the emergence of a new tenement visibility, the technical domain should not be passed over too quickly. Riis's equipment agreed in a remarkable way with the expressive capacity of the photographed subjects, a circumstance of no little importance for the emergence of a new visibility.

Technical Developments

Magnesium flash was Riis's main source of light while photographing during nocturnal expeditions or in dark tenement apartments. The applications he used were either loose powder lit up in a tray or cartridges fired with a flashgun. Although a few portrait studios in England and America had experimented with magnesium flash as early as the 1860s, the smoke and the blazing sharp light required ex-

2. This formulation is, of course, borrowed from Jacques Rancière, cf. *The Politics of Aesthetics* (Continuum New York: 2004), 63.

tensive ventilation and bulky reflectors that discouraged widespread adoption.[3] Prior to Riis, photography with artificial light was explored most successfully in marginal areas such as cave photography and night photography, practices that preoccupied certain devoted amateurs and specialized professionals, but were largely unfamiliar to the general public.

Dry gelatin plates of sufficient light sensitivity for handheld exposures were in 1887—the year before the first Kodak camera—also a relatively new and exciting product, having been invented only in the 1870s. These plates allowed photographers to work quickly, quietly, and on the move with no tripod. Dry plates also allowed photographers to develop their negatives long after exposures had been made. By contrast, the earlier wet collodion technique required that negatives be instantly developed after each exposure. With the advance of gelatin, small handheld cameras emerged on the market, and those were crucial for the speed required for Riis's project. One might say that these developments dramatically altered the range of objects that were possible to photograph. They changed the conditions of photography by making possible other ways of seeing the world photographically. Of course, one such photographic object, which now became otherwise visible, was New York's tenement population.

Phrasing it in terms I have conceptually developed elsewhere, the new photographic technologies opened new photographic spaces.[4] Photographic space is the space that anything photographed must enter into in order for it to appear in a photograph. It is obviously possible to photograph things in such a way that they do not appear at all in the resulting photograph. They have then not entered the space offered by the apparatus. Photographic space is modified by a number of parameters, which can be manipulated to define how a thing to be depicted will translate from a sense-perceptive visibility into a tech-

3. Chris Howes, *To Photograph Darkness, the History of Underground and Flash Photography* (A. Sutton, Gloucester: 1989), 6, 100-1; *Floods of Light: Flash Photography* ed. Martin (The Photographer's Gallery, London: 1982).

4. Dag Petersson in collaboration with Walter Niedermayr, "Photographic Space" in *Representational Machines: Photography and the Production of Space* (Aarhus University Press, Aarhus: 2013), 107-147.

nical one. Photographers use a number of different techniques to control the manipulation of this space. With skill, they design how things may appear photographically, knowing well that it will always differ from how things may appear as perceived, or as painted, sculpted, or drawn. Technology, however, does not determine photographic space, but it offers certain means by which photographers can manipulate it in different, and sometimes new ways. Again, photographic space can be manipulated so that things photographed do not appear at all, or appear only partially, or unrecognizably. No photograph conveys a thing's real existence, its true "having been there," in any ontologically pertinent sense. Photographers design photographic spaces, but although they consistently manipulate space, they do not always care very much about controlling it. Most photographers value the skills required for working with it and for knowing how to see otherwise, and some artists deliberately explore the margins and create spaces of their own. Riis invented a new such space. He seems aware that it has nothing to do with the tenement dwellers as such. Reflecting on his own first attempts, he found that what mattered most was their translation into photographic appearance: "The very blackness of my picture proved later on, when I came to use it with a magic lantern, the taking feature of it. It added a gloom to the show more realistic than any the utmost art of professional skill might have attained."[5]

Photographing at night, at dusk, or inside dark and damp interiors, sometimes with a chemically burning flash, Riis came to design a photographic space that made visible the very darkness in which the paupers lived, worked, idled, hustled, and drank. Even when he worked in ambient light with no flash, there is a darkness that clings to everything that his images make visible. Riis invented a space for darkness to appear, a new darkness that became conditional for apprehending the truth of the tenements "as he saw it". This iconology has obvious paradigmatic roots in the realist *chiaroscuro* of for example Daumier and Goya: a painterly tradition of which Riis

5. Riis, *The Making of an American*, 271.

claimed no knowledge whatsoever. Among photographers in Europe, the loosely defined program of pictorialism had already established a taste for *chiaroscuro*. Developing Henry Peach Robinson's pioneering ideals of artistically created photographs (as opposed to merely recorded images), artists like Robert Demachy, Julia Margaret Cameron, and Oscar Rejlander were already well-known in the late 1880s for their dim and somber work. But theirs is a velvety darkness, softly embracing the motif like satin in a jewelry box, nothing at all like the coarse gloom that let tenement utensils and bodies at menial labor be seen. And as with the painterly tradition, these artists seem to have meant little to Riis—equally little, in fact, as did those acclaimed photographers who opposed the pictorialists on relevant artistic grounds. To the American 'naturalists,' including photographers like Edward S. Curtis, Doris Ulman, and Rudolf Eickemeyr, who admired the vocal and controversial Dr. Peter Henry Emerson and favored a so-called 'naturalistic photography', the pictorialists' unrestrained image manipulations and contrived symbolism were at odds with the realist essence of photography.[6] Their inexorable dispute, being among the most decisive for the burgeoning history of photography, seems to have eluded Riis completely. Apparently without the slightest interest in or knowledge of the works produced by the most influential photographers of his time, Riis went along with some skilled amateur friends (Richard Hoe Lawrence, Henry G. Piffard, Dr. John T. Nagle and others), putting novel and to some extent unfamiliar equipment to work in very difficult and photographically uncharted environments. But however much the gloom and the obscurity of his pictures were dissimilar to anything previously seen in a photograph, and however tenuous the relationship might have been between Riis's target charity audience and those invested primarily in photographic matters, the images he made were nonetheless recognized for their experimentation with the possibilities of photographic representation.

6. Christian A. Peterson, *Peter Henry Emerson and American Naturalist Photography* (Minneapolis Institute of Arts, Minneapolis: 2008).

When Riis, in January 1888, presented one hundred photographs of tenement life to the Society of Amateur Photographers in New York, several of them had clearly been made using flashlight. Many of the audience members were most likely at the time themselves struggling to harness the technology, trying to put it to use within the boundaries of public taste. Riis had, by contrast, immediately applied it without any such aspirations and in conditions (and for purposes) it had not been intended for. With precious little interest in its capacities for pleasing effects, and with little more than a metaphor of "letting in the light"[7] as a startup motivation, he explored flash technologies heuristically and with results that must have failed all common standards for a good photograph. Riis ventured out into the margins of the visible, prompted by a political cause, a convincing metaphor, a novel gadget, technical ignorance, a minimum of patience, and complete lack of self-doubt. Had it not been for the photographic skills of Dr. Lawrence, Mr. Piffard, and Mr. A.D. Fisk, friends who assisted Riis and took several of his first photographs, it is rather likely that the entire project would have shipwrecked on technical difficulties. Together, as a team, they explored the fringes of photography and discovered with the flash a space that—luckily, perhaps—could make emphatically visible one other salient feature of the slums apart from darkness: dirt. Like no other image technology, Riis's flash photographs made dirt visible. In the places where he went, the blazing flash reflected off surfaces like moist skin, plaster, worn wood, linen and paper, highlighting these with a bright matte shade. By contrast, any dirt, mud, mold, and smudges absorbed the light and deepened the stains and blemishes on unkempt faces, dirty clothes and interiors. The flashlight gave a remarkably haptic quality to any rugged surfaces, worn fabrics, piles of grime, accumulating garbage, and general decay. As the light at times came from blazing magnesium powder, which burned for some time in an open pan, certain flash images also contain movement blur. Body parts that are simultaneously smeared out and blemished in the flashlight offered a graphic depiction of corporeal disintegration never seen before, and

7. Riis, *The Making of an American*, 268.

on two iconic levels: on the level of presentation and on the level of representation.

The visible dirt and the ragged surfaces that appear in the image are visual signs: signifiers of recognizable image content or perhaps rather, of represented signifieds. But the dark smudges of depressed coloration are not simply signs. Or rather, they are signs, but they are also very clearly something else. Just like any mere shade, tone, line, pattern, symmetry, grain, frame, shape and occasional color, these dark blotches are also just simply that: an area of darker grey that sensuously presents itself on the print surface. However much photographic conventions strive to conceal the level of presentation, one must see the stain in the picture surface too—and not just the represented smudge that lies beyond it. As a non-semantic image element, a part of the physical picture surface, it brings to the fore the third articulation of the image. New technologies were vital in the process of inventing novel means for their fabrication. Photographic visuality changed with technologies that allowed an otherwise manipulable light-differentiation. Making it possible thus to extend photographic space in new directions, many well-known things suddenly became differently visible. In this sense, one may analyze how a particular new visuality emerged with Riis's photographs, one that translated poorly into wood engravings and line drawings. The privileged medium for its public dissemination was the illustrated lecture, where the darkened hall or church and the enormous size of the projections added further force to the new non-semantic impressions.

The new visuality that was made possible with a modified photographic space affected not only how things were made visible in a single photograph. It also gave credence and support to a certain narration. Photographing into dark lodging rooms with a portable flashlight produced the impression of spaces lighted up for inspection. A popular trope often used in visual depictions of tenement tours or health inspections centered on the lantern that illuminated the obscure hovels. The light it cast represented not merely a necessary condition for inspection and discerning analysis; it was also a symbol

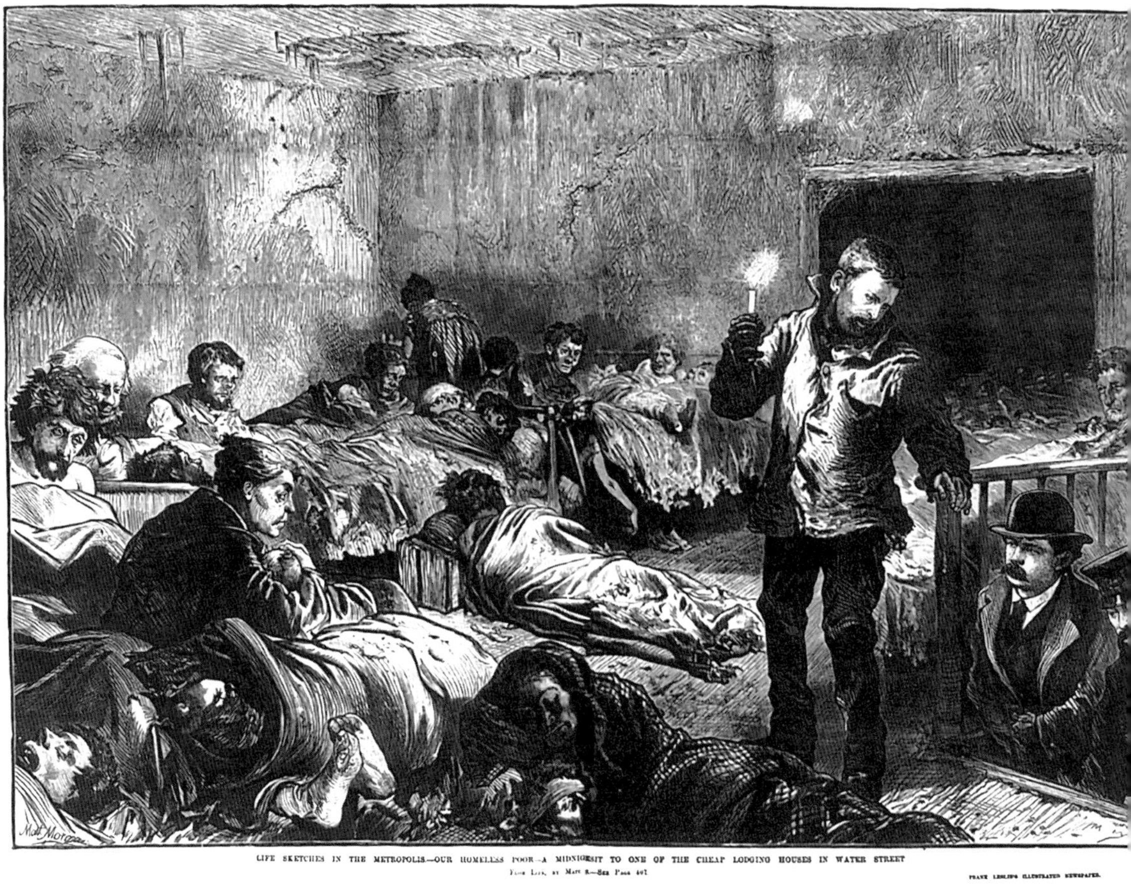

Figure 35. Matthew Sommerville Morgan, "A Midnight Visit to one of the Cheap Lodging Houses in Water Street" in *Frank Leslie's Illustrated Newspaper*, March 9, 1872.

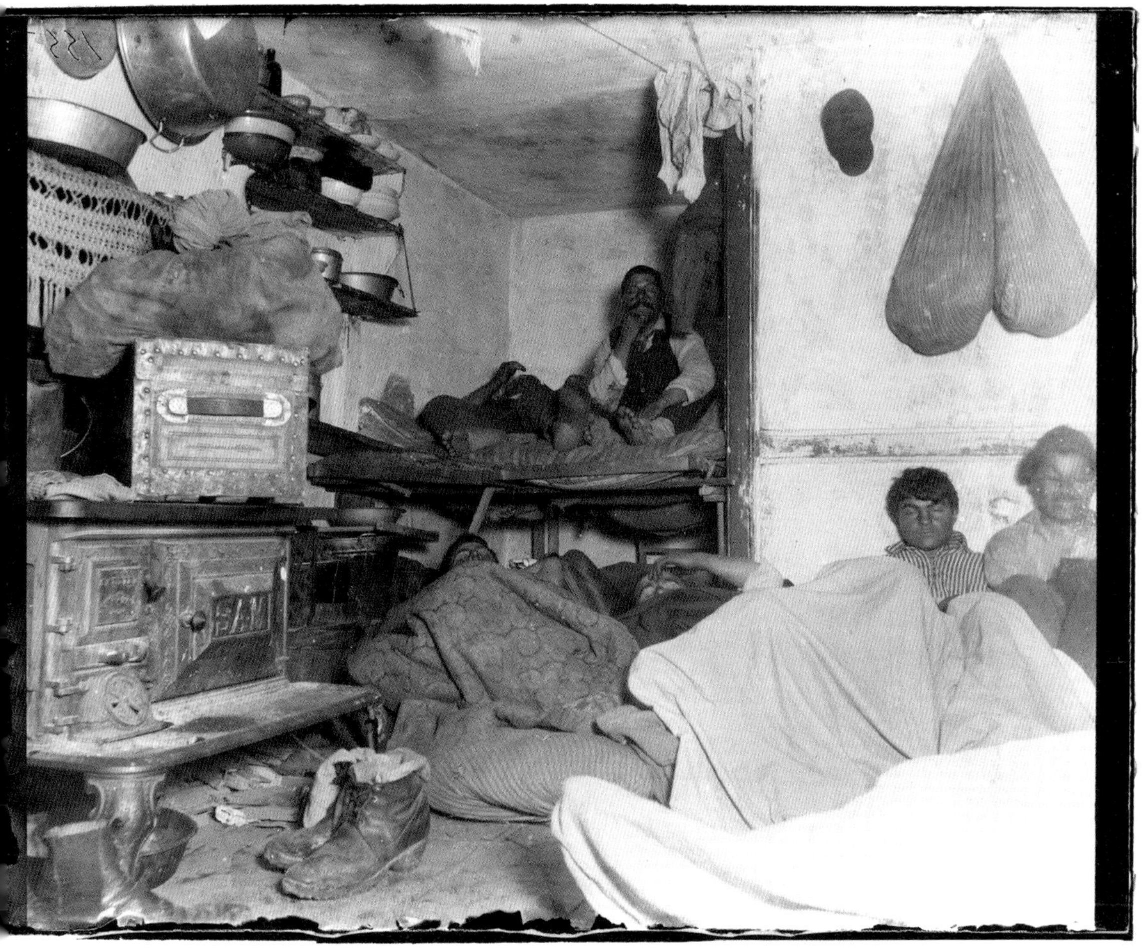

Figure 36. Jacob A Riis, "Lodgers in a crowded Bayard Street Tenement", or "Five Cents A Spot," [90.13.4.158] 1889. MCNY.

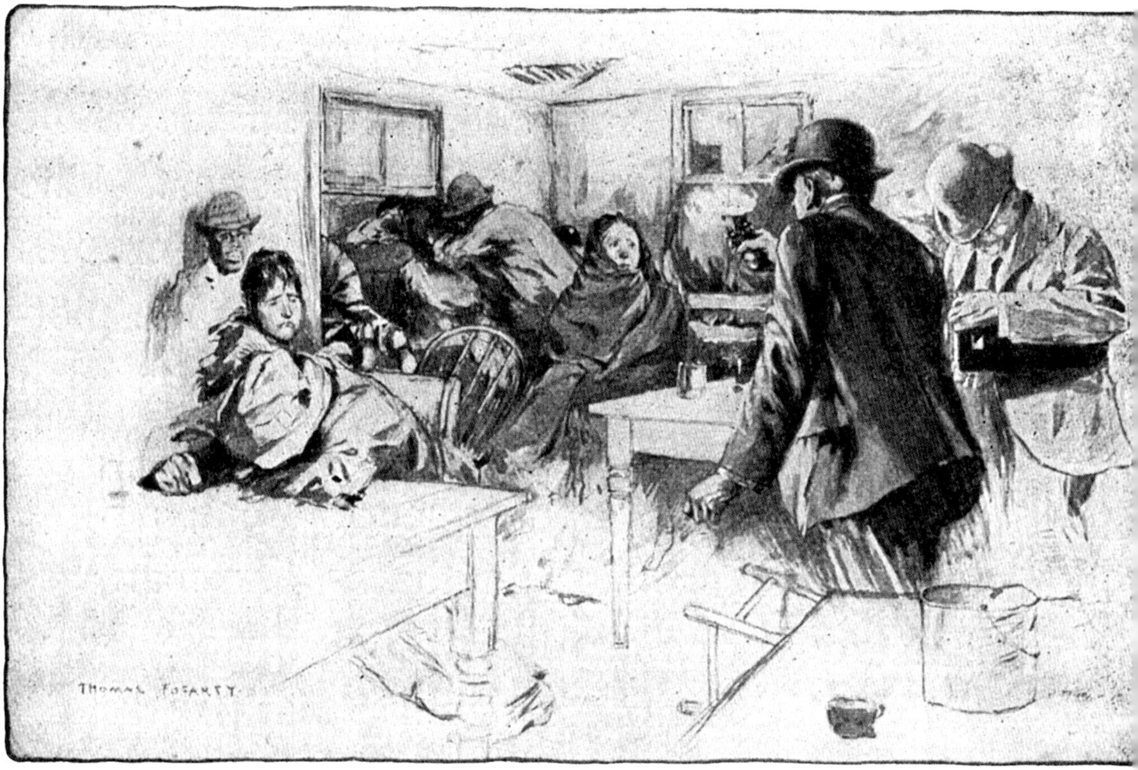

Figure 37. Thomas Fogerty, "The tenants bolted through the windows," from *The Making of An American.*

of the brightness, hope, and justice that reformers brought into the slums. It is easy to find examples in the popular press: one image depicts an aid worker silhouetted against a bright doorway that leads into a dark dump; another shows a policeman aiming his torch underneath a pier where dock-rats or homeless congregate; a third one pictures a health inspector holding up a lantern better to see into an overcrowded attic. This common visual trope of opening a door, or casting a light upon the darkness was often verbally underscored in Riis's lectures. Before a new slide he would say: "Let us go into one of the alleys [...] and see what goes on there at three o'clock in the morning"; "We will go inside and see what it looks like"; "Let us go upstairs and take a look." With Riis's application of flashlight, this narration would dramatically cast the audience in the role of first person observer and thereby deepen the performative effect of his tenement analysis. The conservative triangle literally grasped the audience as they followed the guided tour. Viewers went inside the family homes of the poor, recognized their labor situation, and acknowledged by force of persuasion the existential brotherhood of mankind.

With regard to Riis's photographic visibility of dirt, it can be said to have belonged to a paradigmatic order which also included other experimental efforts with artificial light, such as cave photography, high speed photography, and night photography. Such experiments tended to feature a similarly soiled effect, with the typically raw and craggy appearances outlined by sharp shadows looming behind illuminated objects. As already mentioned, this paradigmatic order included a number of visual properties that most portrait clients and studio photographers were keen to avoid, however much both would have preferred shorter exposure times and studio facilities devoid of scorching skylights. The unflattering effects of a blazing magnesium flash on human features could only be avoided by bulky bounce contraptions or diffusion devices, which, combined with the massive amounts of smoke generated from magnesium combustion, is said to have delayed the general introduction of flash in portrait studios.[8] But the harsh light

8. Pierre Bron and Philip L Condax, *The Photographic Flash: A Concise Illustrated History*, (Bron Elektronic, Allschwil: 1998).

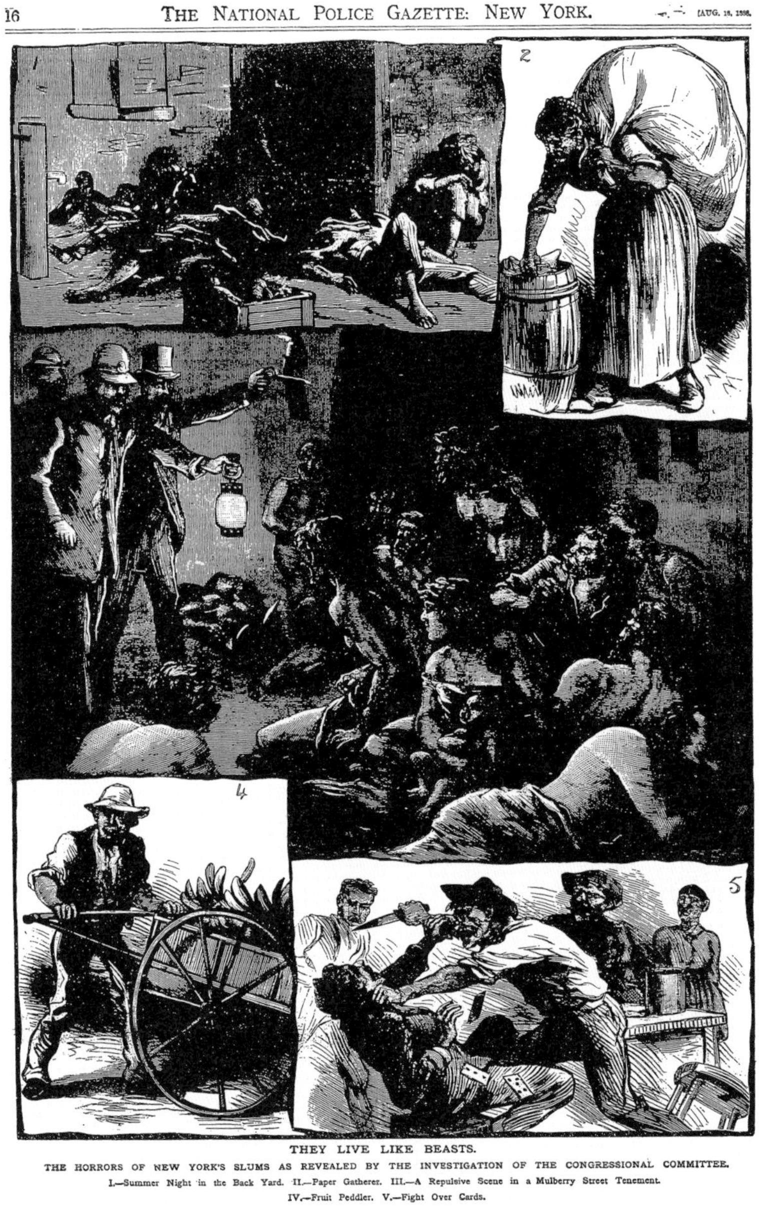

16 THE NATIONAL POLICE GAZETTE: NEW YORK. [AUG. 18, 1888.

THEY LIVE LIKE BEASTS.

THE HORRORS OF NEW YORK'S SLUMS AS REVEALED BY THE INVESTIGATION OF THE CONGRESSIONAL COMMITTEE.

I.—Summer Night in the Back Yard. II.—Paper Gatherer. III.—A Repulsive Scene in a Mulberry Street Tenement.

IV.—Fruit Peddler. V.—Fight Over Cards.

Figure 38. Anonymous, "They Live Like Beasts," from *The National Police Gazette*, Aug. 18, 1888, 16.

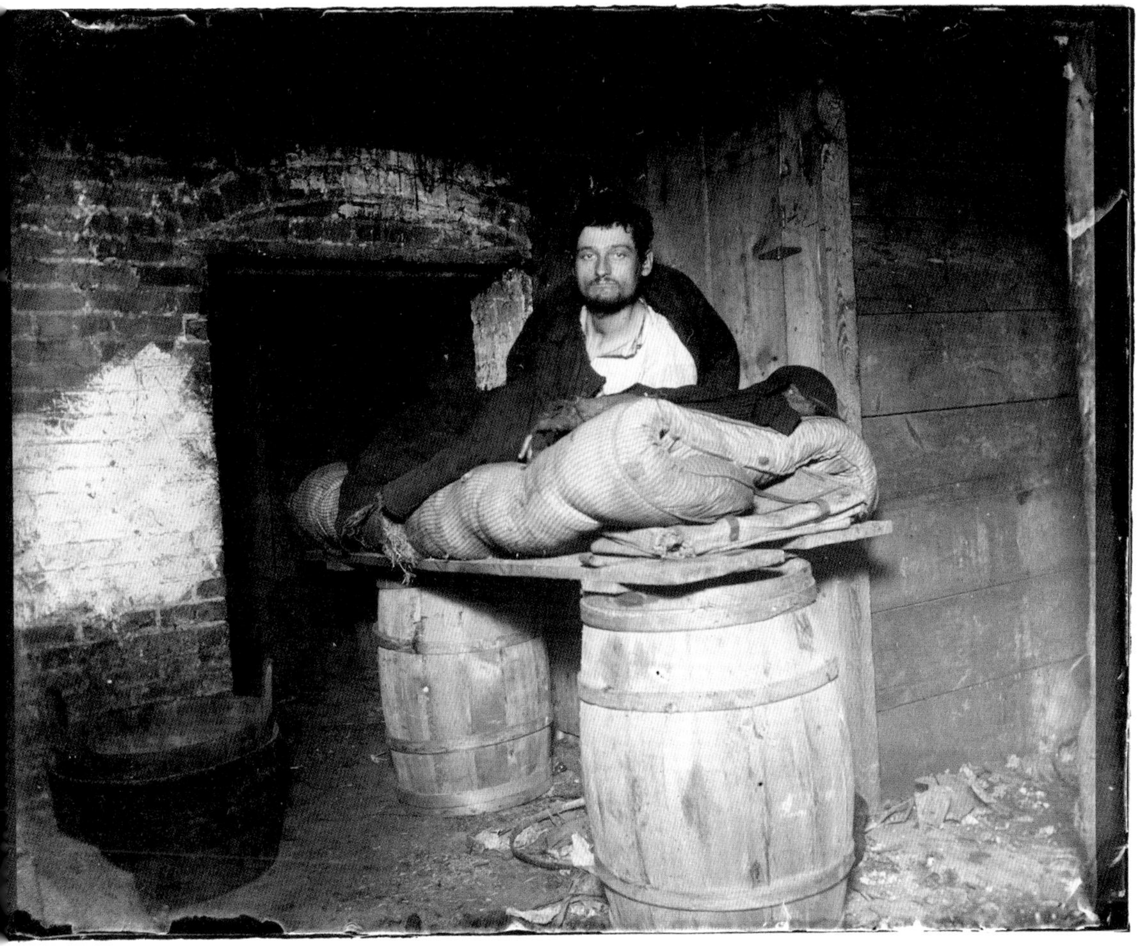

Figure 39. Jacob A. Riis, "Slept in that Cellar Four Years," [90.13.4.207] 1892. MCNY.

served Riis's endeavor perfectly and offered a powerful niche in the margins of the photographically visible.

With regard to how this non-semantic paradigm impacted on the possibilities for syntagmatic constructions and narrations, the example recounted above (of casting a light into the tenement obscurity) was perhaps among the simpler ones. A much more complex kind of paradigmatic impact with greater implications for the mutation of tenement visibility, was wielded from the generic representations of poverty associated with the entertainment industry.

At the time, a cultivated common curiosity about physiognomic otherness laid the grounds for a thriving entertainment industry. New York's downtown tenements provided more in this respect than a popular lineup of spectacular sites for slum tourists. Cheap theaters staged spectacular melodramas with plots often set in the tenements; dime-museums portrayed tenement intemperance in gory *tableaux vivants*, and of course the weekly press entertained continually with illustrated causeries from the immigrant neighborhoods. On a grander scale, Coney Island showcased touring exotic tribes from around the globe along with an in-house cadre of human abnormalities. Freak shows, museums, and touring circuses provided a regular staple of family amusement, showcasing cleverly orchestrated displays of the odd, the ghastly, and the pitiful. Riis often and clearly dissociated himself from this plebeian entertainment industry, but a cartoon pasted into his own scrapbook suggests that he was well aware of connections commonly drawn between sideshows and his own performances. The cartoon even speaks of a stronger kinship between Riis's lectures and the entertainment industry than one would think he was keen to admit. It does not suggest, however, that his charity lectures were perceived as a mere freak show, or as unequivocal exploitation of the poor. However, a clear connection to a popular industry fraught with contradictory values and problematic regulations of conduct must be acknowledged.

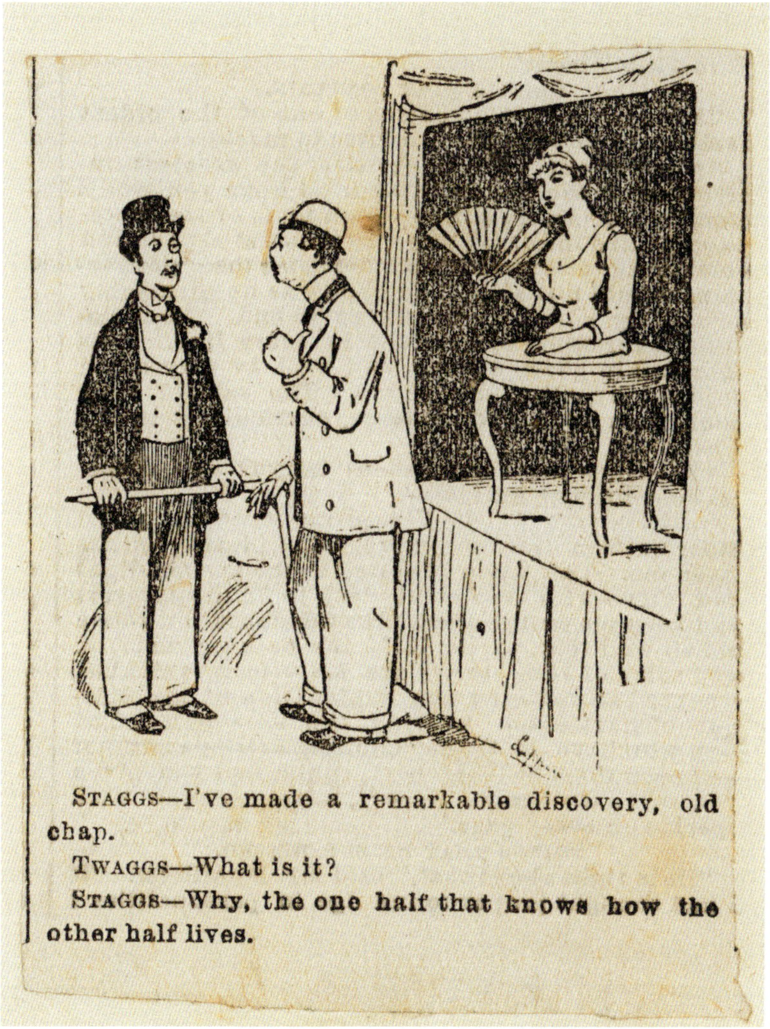

Figure 40. Unidentified artist, Cartoon from Riis's scrapbook, page 24.
Library of Congress.

Riis and the Entertainment Industry

In spite of Riis's explicit contempt for the sordid entertainment industry, many historians and commentators have found reason to emphasize Riis's own talents for amusing his audience. Daniel Czitrom, being one of the more recent, speaks of Riis's "vaudeville model"[9] and describes how he employed "humor and an appeal to the exotic to reassure his readers and reinforce their sense of superiority."[10] The exoticism and racism that are glaring features of his work today were first pointed out in the 1980s as being evidence of dubious priorities on Riis's part, even signs of compromised commitment to the tenement dwellers.[11] But this interpretation is to some extent anachronistic. Riis was not considered racist in his own time, nor were objections raised against his inclination for the exotic and the repulsive. In a charity context, however, Riis's piggybacking on popular visual stereotypes and exotic curiosities associated with cheap entertainment venues were indeed controversial and seem to have generated public attention. A distinct flavor of entertainment to Riis's performances helped most certainly to individuate the visceral gloom and darkness of his photographs; it also modified the atmosphere of reform activism and distinguished the author from mainstream contributors to the saturated charity market. To get a better grasp on this, a wider contextualizing perspective must be obtained.

Looking at the entertainment industry in New York in the 1880s, one soon finds that spectacular views of poverty and social otherness were not uncommon. If there was a disturbing element to Riis's photographs, it did not derive from their raw and realistic display of misery and otherness as such, but rather from their presence in a charitable setting. Traffic in the reverse direction—from charity to

9. Daniel Czitrom, "Jacob Riis's New York," 87.
10. Ibid., 18-19.
11. Cf. Martha Rosler, *The Contest of Meaning: Critical Histories of Photography* ed. Richard Bolton (MIT Press Cambridge MA.: 1989). Also, Sally Stein, "Making Connections with the Camera: Photography and Social Mobility in the Career of Jacob Riis," in *Afterimage*, 10:10, 1983.

entertainment venues—was neither shocking nor uncommon. The curiosity industry, spearheaded by P.T. Barnum's *American Museum* and supplemented by a train of smaller dime museums and circuses, borrowed habitually from charity in order to fig leaf potentially disturbing displays behind educational intentions. "Moral Amusement" might include, for example, a deterring wax tableau of an intemperate tenement family or a wholesome lecture or stage melodrama with explicit reference to vicious habits.[12] Other amusement venues that capitalized on the slums, such as guided tenement tours, attracted respectable patrons with similar promises of insight and learning. In fact—some say—it offered nothing but a spectacular opportunity to gawk at subhuman living conditions. Middle class patrons without the opportunity or the courage to visit the slums in person could rely on a multitude of publications that offered gruesome armchair experiences of the lower wards on a similar pretext. The suggestion that these techniques of looking at urban poverty had ties to the circus and the freak show is supported not only by the many flaneuring causeries in newspapers and occasional appearances of destitutes in circuses and cheap museums; the mere title of the "City Sideshows" page in *The National Police Gazette* supports the affinity quite literally. But to introduce these gazes into charity was nothing short of scandalous.

Cheap theaters were at the time considered an even more unseemly form of entertainment than the freak show. Here, the mob mingled dangerously close with the upper classes while enjoying gaudy spectacles and popular stage melodrama. The particular staple of plays known as melodrama were written and produced to draw a crowd and would typically run for a month or two in houses like Niblo's Garden, the People's Theater and Thalia Theater (which occasionally played in German). The genre typically entertained with a simple plot, popular songs, impressive décor, and hair-raising stunts. Judging from reviews in *The New York Dramatic Mirror* from the time, it appears that the city's tenements were frequently used as settings for melodramatic plots. It is easy to find reviews of plays like

12. Andrea Stulman Dennett, *Weird and Wonderful: The Dime Museum in America* (New York University Press, New York: 1997), 54-55.

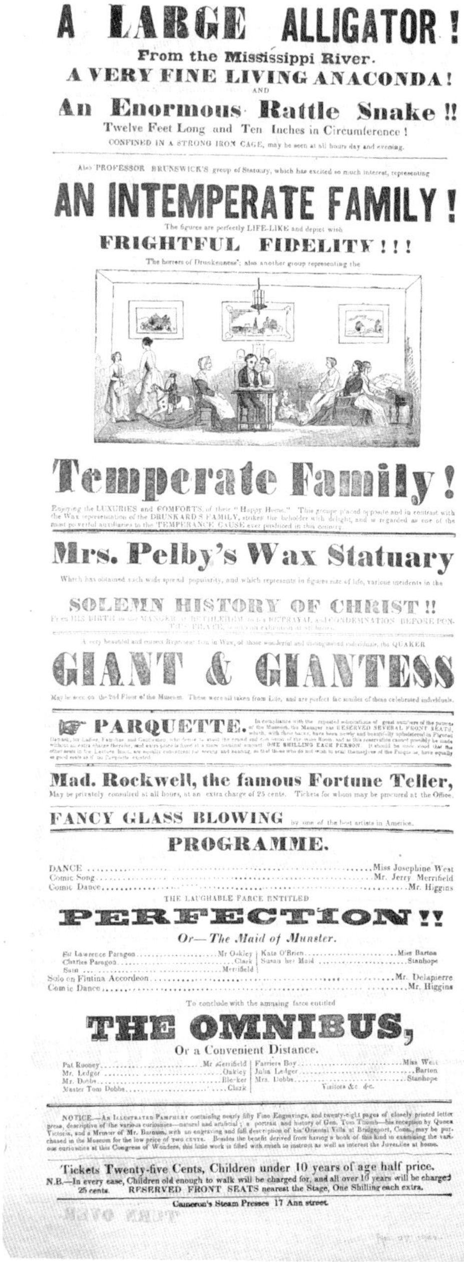

Figure 41. Poster for P.T. Barnum's *The American Museum*, 1849. New York Historical Society.

"The White Slave", "Lost in New York", "After Dark", "Out in the Streets", and "Children From the Ghetto." A little research on one of the most celebrated melodrama instructors and playwrights, Mr. Edward Harrigan, reveals that the characters in blockbusters like "Reilly and the 400" and "Waddy Googan" were modeled after first-hand tenement observations. Occasionally, these characters were subsequently modified according to public signs of approval or disliking.[13] In some cases the plot was set in a tenement neighborhood no more than a few blocks away from the theater. And for the plot, a clandestine love affair across class divisions, or a case of mistaken identity would suffice to propel the bourgeois hero(ine) into the horrors of the slums, where blood and thunder paved the way for a happy ending.

While these popular venues were expected to offer garishly entertaining peeks into the disorderly tenements, the establishments and associations that hired Riis for an evening were certainly not. No fearsome, loathsome, or scurvy displays were expected to overwhelm or shock their audiences. Although both types of establishments welcomed the same individual patrons, and although both dealt with basically the same subject matter, the cleft between their visibilities was unmistakable. But as the border that separated the two was permeable in only one direction, charity managed to preserve its sincere and earnest reputation, thus remaining entirely unsuitable for pranks, exaggeration, and daring visuals. Charity was not, however, devoid of emotional content. Sentimentality and pity belonged no less to charity events than to popular melodrama, albeit with the difference that charity reserved such pathos for acts of virtue, care, and forgiveness whereas in melodrama it was more often associated with relief from reason and responsibility.

Riis's excursus into the entertainment industry must have implied a risk. Not only were the theatres and circuses considered morally inferior to the charity venues that Riis performed at, but the grime

13. Cf. *Scrapbook of Edward Harrigan's Theatre Comique, 514 Broadway*, New York Public Library, Edward Harrigan Papers, MWEZ n.c. 4526; see also "A Chat with Harrigan," in *New York Dramatic Mirror*, April 27, 1889.

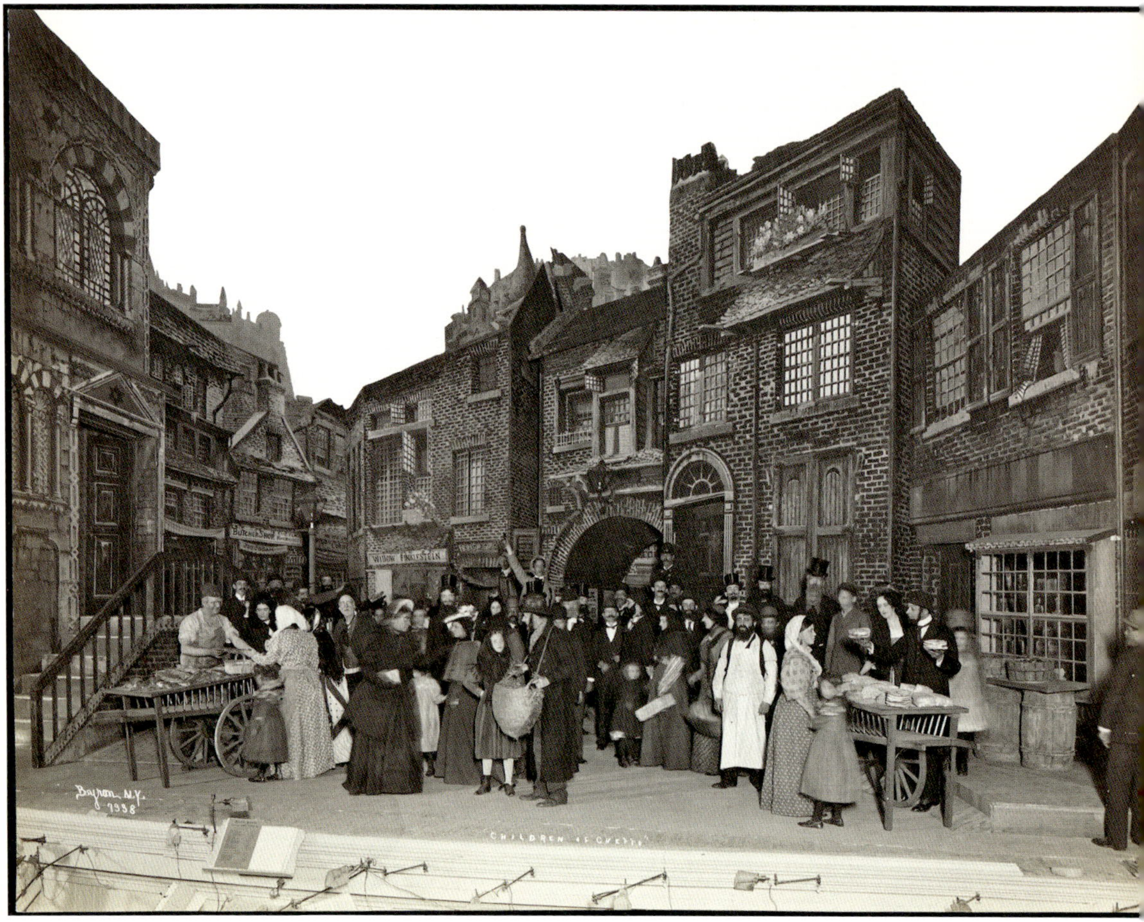

Figure 42. Byron Co., "The Children of the Ghetto," [43.98.166] 1899. MCNY.

and the human denigration that some of his most controversial photographs laid forth surpassed even the most abhorrent displays at the most tawdry venues. Did he risk rejection? Undoubtedly, but he also protected himself. The visualities that he discovered on the fringes to the entertainment industry offered new and unique opportunities for narration, not least as their organization of gazes already maintained a measure of resilience to objections against the overtly distasteful. Five visualities, already striding the gulf between reform and the entertainment industry, were instrumental in mutating the charitable image of the poor. These five were capable of affecting the performative image-word constructions during lectures. One may identify, a) a clearly dramatic disposition of dominant viewer and subdominant viewed; b) a corporal and often violent orchestration of bodily harm—invariably in view of a final redeeming moment; c) a discernible staging or posing of bodies for display (Riis's street boys sleeping outdoors and gang members mugging a victim are directly quoted from theater plays); d) a sense of extraordinary and exclusive access to places that are culturally secluded or prohibited; and e) a sense of timing and coordination between Riis's performance onstage and the slide projector operator, a non-semantic element in its own right that Riis appropriated from entertainment practices.

Conventional charity lectures offered by contrast a strictly verbal experience. To the extent that pictures were at all used, they were stereotypically sentimental or religiously symbolic, numbingly virtuous by content and delivered with a minimum sense of stage finesse. Riis's five fringe visualities affected the verbal-visual apparatus and made his narratives transcend the charity-entertainment divide. This was nothing short of revolutionary. To succeed in introducing them he made use of four tactical measures. Each helped in different ways to integrate the theatrical fringe visualities into his charity performance and thereby to individuate the Other Half as a new visibility of tenement poverty. These tactical measures were instrumental for the resilience of the new mutant. The measures employed to rear his tenement visibility were of course not themselves non-semantic ar-

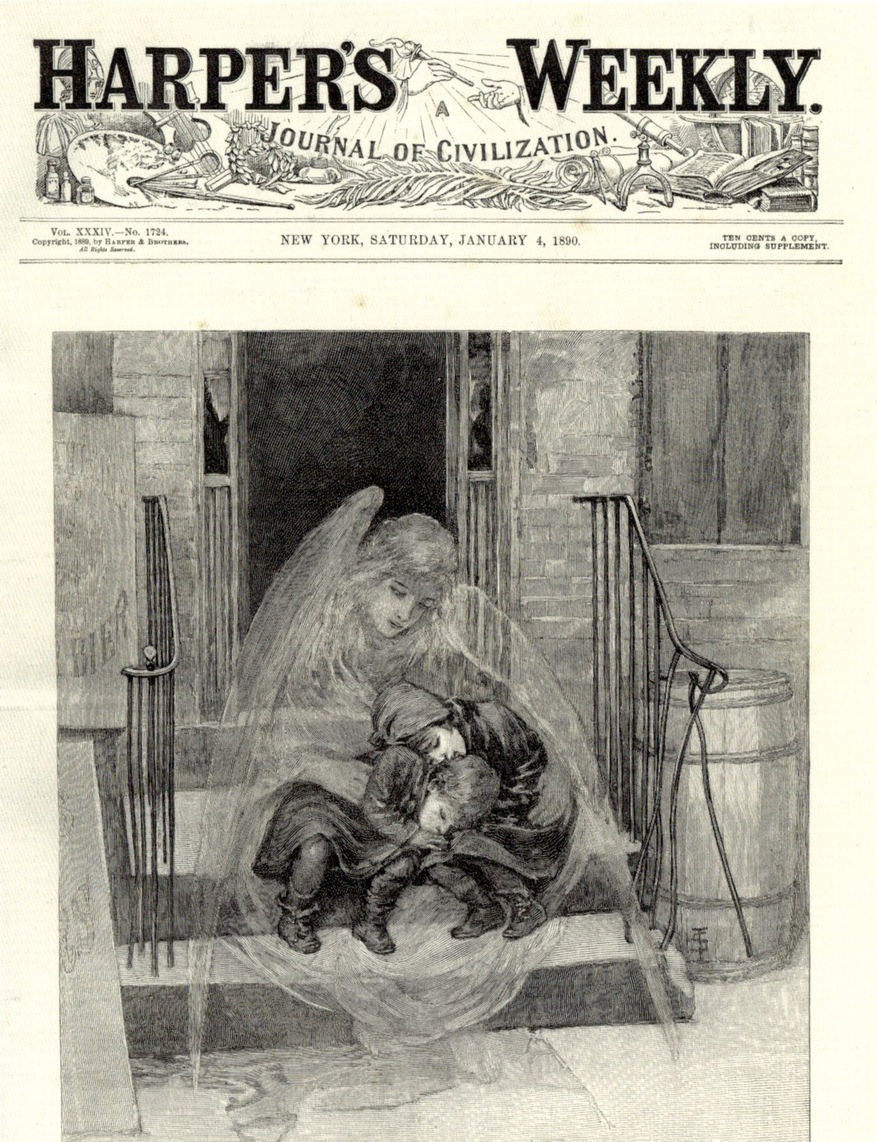

HARPER'S WEEKLY.
A JOURNAL OF CIVILIZATION.

Vol. XXXIV.—No. 1724.
Copyright, 1889, by Harper & Brothers.
All Rights Reserved.

NEW YORK, SATURDAY, JANUARY 4, 1890.

TEN CENTS A COPY,
INCLUDING SUPPLEMENT.

"UNTO ONE OF THE LEAST OF THESE."—Drawn by Jessie Shepherd.—[See Page 11.]

Figure 43. Jessie Shepherd, "Unto One of the Least of These," in *Harper's Weekly*, Jan. 4, 1890.

ticulations. But as tactical means, they had all been tried elsewhere and proved viable for managing conflicts between incompatible visualities.

1) An alternating rhythm between spectacular gore and sober images made sure that Riis was not suspected of seeking mere scandal or effect. Not all of Riis's photographs were provocative or outrageous. Images like "Two Ragamuffins", "The Florence Mission" or "Prayer Time in the Nursery" challenge no charity conventions. Their composition is harmonious, the motif is clearly focused with the main subject posited in an ordered and commendable milieu. Even images like "Street Arabs in Sleeping Quarters" maintain the sentimentality of staged charity and show nothing of the explicitly chaotic character of "A Downtown Morgue", "Overcrowding: Five Cents a Spot" or "A Flat in Hell's Kitchen". By contrast, these images' bewildering disarray of human bodies, furniture, and utensils, all more or less worn, broken or mended, some overexposed, distorted, or unfocused, would certainly be considered appalling, but in a truly remarkable way also paradigmatically correlated with the orderly charity images.[14]

14. It may be apposite here to recall what Bonnie Yochelson has already said with regard to interpreting Riis's images. They were not made in a conscious attempt to introduce baroque compositions or corporal effects in photography. At times, his photographs turned out disorderly because Riis and his team of photographers worked under very challenging and unfamiliar circumstances. When his photographically skilled partners got exhausted from the late night raids, Riis learnt the basic craft himself and pushed on with his experiments. He often found himself without the time or the opportunity to arrange his subjects before the camera: for example, an early publication remarks apologetically, "The first view taken, or rather stolen, for there could be no posing for effect." Photographing at night in hostile situations under police escort meant reduced possibilities to arrange anything; the shots came out as best they could. Interestingly, Riis seems not to have cared—at least not initially. He believed in the persuasive quality of the camera, and took the images at face value, often rather satisfied with the expressive qualities from occasional mishaps. With time, however, it seems that Riis developed a limited tolerance of chaotic images: a story in *The Children of the Poor* describes how a gang of unruly children prevented him from taking a picture as they would not stop pestering him.

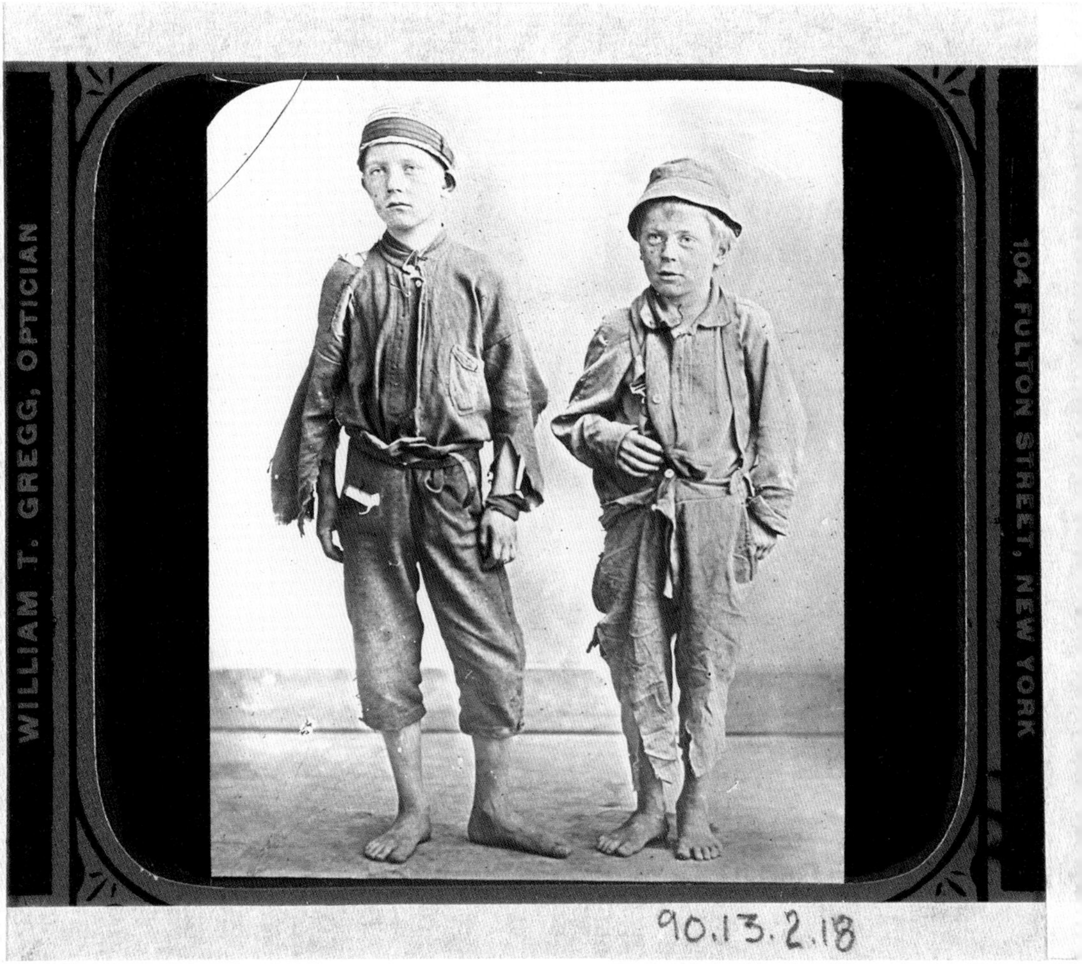

Figure 44. Jacob A. Riis, "Two ragamuffins," [90.13.2.18] ca. 1890. MCNY.

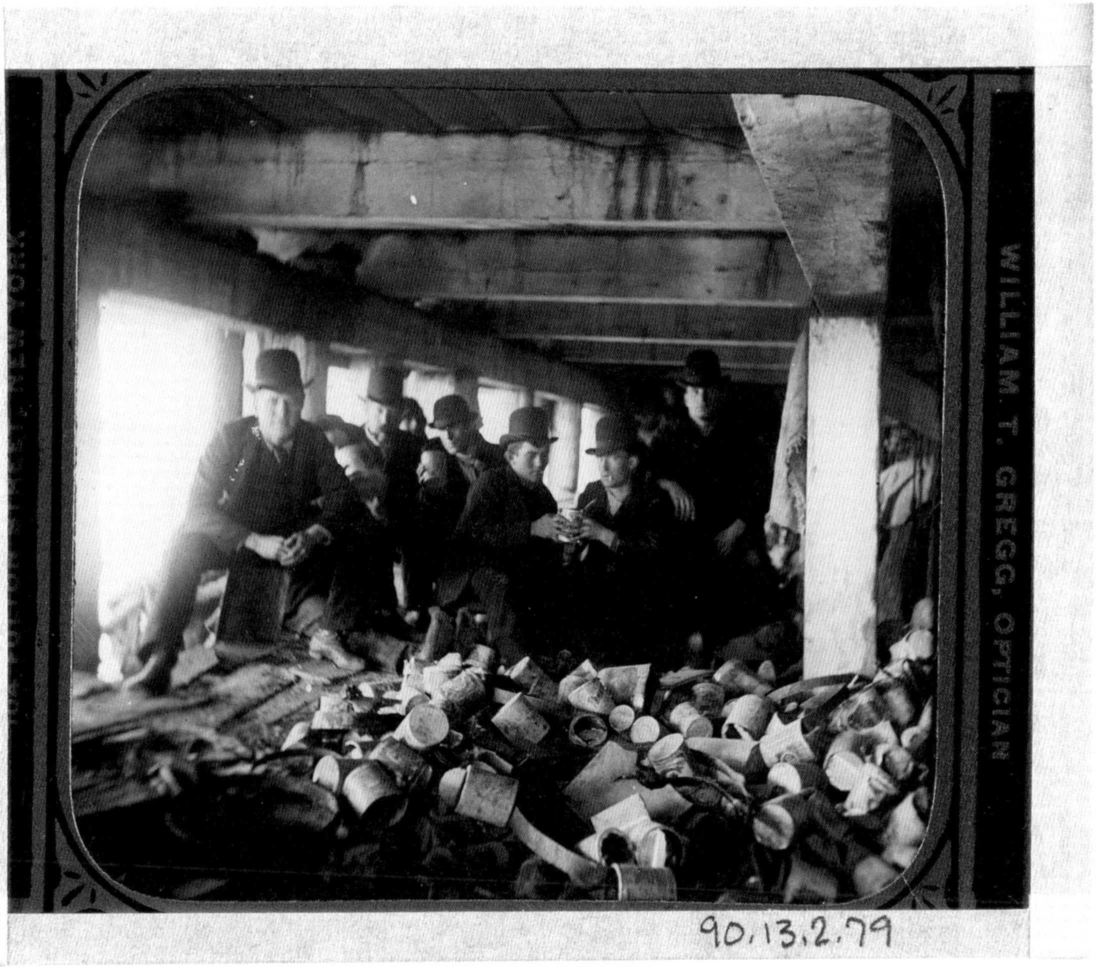

Figure 45. Jacob A. Riis, "Dockrats in Quarters," or "Short Tail Gang (Corlears Hook) Pier at Foot of Jackson Street, now Corlears Hook Park. Photographed from the Police Boat," [90.13.2.79] 1887. MCNY.

Constant rhythmic shifts between conflicting visualities, alternating within a single syntactically coherent series: this helped to protect the illustrated lecture from being condemnable as scandalous. Riis often composed the slides as abrupt juxtapositions of extremes rather than as bridged transpositions, and although one might detect in the reconstructed lecture an increase of chaotic images toward the final part, both types are present throughout.

This first tactical measure depended on establishing a single syntactic continuity out of images that conventionally belonged within two distinct visibilities, and with visualities at odds with each other. To create this cohesion, Riis emphasized certain non-semantic articulations that both visibilities might conventionally employ, albeit for different affects. The Montgomery Guard sequence from the second part of the reconstructed lecture may reveal how it works. Riis put together a syntagmatic set of six images that belong to distinctly different visibilities, but in such a way that some of their non-semantic elements begin to relate. It begins with "Two Ragamuffins," which is clearly within the charity visibility. The leap to "A tramp's nest" could hardly be more distressing, and the next freakish view, of "A Black and Tan Dive" is equally grim. Then "Dock Rats" appears as if taken directly from a theater play, showing a group of gang members in bowler hats posing menacingly under the piers among beer cans and debris. Their apparent posing is not here a sign, it does not refer to anything, but as a visual order of bodies it helps to reconcile in some sense the visibly established cleft between salvaged children and parents lost, as both follow the distinct display convention of posing for the camera. An articulation of posing appears, however different meanings their distinct visibilities may evoke. Therefore, when Riis then switches to the thugs of The Montgomery Guards, the non-semantic articulation of the image series affects the singular picture with a distinct sense of instructed order. Thugs pose for the camera, and more importantly, they pose for us, *as* thugs. Particularly in the second image of these boys, pranking in front of the camera and showing how they would go about robbing a sleeping drunkard, the

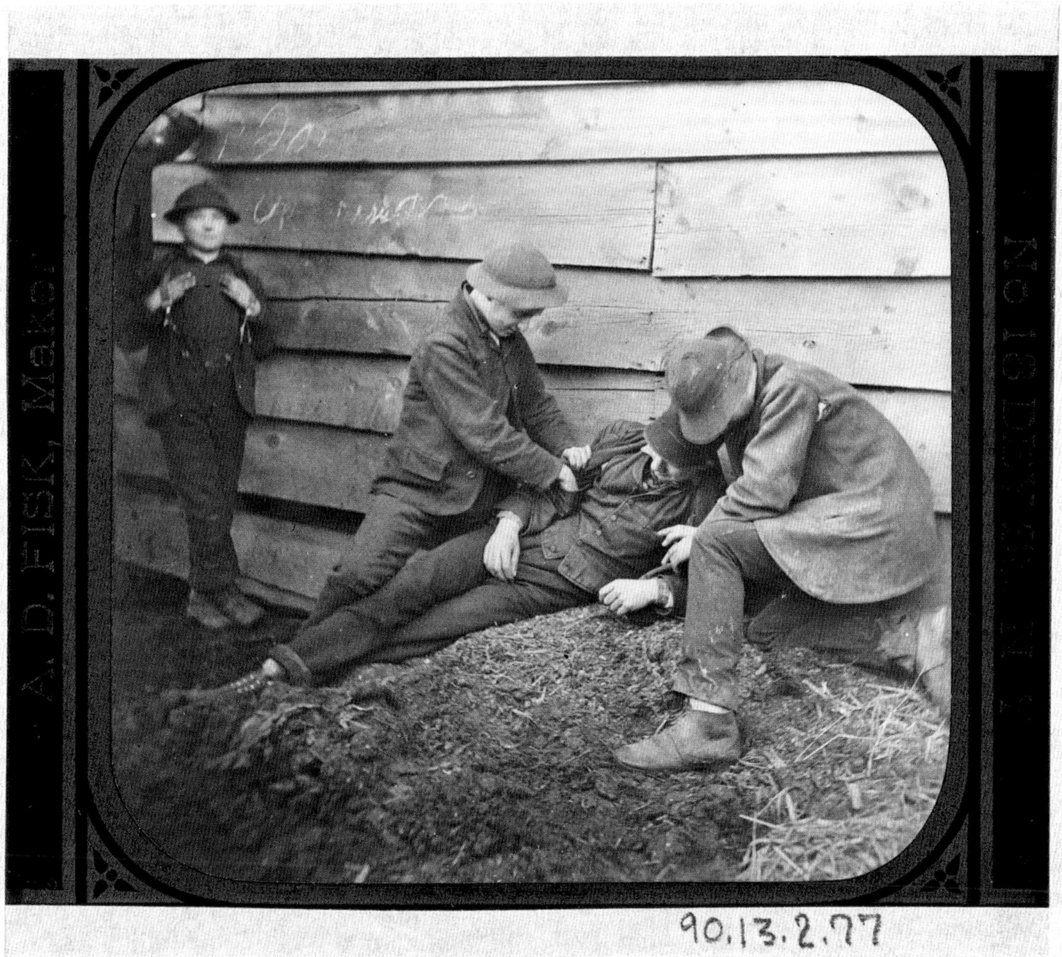

Figure 46. Richard Hoe Lawrence and Jacob A. Riis, "Showing their Trick. Hell's Kitchen Boys," [90.13.2.77] 1887. MCNY. These boys are identified as members of a gang known as The Montgomery Guards in the lecture "The Other Half and How They Live." How the picture was made is recounted in *How the Other Half Lives*, 222.

jovial theatricality has such a profound effect on the semantics (the actors' comrades looking on close by, consciously almost in the frame, so childishly happy playing their games) that the whole sequence begins to speak to the sentimental hearts of the charity genteel. But then it has to be noted that this photograph is one that certainly does not belong to the visibility of charity. Thus, something new appears: that there is apparently more to posing than mere spectacular, theatrical menace—and it is in this childish, charitable sense of posing that the non-semantic element relates the "Montgomery Guards" paradigmatically to "Two Ragamuffins." They become variations of the same series. It would be possible here to extend the analysis to include other image series as well, and eventually to show that the whole lecture constructs a single syntactic series out of similar shifts between conflicting visualities.

2) The second tactical measure may help to explicate how Riis's visibility could begin to gain public ground. Cultural historians studying the shadier segments of the entertainment industry during the late 1870s and early 80s have noted several signs, mainly from larger cities, of a conflict developing between increasingly daring amusement venues and bourgeois moral sensitivities. Complaints of moral corruption spreading from the circuses and dime museums grew increasingly belligerent and widespread as the amusement industry explored new daring routines. Robert Bogdan, author of the seminal study *Freak Show* notices a delayed popularity decline: "Starting in the 1870s, dime museums proliferated, reaching their peak in the 1880s and 1890s" after which, he adds, a sharp decline sets in that continues throughout the twentieth century.[15] Andrea Stulman Dennett, who has chronicled the dime museum in America, also documents several examples of outspoken hostility against the more aggressive museum displays, prompted by internal competition.[16]

15. Robert Bogdan, *Freak Show* (University of Chicago Press, Chicago: 1988), 35-38.

16. "The Society for Prevention of Cruelty against Children, for example, lodged an official complaint against museum exhibition rooms in January 1891. A year later, on February 1, 1892, the licenses for stage performances at a number of museums and concert halls officially expired." Dennett, *Weird and Wonderful*, 59.

While Riis was in the process of working out his first lectures, a growing number of the reformers and charity workers that he sought to address would support the rising antagonism and promote increasingly austere moral views within the philanthropic community. Riis's hopes of awakening the community with stunning photographs may seem to have been out of touch with the audience's sentiments from the start. From what he himself recounts of the first months of building up a philanthropy career, prospects certainly looked dim; Riis was consistently met with reluctance and disapproval from the churches and the philanthropic communities he initially approached. He interpreted their disinclination as wariness against his profession as a police reporter,[17] and he explains that he needed vouching. A kind of authorization would be the second tactical measure for integrating fringe visualities: an ecclesiastical approval that he eventually got from the superintendent of the New York City Mission, Rev. A.T. Schauffler, who in February 1888 became a kind of agent for Riis.[18] Schauffler managed to get his show into the Broadway Tabernacle, where two important representatives of the reform movement, Rev. Parkhurst and Josiah Strong, were present.[19] Schauffler and Parkhurst had collaborated at least since 1881, when Parkhurst had invited the superintendent to lecture at the Madison Avenue Presbyterian Church on the topic of work done at the Bowery City Mission.[20] Both of them were important allies, but according to Bonnie Yochelson, the breakthrough came in May 1888 with a lecture that Riis gave on invitation by Rev. Lyman Abbott at the Plymouth Church in

17. Riis quoted in an untitled clipping from *New Bedford Mercury*, January 1st, 1889: "The reason assigned in every case for the refusal to let me into the churches was that I am a newspaper man and a police reporter at that." LC, Riis papers, box 4.

18. Schauffler to Riis, letter dated February 29, 1888; LC, Riis papers, box 12. See also Schauffler, Letter of recommendation, dated March 3, 1888.

19. Cf. Yochelson and Czitrom, *Rediscovering Riis*. There is a slight discrepancy between Yochelson and Czitrom on the issue of Schauffler's role in promoting Riis (88-89 and 144-45): whereas Czitrom argues that Schauffler got involved "after seeing the lecture at the Broadway Tabernacle", Yochelson suggests that Schauffler's support secured Riis an invitation to speak. As nothing important depends upon settling the issue I leave it undecided.

20. "Phases of New York Life," in *The New York Times*, Jan. 10, 1881, 8.

Brooklyn. This performance led to the assignment of two full-page articles in the *Christian Union*, the launch pad from which "Riis entered the realm of New York's clerical and charitable elite."[21]

Whatever reasons these men had for going against the grain—we know nothing about it—their support and their respective influence were crucial for introducing Riis's occasionally disturbing images into the city's respectable charity institutions and churches. Their endorsement may not have neutralized the appalling photographs as much as ratified a moral position for them. Their ratification, or authorization of moral wholesomeness is important to take note of. To secure legitimacy through established authority is of course common when introducing something new and challenging to a saturated and hierarchical market, but in the case of Riis, who preferred to portray himself as a self-made man with a unique reform agenda, leaning on ratification from higher authorities was not uncomplicated.

Despite the waning popularity of crude entertainments among the constituencies that were to make up Riis's target audience, Abbott, Parkhurst, and Schauffler decided to vouch for his performances as proper church entertainment. One explication for their support is close at hand: much like the vocal pious protesters against Sunday newspapers also bought them and read them, it is conceivable that the growing discontent with ignoble venues had not yet begun to reflect in declining allure. A growing ambiguity about the dangers of lesser entertainment (whether their carnal and curious displays were deplorable in kind or perhaps tolerable as educational handmaid in the battle against various evils) would have worked in Riis's favor. Entertainment was an intensifying public concern, and even more so the closer it got to the role of education. Higher authorization was solicited and granted as a tactical measure to avoid scandalizing venue owners and audiences. Riis's corporally violent impressions were at odds with mainstream charity, but his sponsors might have recognized possibilities in exploiting the ambiguity for rhetorical advantage.

21. Yochelson and Czitrom, *Rediscovering Riis*, 145. I have been unable to verify this performance.

3) The third tactical measure that helped to integrate the five fringe visualities was verbal in its mode of expression and operated as a protective filter against the visibility of cheap drama. This one did not emerge from the conflict between gross entertainment and pious charity; in fact, it derived not from a visual conflict at all, but from one pertaining to journalism and academia. Riis paid minute attention to facts, names, dates, places, and above all, to statistics. Cool numbers would contrast the wealth of outrageous images, and they seem to have assisted in preventing the most forbidding views from antagonizing the audience. But whereas a general application of facts derived from journalism, its tactical function during lectures was only effective relative to Riis's particular lecture setting, which, as I shall return to as the fourth tactic, appeared somewhere in-between established conventions. What distinguished these conventions from each other had to do with conflicting visualities, and it is from Riis's negotiation of this conflict that the tactical function of statistics evolves.

From Riis's very first lecture at the Society of American Photography, reviewers seize upon the abundance of "facts,"[22] "statistics,"[23] and the lecturer's intent to "picture to the audience the exact conditions" of tenement life.[24] Riis was not casual about numbers. An irritated note in the margins of his scrapbook, next to a review that had misrepresented his figures, reads, "Nonsense. Never said anything of the kind." In the spring of 1888, Riis was regularly commended for his extensive knowledge and for communicating a wealth of indisputable figures. *The World* even described the rhetorical effect in minute detail.

> Before the gas was turned down, Mr. Riis gave a few figures, taken from the Board of Health records. He said that New York contained 31,534 tenements in which 1,016,365 persons found what they called homes. The worst overcrowding is below Fourteenth Street, and some of the worst tenements are in

22. *New York Tribune*, January 26, 1888.
23. *New York News*, Jan 27, 1888.
24. *The Photographic Times*, Feb 3, 1888.

> Harlem. In London the most populous area contained 170,000 to the square mile; in New York the figure was 290,000 to the square mile. There were in the United States 350,000 professional criminals of whom one-third were under twenty years old and one-half under twenty-one. To show how people are huddled together in some parts of New York, Mr. Riis cited a house in Crosby Street, where a young man and his wife disheartened with their hopeless struggle against starvation had committed suicide together. Here were four rooms in the top floor of a house which originally was a private dwelling. Each room contained a family who paid $5 a month to a Christian lady in Massachusetts.[25]

In May, the *New York Star* misrepresented Riis as "Professor" (what he merely underlined) and the *Tribune* reported that his "practical observations" "told the truth," "traced an evolution," and gave "a realistic assurance" of the dark side of town.[26] The audience's interest is reportedly "serious and sympathetic" and not at all similar to a vaudeville performance. In other words, many reviewers had already recognized convincing research and scholarly rigor behind Riis's performances.

These virtues should not be mistaken for journalistic ones. They were not background for news, but fronted as social diagnostics in their own right. Nonetheless, the scholarly qualities attributed to Riis had little to do with his diction, which was too full of innuendos, ironies, and leaps into sentimentality to be perceived as properly academic. Rather, it rested on the one hand on the sheer wealth of data, names, and factual information delivered piecemeal in intense passages. Their contribution was of course rhetorical, but also tactical insofar as they established a factual and objective atmosphere, which in turn protected the five theatrical fringe visualities from inviting the strong entertainment visibility into Riis's performance.

25. "How They Live and Die," *The World*, April 27, 1888; LC, Riis Papers, box 4.

26. "Pictures of Opium Dens," in *New York Star*, May 11, 1888; "How the Other Half Lives," in *New York Tribune*, May 11, 1888; both clippings from LC, Riis Papers, box 4.

Now, Riis's scholarly reputation rested also, on the other hand, on the formal lecture setting that he had developed. It provided the necessary framework for his numbers and statistics to operate rhetorically, and it served therefore as the most active tactical instrument for integrating non-semantic articulations.

4) The fourth tactical measure was complex; it developed alongside a new lecture format that Riis tried to advance and situate among conventions already in place. Riis appropriated and adjusted constitutive elements from at least three different established lecture formats, each with its own visualities. As we shall see, appropriation and adjustment were techniques to actively and successfully integrate the five non-semantic articulations that would support a new performative narrative and protect it from pious protesters. Once again, these articulations were: a) the dramatic dominance of beholder over beheld; b) the orchestration of harm in view of redemption; c) a discernible posing of bodies; d) exclusivity of access to secluded places, and e) the crucial visuality of timing between on-stage events.

Riis and the Visual Mode of Lecturing

When Riis's Washington DC lecture was reconstructed in 2008 for the *Jacob A. Riis* exhibit at the National Museum of Photography in Copenhagen, it was also a research experiment conducted in view of discerning the non-semantic visuality of the lecture. Among other things, it became evident that the lecture was craftily composed, and that the visual elements were leading the narrative. Rhetorically, the lecture appeared very confident—as an established mode of address, much like a film documentary today, and in no sense immature, experimental or undeveloped. This is worth noticing in view of the circumstance that Riis's rival reform lecturers abstained consistently from performing with illustrations.

Riis's position amongst other reform lecturers appears to have rested on little else than a common topic and political ambition. Subject matter he obviously shared with other peers but in terms of performance, his was of a different nature. As already touched upon, peer philanthropists lectured without illustrations: Josiah Strong, Stephen Smith, Josephine Shaw Lowell, Felix Adler—none of the great reformists have left any trace of visual aids. Even so, illustrated charity lectures were not invented by Riis. Less prominent performers who entertained in smaller churches, in local community halls, and sometimes also in their private homes often used a magic lantern to invigorate their message. These sessions relied typically on ready-made manuscripts and slides available on subscription. The Polyopticon magic lantern, for example, was advertised in *The Ladies' Home Journal* in 1889 as a perfect contrivance for home entertainment or smaller lecture venues, and it was available with a set of slides featuring, among other available topics, "Illustrations of a Temperance Lesson."[27] These slides have not been preserved, but in view of their intended use, they probably offered generic imagery that corresponded to illustrations in popular monthlies: these would certainly fend off any narrative challenges or visual embarrassments. Compared to Riis's performances, their visual norm was reassuring, value-confirming, and, if anything, the perfect opposite of his provocative charity activism. However, within this popular domain there was already established a melodramatic dominance of viewer over viewed. There were also reliable techniques for showcasing the physical harm to be expected from intemperance and disease, invariably overlaid by prospects of final salvation.

Another, quite different genre of public address appears to have been closer to Riis's performances: the ethnographic lecture. At the time when Riis began photographing, advertisements for illustrated lectures on exotic cultures and ancient civilizations appeared frequently in the daily press. Private adventurers and university schol-

27. A lantern advertisement for the Electro Radiant Magic Lantern, published 1885 in *Zion's Herald*, explicates the intended use and cultural belonging of the device. The manufacturers "particularly recommend this Lantern to all societies who have occasion to raise money for charitable and other purposes." The lantern is promised to "'draw' with the combined power of the Theatre, the Circus, Prestidigitateur, the Country Fair, the Temperance Crusade, and the Camp meeting."

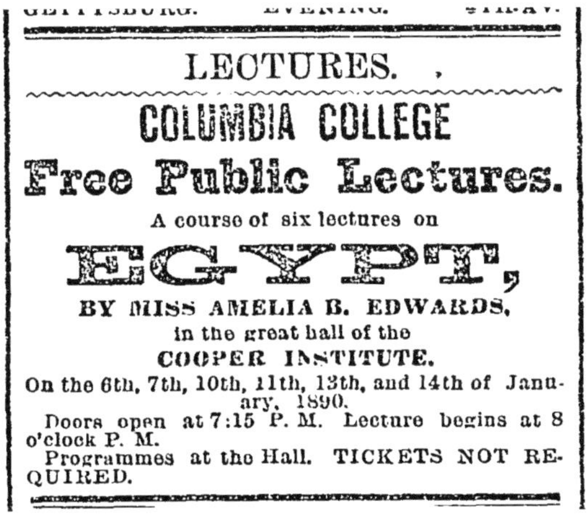

LECTURES.

COLUMBIA COLLEGE

Free Public Lectures.

A course of six lectures on

EGYPT,

BY MISS AMELIA B. EDWARDS,

in the great hall of the

COOPER INSTITUTE.

On the 6th, 7th, 10th, 11th, 13th, and 14th of January, 1890.

Doors open at 7:15 P. M. Lecture begins at 8 o'clock P. M.

Programmes at the Hall. TICKETS NOT REQUIRED.

Figure 47. Advertisement for Anthropological lecture, *New York Times*, Jan. 1, 1890, page 7.

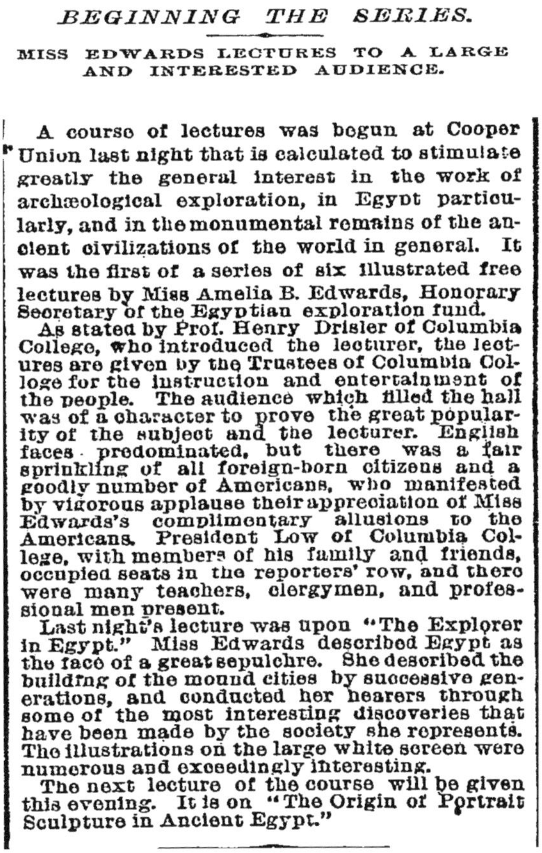

BEGINNING THE SERIES.

MISS EDWARDS LECTURES TO A LARGE AND INTERESTED AUDIENCE.

A course of lectures was begun at Cooper Union last night that is calculated to stimulate greatly the general interest in the work of archæological exploration, in Egypt particularly, and in the monumental remains of the ancient civilizations of the world in general. It was the first of a series of six illustrated free lectures by Miss Amelia B. Edwards, Honorary Secretary of the Egyptian exploration fund.

As stated by Prof. Henry Drisler of Columbia College, who introduced the lecturer, the lectures are given by the Trustees of Columbia College for the instruction and entertainment of the people. The audience which filled the hall was of a character to prove the great popularity of the subject and the lecturer. English faces predominated, but there was a fair sprinkling of all foreign-born citizens and a goodly number of Americans, who manifested by vigorous applause their appreciation of Miss Edwards's complimentary allusions to the Americans. President Low of Columbia College, with members of his family and friends, occupied seats in the reporters' row, and there were many teachers, clergymen, and professional men present.

Last night's lecture was upon "The Explorer in Egypt." Miss Edwards described Egypt as the face of a great sepulchre. She described the building of the mound cities by successive generations, and conducted her hearers through some of the most interesting discoveries that have been made by the society she represents. The illustrations on the large white screen were numerous and exceedingly interesting.

The next lecture of the course will be given this evening. It is on "The Origin of Portrait Sculpture in Ancient Egypt."

Figure 48. Ensuing lecture review, *New York Times*, Jan. 7, 1890, page 3.

ars competed on a burgeoning infotainment market, and many relied on photographic slide projections for an edge. As Elizabeth Edwards has shown, it was common for these scholars and lecturers to distribute photographs amongst each other for making slide reproductions. Projections were then used to add an "affective tone" to the public event.[28] Although research remains to be done on the subject of anthropological entertainment, one may still glean from the contents of certain archives what type of images the patrons may have seen.[29]

Much like Riis's images, ethnographic photography habitually portrayed daily labor, leisure, and commercial activities in foreign parts of the world. Frequent are also group portraits, individual portraits and images of objects, tools, houses, and crowded public places. But while Riis's images appear with a peculiar kind of raw and unpolished sensuous quality, the photographs preferred by ethnographers have a smooth tonal range and are generally technically accomplished. Important non-semantic overlap may by contrast be discovered in their dissemination. The darkened large hall with one or two domineering projections; the disembodied narrator voice; the narrative primacy of visuals over diction; the mandatory introduction speech given by an esteemed peer; the conventions of advertising prior to an event; the weight of the hosting institution; the dress code and social rituals amongst audience members. When Riis entered the lecture business, these perceptible elements were already in place as a framing device for the public's contact with academia and for an enlightened discourse on, among other topics, social and cultural abnormality.

As it were, these popular lectures were not properly academic.

28. Elizabeth Edwards, *Raw Histories*, 44-45.

29. Cf. the online collection of lantern slides at The George Eastman House, http://www.geh.org/ (accessed on 12 August 2015); in New York are important slide collections at the Anthropology Division of the American Museum of Natural History and in the Photograph Study Collection of the Department of the Arts of Africa, Oceania and the Americas at The Metropolitan Museum of Art.

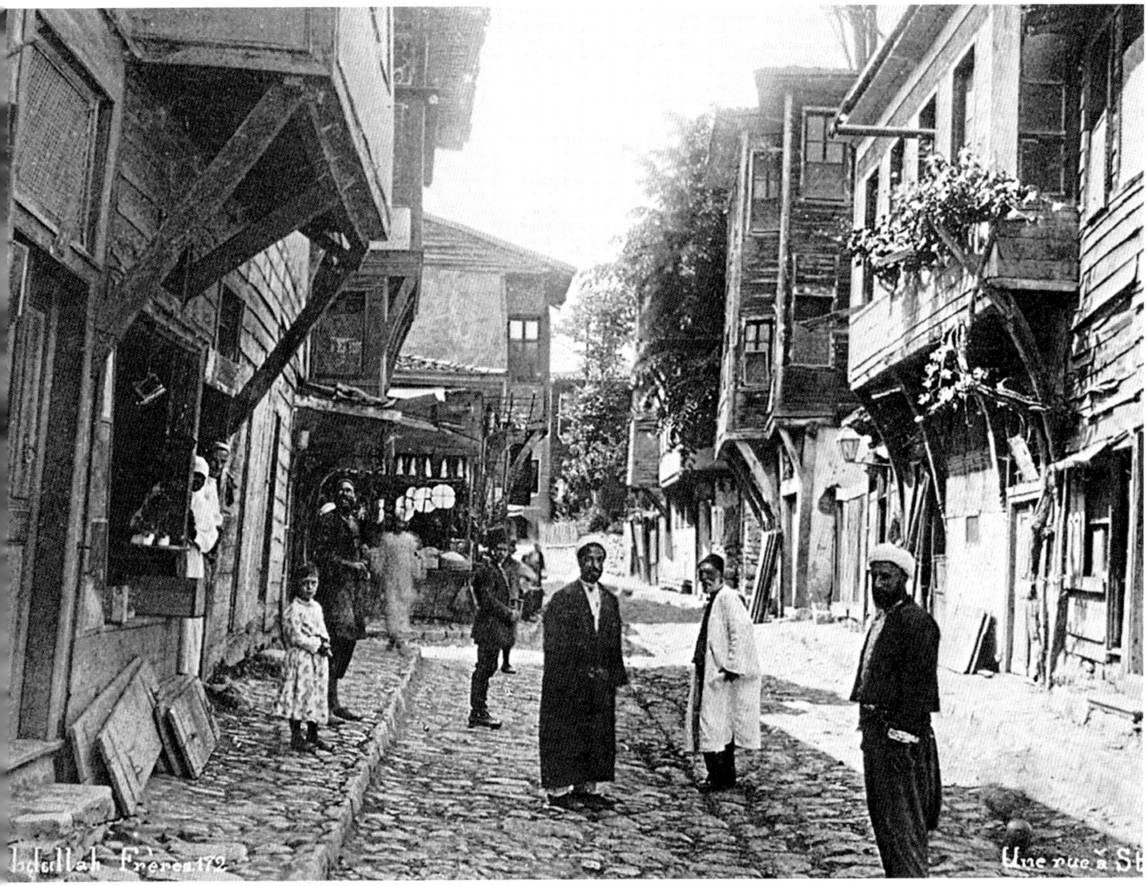

Figure 49. Abdullah Frères, "A Street in Istanbul," (1870), reproduced in Engin Çizgen, *Photography in the Ottoman Empire 1839-1919* (Haset Kitabevi, Istanbul: 1987).

Their framing devices presented neither formal specimens nor scholarly examples but rather something in-between a roman à clef character and a case exhibit. Furthermore, their mandatory exoticism veered irrepressibly toward the mythical and the fantastic, what no performer could refuse a demanding audience. Riis's lectures, which were a fortuitous combination of minor charity routines and popular academia, appropriated from the latter a dramatized staging of human bodies and exclusive access to the mystical domains of the foreign Other. With regard to his wealth of facts and statistics, it seems that the visual conventions of academia gave them their proper context and due credence. Designed to accommodate a popular academic framework, Riis's otherwise agitative performance was even found suitable for the Bickmore lecture program at the American Museum of Natural History, a series that was pronouncedly academic in educational purpose and tone of address.[30] Of course, an academic framing implied restrictions on normative content. Innuendos, accusations, and proposals for improvement should only be expressed implicitly, or cautiously toward the end, in accordance with academic principles. It should be noted that popular ethnographic lectures maintained established hierarchies of ethnicity; they also preserved scholarly delimitations of subject matter and, above all, their adherence to academic protocol inoculated the public performer from the entertainment industry. Restrictions on content applied to less prominent private performers as well. Sets of ethnographic slides were also available for home entertainment; when deprived of the scholarly ceremonials of larger events, these minor gatherings were rather similar to small-scale charity performances. However, and once again, none of the lecture formats described above would include Riis's call for activism or his performative appeal to moral improvement.

To visually underscore this essential appeal, Riis added a simple and very alien ingredient, but an extraordinarily powerful one, to his blown-up charity-ethnographic lecture event. This was something far

30. Riis presented "How the Other Half Lives" on Dec. 11, 1893 at the Museum of Natural History as part of the Bickmore lectures.

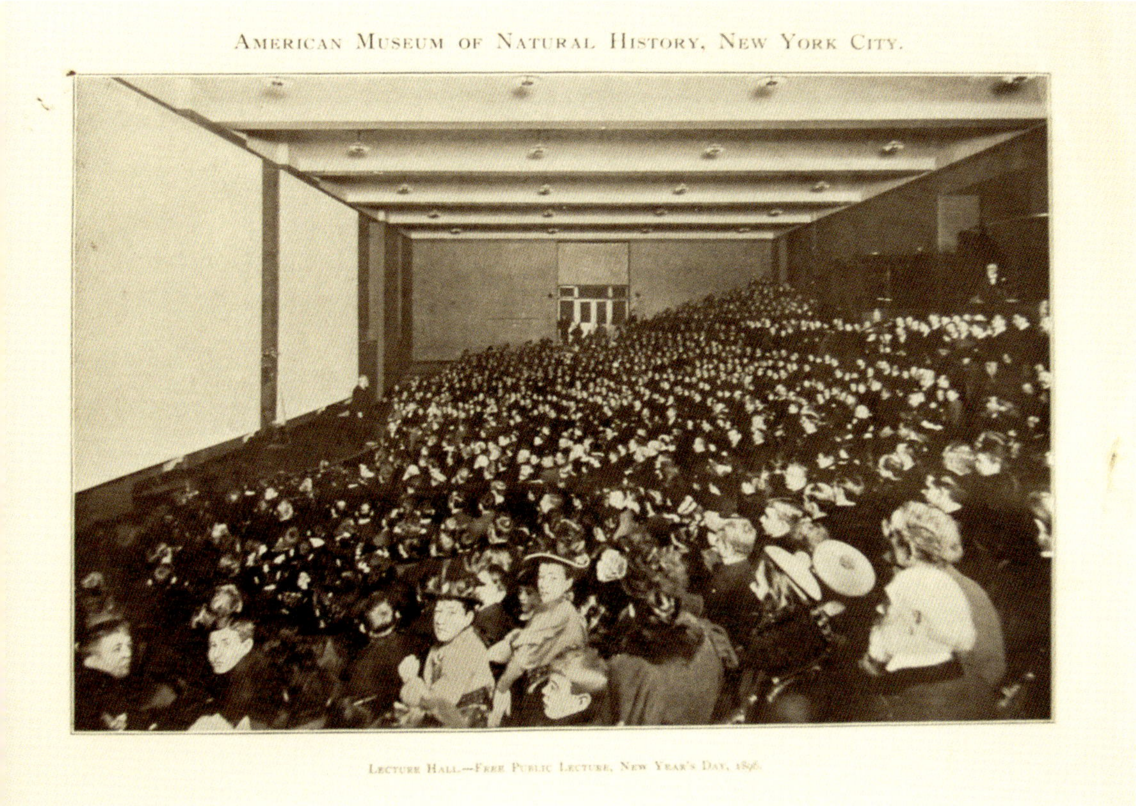

Figure 50. Anonymous photographer, "Lecture Hall—Free Public Lecture. New Year's Day, 1896." American Museum of Natural History.

more sophisticated than mimicking with his flash the often depicted lantern, which in many popular illustrations illuminated the tenement misery. Impacting ethically on his audience was, as we have seen, a matter of performative rotations of the conservative triangle. These movements were obviously semantically induced, but there were important non-semantic stimuli involved in conveying the movements unto the audience. One such paradigmatic impulse was appropriated from an altogether different visibility, one belonging to an enterprise with which charity had few agreements.

The source of this performative, non-semantic stimulant can be traced to commercial advertisement, an area that for a long time already had employed the magic lantern as a public media device. Riis became acquainted with the advertising potentials of the magic lantern already in 1877, while embarking on a brief business adventure with a friend. Those experiences taught him the conventional methods of shepherding consumer feelings and opinions toward a desired goal. One of the most common advertising ploys at the time was a two-part argument based on associating a given product with relief from distress. The first part of the message reminded potential customers of some ailment or problem for which the second part, with a hefty emphasis on the commodity brand, offered a solution or relief. This simple syntagmatic operation would visually be associated with non-semantic elements to further emphasize the advantages offered with the product. A most important feature of the scheme was timing. The rhetorical power of the turn from problem to solution depended on an acute sense of when, and how, to best satisfy. Riis occasionally marketed his cause in a similar way, or at least with non-semantic elements put to similar use. For example when during a lecture presentation he let a disastrous interior view (*Upstairs in Blind Mans's Alley*) be followed by a lovely photograph of a small crowded classroom, accompanied by the following appeal: "Now, friends, there you have some of the Christian work that you represent. Somebody went down into that slum and settled there and made

31. Riis, "The Other Half and How They Live," 409.

a home among those people and said, 'Come, brother, let me help you.'"[31] The syntagmatic construction is simple enough to see. More covertly, perhaps, is the timing and composition of non-semantic image elements, which, acting sensuously upon the affirmation of neighborliness, served immediately to strengthen the audience's will to honest reform initiatives. The darkness of a blind man's loft is effectively battled by the sudden brightness of the ensuing slide, as if illuminated by the confidence and the hope glittering in children's eyes. Similar tropes are prevalent and their habitually cheerful finale prevents an otherwise sensational gloom from dominating the performance.

Riis's lecture was not advertisement. It borrowed a couple of non-semantic features from advertisement to help foster a common desire for social engagement and individual improvement. Rival charity lecturers were barred from similarly underscoring such ambitions, primarily by dint of their comparably restricted visual repertoire. Five modified visualities were instrumental in mutating the image of New York's tenement population. They let words and images interweave in different and exciting ways during Riis's lectures without reducing his stories and spectacular photographs to a mere spectacle. They were instrumental in individuating the Other Half as a unique visibility, a new way of seeing urban poverty, thus certainly assisting Riis in the task of persuading his audience. This he could achieve without resorting to superlatives and heavy-handed diction, what in turn allowed a trustworthy and more congenial address than his peers were able to afford.

Conclusion

Riis explored a multitude of ways of making tenement life visible. Borrowing and modifying from sources more or less compatible with conventional charity, Riis took advantage of new and already established techniques to orchestrate a novel relationship between beholder and the photographically depicted. The tenement population was then no longer visible in the way that reformers knew from before. For sure, the change was not exclusively due to the inventive use of novel photographic technology—although it played an important part. Equally important were paradigmatic trajectories attracted from the entertainment industry, operating in Riis's work next to more readily adaptable conventions, invited in from otherwise earnest and somber illustrated lecture formats.

Whereas Riis's syntagmatic relationships altered the significance of the tenement problem, suggesting different meanings and perhaps deeper values, his paradigmatic hospitality established relationships to faraway practices, practices whose values and visual orders provided a curious atmosphere to his message and situated it in a unique cultural niche. These values—paradigmatically exclusive for The Other Half—were crucial for establishing Riis's position within the overall charity and reform movement. Together, the syntagmatic and paradigmatic trajectories individuated a new mode of addressing the tenement problem, and soon they engendered a new visibility. The tenement population appeared, iconographically speaking, in a different light, in a new kind of picture. A minor reorientation had taken place between beholder and subject.

The mutation of visibility and the mutation of discourse that produced The Other Half meant that New York's tenement population could be understood in new ways. Riis made them appear once again, now more intriguing and more complex, meaningful in other ways, but still recognizable. He made their social progress a palpable moral concern for the reader and the spectator, and he made it a desirable business to assist a civil brother in need. The Other Half was a remarkably influential concept—less, perhaps, an incitement to actual reform initiatives than a new public concern with the power to raise debates for more than a century ahead.

Index

Name index